Summer & Fall
WILDFLOWERS
of New England

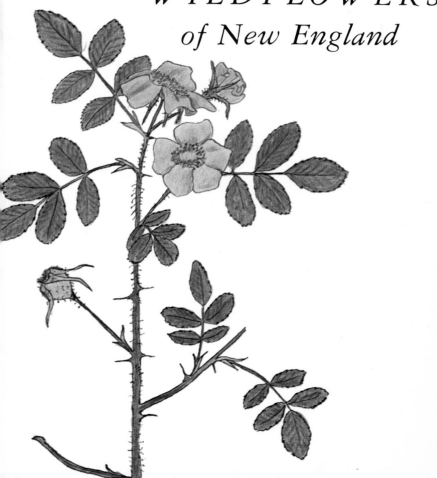

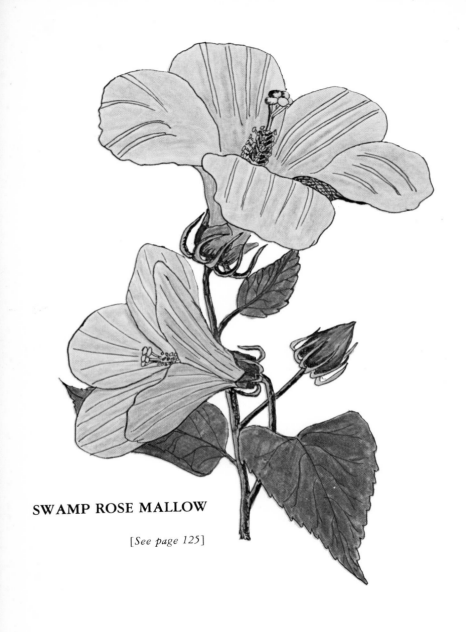

SWAMP ROSE MALLOW

[*See page 125*]

Summer & Fall
WILDFLOWERS
of New England

By

Marilyn J. Dwelley

DOWN EAST ENTERPRISE, INC.
CAMDEN/MAINE

Summer & Fall
WILDFLOWERS
of New England

ISBN 0-89272-020-4

4   6   8   9   7   5   3

Down East Books / Camden, Maine

Preface

      The flowers contained in this book are those which grow in New England and bloom from mid-June on. For those flowers which bloom earlier, see *SPRING WILDFLOWERS OF NEW ENGLAND* by the same author. The flowers are arranged by color and are grouped into the following sections:

1. **White Flowers**
2. **Pink or Red Flowers**
3. **Orange Flowers**
4. **Yellow Flowers**

5. **Green Flowers**
6. **Blue**
7. **Lavender or purple**
8 **Brown**

  Because some flowers vary in color or have two prominent colors they may be in two different sections. Some flowers have colors that are difficult to put into either section, therefore it may be necessary to look in more than one section to find it. For example, should you find a flower which looks lavender to you and you can not find it in that section, you will probably find it in the pink section.

  Within each color group, the flowers are arranged by families. The arrangement of families corresponds with that in the 8th edition of *Gray's Manual of Botany*. Within the families, the flowers are listed according to Gray's order whenever possible. This order may be slightly disrupted when several flowers have been placed on the same page.

  As my authority, I have used *Gray's Manual*, and when there is a discrepancy in the Latin name given to a certain flower in various texts I have used, I have listed the one given in Gray's. Some Latin names given in older texts have been updated. In some instances, two different Latin names have been given as an aid to the reader who might be trying to locate the flower in other texts.

I would like to thank Dr. Charles D. Richards of the Botany Department at the University of Maine in Orono for all of his help and for the time spent in checking my work for errors.

Thanks should also go to many of my friends in the Josselyn Botanical Society who have helped me locate and identify specimens, and who have loaned me some of their slides of wildflowers.

Special thanks should also go to those people at *Down East Enterprises,* especially Leon Ballou, who had faith enough in my work to accept the responsibility for printing and distributing both of my books on wildflowers.

Sincerely,

Marilyn J. Dwelley

Contents

Glossary

anther	The top or fertile part of the stamen.
axil	The angle formed where the leaf is attached to the stem.
basal	Located at the base of the plant.
blade	The large part of the petal or leaf.
bloom	A whitish powdery covering — sometimes rather waxy in nature.
bract	A small modified leaf — usually under the flower.
calyx	The whorl of sepals.
compound leaf	A leaf divided into smaller leaflets.
corolla	The whorl of petals.
entire	Without teeth or divisions.
keel	A central ridge of a flower, petal, or leaf — like the keel of a boat.
mid vein	The central vein of a leaf running from base to tip.
pedicel	The stem or stalk for an individual flower.
peduncle	A primary flower stalk supporting either a cluster of flowers or a solitary flower.
perfoliate	The stem passes through the leaf.
petiole	The stalk on a leaf.

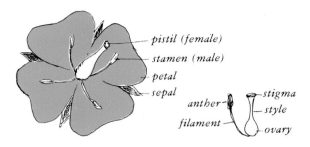

pistil (female)
stamen (male)
petal
sepal

anther—
filament—
—_stigma_
—_style_
ovary

pistillate	A flower containing only pistils.
raceme	An unbranching flower cluster where each flower is on its own stalk.
sheath	An organ or part of the leaf which surrounds the stem.
spadix	A spike of flowers on a fleshy stem — as in the Arum Family
spathe	A large leaf-like bract which encloses a spadix or another type of flower cluster.
spatulate	Broad at the tip and tapering towards the base.
spike	A flower cluster where each flower is _not_ on its own stem, but is attached directly to the main stem.
staminate	A flower containing only stamens.
stipules	A pair of small leaf-like appendages at the base of the leaf stalk.
succulent	Juicy or fleshy.
tendril	A twisting thread-like end used for climbing.
umbel	A flower cluster where all the flower stems start at the same point.
whorl	Three or more leaves in a circle around the stem.

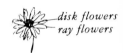
—_spur_

—_disk flowers_
—_ray flowers_

—_corolla_
} _calyx_

—_stipules_

WATER PLANTAIN
Alisma trivale
Water-Plantain family

Water Plantain grows in shallow water in swamps or ditches or along muddy river banks — sometimes growing in wet sand. It reaches a height of from six to eighteen inches.

Long-stalked oval leaves are in a clump at the base of the plant, and a very branching flower stem rises from the center of this cluster. The leaves are sometimes indented at the base, and the leaf stems (petioles) may be up to a foot long. The flower stem is sometimes shorter than the leaves, but usually it stands tall above the leaf cluster. The small, white flowers are about one fourth inch broad. They have three green sepals, three waxy white petals, six stamens, and resemble miniature arrowhead flowers. The flowers are arranged in whorls of four or more on the stem.

ARROWHEAD
Sagittaria latifolia
Water Plantain Family

There are some sixteen species of Arrowheads in our area, but most are quite similar to the one shown. The leaves on most species are deep, lustrous green and are distinctively arrow-head shaped. Most arrowheads grow right in sluggish or quiet water of streams, marshes and ponds to a height of from four to forty inches. The pure white flowers with three round, waxy petals are on erect flower stalks. Usually the flowers are arranged in whorls of three each. The lower whorl contains female flowers and the upper whorls contain only male flowers. There are three bracts below each whorl of flowers.

1

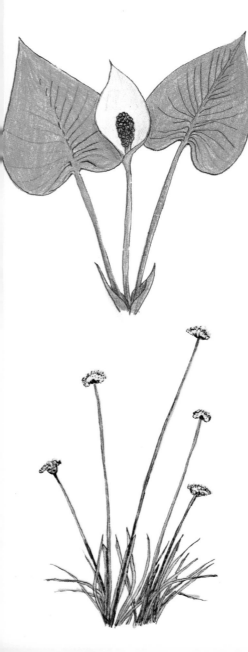

WILD CALLA
Calla palustris
Arum Family

This is a slender plant which grows from five to twelve inches in height. It is often called Water Arum. It used to be plentiful in bogs and swamps of New England, but draining practices and new highways have almost eliminated this plant. The outer surface of the spathe is green and the inside of it is a waxy-white. This beautiful spathe is often mistaken for a flower, but the true flowers are clustered together at the end of the greenish yellow spadix inside of the spathe. This cluster of tiny flowers called the spadix is usually from one to two inches long. The beautiful dark green heart-shaped leaves, which often reach a width of four inches, stand above the water in which the plant grows. After the spathe dries up, a cluster of red berries appears which is quite similar to that found on the Jack-in-the-pulpit.

PIPEWORT
Eriocaulon septangulare
Pipewort family

Pipewort has some other interesting common names which really are more descriptive of the plant: White-Buttons, Duckgrass, Hat Pins, and Seven-Angled Pipewort. Pipewort grows in still water on shores of ponds, lakes, and slow-moving streams — usually where the soil is sandy. The small tufted plant is usually less than nine inches high, but its height depends upon the depth of the water in which it is growing. Tufts of awl-shaped leaves — from one to three inches in length — are at the base of

2

the plant. These leaves are usually submerged in water and only the flowering stem (scape) is visible above the water. This scape is leafless and has seven grooves in it. On some plants this scape is stiff and non-bending, while on others it may be soft and fragile. Tiny flowers are in small, flat, white, woolly heads at the summit of the scape. The flowers are interspersed with numerous bracts.

Ⓐ MUD PLANTAIN

Heteranthera reniformis

Pickerelweed Family

See page 272 in the blue section for details.

DEVIL'S BIT

Chamaelirium luteum

Lily Family

Other common names for this plant are Blazing-Star and Fairy-Wand. It grows in moist woods, bogs, and thickets to a height of from one to three feet. It is a very slender plant with a tuft of basal leaves and a white tightly-packed spike of flowers. This is one of the flowers which has the male (staminate) and the female (pistillate) flowers on separate plants. The staminate flower spike tapers at the tip and often droops or tips to one side. The pistillate spike is shorter, straight, and blunt at the tip. The individual flowers in the spike are very small, white, and have six very narrow petals and sepals.

FALSE ASPHODEL

Tofieldia glutinosa

Lily Family

This plant grows in bogs, marshes, or on damp ledges to a height of from six to twenty inches. It has a hairy stem with black glands on it. The linear, grass-like leaves are tufted at the base and are one-half to two-thirds as long as the flower stalk. There is a small leaf-like bract midway on the stalk. The small flowers have whitish or greenish concave sepals and petals. They are in a close spike at the top of the plant, and each flower is singly attached to the stem.

WILD LEEK or RAMP

Allium tricoccum

Lily Family

Wild Leek grows from a slender bulb in rich woods. It reaches a height of from six to twenty inches. In the spring two or three onion-scented leaves appear. These may be one or two inches wide and from six to twelve inches long. The leaves are narrowed at the tip and taper to a long leaf stem (petiole). These leaves wither away before the flowers bloom.

The flower stem has two papery bracts which enclose the flower cluster at first. As the flowers mature, these two bracts open and fold backwards. The numerous flowers measure from one-fourth to one-half of an inch and are arranged in a single hemispherical cluster at the top of the rigid flower stalk. Each flower has six oblong sepals and petals.

FALSE SOLOMON'S SEAL

Smilacina racemosa

Lily Family

This plant grows in moist woods and is from one to three feet tall. It has a crowded panicle of small white fragrant flowers. The stem is gracefully curving and has alternate oval pointed leaves. The leaves are three to six inches long and are coated with fine hair on the underside. The flowers have six petals and the stamens are quite prominent — giving a fuzzy appearance to the cluster of flowers. The fruit is first whitish and speckled with brown, but later turns ruby-red.

STARRY FALSE SOLOMON'S SEAL

Smilacina stellata

Lily Family

This plant is from eight to sixteen inches high and has eight to ten star-shaped flowers at the top. It grows on moist banks and is similar to the plant at left. Leaves clasp the stem.

THREE-LEAVED FALSE SOLOMON'S SEAL

Smilacina trifolia

Lily Family

This plant is found in cold bogs or cool woods. It is from two to six inches high and has from two to four leaves — most frequently three. The leaf bases taper and sheath the stem. The flowers have six points, and are produced in a few-flowered raceme at the end of the stem.

COLICROOT or STARGRASS

Aletris farinosa

Lily Family

This plant has a cluster of narrow basal leaves about eight inches long around the leafless flower stalk. Colicroot grows in dry sandy or peaty soil to a height of from one and one-half to three feet. At the top of the stem is a raceme of small, rough, white flowers, on short flower stems (pedicles). The sepals and petals are joined together to make a tubular, six-toothed flower with a swollen base. Each flower is nearly one-half inch long.

SHOWY LADY'S SLIPPER
Cypripedium reginae
Orchid Family

This is perhaps our largest and most showy wild flower. It has a stout hairy stem which is leafy up to the top. It is usually from one to three feet high. The large leaves are from three to eight inches long, and the plant bears from one to three flowers. The sepals are round or oval and very waxy white in contrast to the inflated lip which is variegated with crimson and white stripes. The lip is from one to two inches long. This orchid grows in swamps and open wet woods, and has been so largely picked that it is close to extinction in some areas. Do not pick any members of the orchid family.

SMALL ROUND-LEAVED ORCHIS
Orchis rotundifolia
Orchid Family

This orchid is about eight or ten inches tall and grows in bogs, spruce forests, cold woods, and places where there is a peaty soil. It has only one broad oval basal leaf which is from one to three inches long. There are one or two scales sheathing the stem below the leaf. The flower is white with the larger bottom petal spreading and three lobed. The large white petal is spotted with purple or magenta. There are usually from five to ten flowers at the top of the stem, and each flower has its own small green bract beneath it.

(A) WHITE FRINGED ORCHIS
Habenaria blephariglottis
Orchid Family

White Fringed Orchis — our most exquisite white native orchid — is a tall orchid which grows in swamps, wet bogs, or peaty soil, especially along the coastal plain. It varies in height from one to over three feet, but it is usually about eighteen inches or so. It has a tall leafy stem and an elongated cluster of pure white flowers. There is a lance-shaped bract or modified leaf beneath each flower. The leaves vary in form from ovate to elliptic or lanceolate, but the upper leaves are merely pointed bracts. The bright white to creamy white flower has spatulate petals which may be toothed at the tip. The narrow, oblong lower lip is deeply fringed at the edges. Each flower has a spur about an inch long.

(B) HELLEBORINE
Epipactus helleborine
Orchid Family

Helleborine is a leafy-stemmed orchid which grows in woods and thickets and on roadside banks. It will usually spread once it becomes established. It may reach a height up to four feet. The leaves are conspicuously nerved and clasp the stem at the base. They vary in width, but are long and pointed. The small flowers are arranged in a loose, elongated cluster at the top of the stem. Each small flower is in the axil of a long, narrow bract. The sepals and side petals are about one-half inch long. They are greenish-white, but may be tinged with madder or rose. The lip forms a sac with a triangular tip which is bent back under the sac.

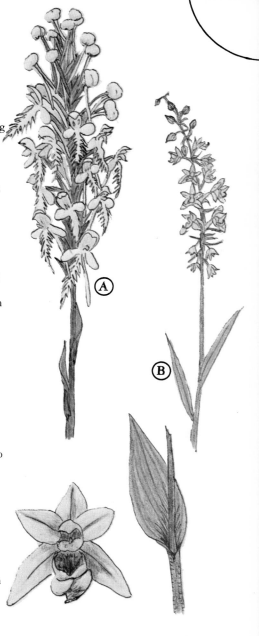

8

NODDING LADIES'-TRESSES
Spiranthes cerna
Orchid Family

There are eleven species of Ladies'-tresses in our area, but all are quite similar to these shown here. Though *S. cerna* is one of the tallest, all have similar flower spikes surrounded by a tuft of sword-like leaves at the base of the plant. Nodding Ladies'-Tresses grows in full sun in bogs, wet woods or along shores to a height of from six to twenty-five inches. It is also called Pearl-twists and Screw-augers because the arrangement of small flowers appears to twist around the stem. On this plant, the small white, fragrant *flowers arch downward.* The upper sepal and two side petals are arching and form a hood over the lower lip which may be toothed or crisped at the margins. The flowers are hairy at their base and are tightly clustered on a slender terminal spike which may be *spirally twisted.*

FRAGRANT LADIES'-TRESSES
Spiranthes cerna var. odorata
Orchid Family

This ladies'-tresses is similar, but smaller, has pointed lips, and a *strong vanilla fragrance.* The side sepals are shorter than the hood, and the lip is veined and shades from white to yellow-green. The flowers are horizontal on the spike, and *do not arch downward.*

SPRING LADIES-TRESSES
Spiranthes vernalis
Orchid Family

This ladies-tresses blooms earlier
than most. It grows in wet meadows,
bogs, and marshes and along the coast.
It has a slender stem from six to
thirty-six inches tall and very slender
basal leaves which are sometimes up to
a foot long. The flowers are entirely
white or yellowish-white, but have red
hairs on them. Each is about one-half
inch long and is very fragrant. The
flowers are close together in a dense
raceme which is often twisted into a
spiral. It is very downy with fine,
simple hairs.

WIDE-LEAVED
LADIES'-TRESSES
Spiranthes lucida
Orchid Family

This orchid is from five to twelve
inches tall and grows in damp woods,
marshes, and along wet shores. It has
from three to five basal leaves that are
lance shaped. From ten to fifteen
flowers are crowded into a dense spike
with small scale-like leaves beneath the
flowers. The flower is white, but the
lower, round, waxy lip has a broad
spot of yellow in the middle.

10

CREEPING or DWARF RATTLESNAKE PLANTAIN
Goodyera repens var. ophioides
Orchid Family

This orchid produces slender runners. The basal leaves are dark, blue-olive green and the veins of the leaves have showy whitish markings. The leaves are usually five-nerved. The greenish or creamy white flowers are in a one-sided arrangement at the top of the flower stem. They are only about one-eighth of an inch long and the lower sac-like lip of the flower has a recurved, wavy margin. The orchid grows in damp, cool woods, usually where there is some moss. It is most often found under hemlocks and spruces. It is seldom more than ten inches tall.

CHECKERED RATTLESNAKE PLANTAIN
Goodyera tesselata
Orchid Family

This downy orchid has mottled dark and light green leaves at the base of the flower stalk. It has a stouter stem than *Goodyera repens* above. It grows in dry coniferous or deciduous woods, especially on hillsides in the woods. The plant grows to a height of from six to sixteen inches and has rather fleshy leaves about three inches long. A "lacy" pattern on the leaves is formed by the interlacing of veins bordered by pale green.

The two-lipped white flowers are about one-fourth of an inch long. They are loosely arranged on the flower stem — either on one side or spiraling around it.

WHITE ADDER'S MOUTH

Malaxis brachypoda

Orchid Family

This orchid grows in damp woods and bogs to a height of from four to eight inches. There is a single, wide, pointed leaf at the base which clasps the stem. The flowers are greenish white and are arranged in a very slender tapering raceme. The horizontal petals are long and slender, but the lower lip is broadly heart-shaped and tapers to a long point. The top middle sepal stands erect behind the lip, but the bottom two sepals come out from behind the lower lip of the flower.

LIZARD'S TAIL or WATER DRAGON

Saururus cernuus

Lizard's-Tail Family

The Lizard's Tail grows in swamps, marshes, and in shallow water to a height of from two to five feet. The stem is very branching, but usually there are only a few flower spikes. Often, the branches without flower spikes are taller than the branches containing the spikes. Minute white flowers are fragrant and are arranged in a spike-like raceme which curves or droops down at the tip. The leaves are very large and heart-shaped. Each leaf has its own long leaf stalk (petiole). The leaf stalk forms a sheath around the main stem at the point where it joins the main stem.

12

BASTARD TOADFLAX
Comandra umbellata
Sandlewood Family

Toadflax grows in dry soils, stony and sandy thickets, or open woods to a height of from six to eighteen inches. It has numerous leafy stems and spreads by means of underground creeping stems which are parasitic on roots of woody plants. The narrow leaves are attached singly and have no teeth. The leaves are football-shaped and may be either blunt or pointed at both ends. The inset shows the detail of the underside of the leaf. It is paler in color than the top side and has a yellowish midvein and side veins. The numerous greenish-white or purplish flowers are clustered at the stem summits. There are no petals, but the five sepals form a funnel-like base which encloses five hairy stamens and a pistil. The pistil is joined to the sides of the surrounding funnel-shaped calyx.

NORTHERN COMANDRA or GEOCAULON
Geocaulon lividum or *Comandra livida*
Sandalwood Family

Geocaulon is a small, smooth plant with a thread-like brown, creeping rootstalk and an erect non-branching stem. It grows in moss or damp humus — usually at higher altitudes of New England. It grows to be from four to twelve inches in height. The soft, thin, pliable leaves are elliptical in shape. They are alternate on the stem and have short leaf stalks (petioles). These leaves may sometimes be purplish or pale-lead colored. The flowers are on flower stalks — usually one on each stalk. Each plant has from two to four

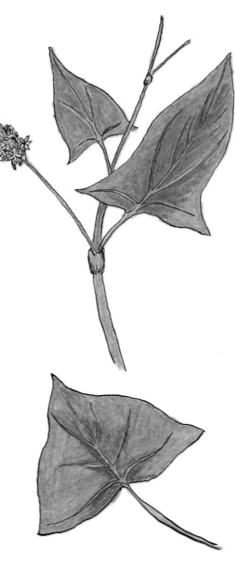

flowers. There are *no true petals*. The bronze or greenish-white, triangular, petal-like lobes are really the sepals. The central flower on the plant has both male and female parts, but the other ones are staminate (male only). The scarlet fleshy fruit is edible.

BUCKWHEAT

Fagopyrum sagittatum

Buckwheat Family

Buckwheat is a rather fleshy, smooth plant which has spread from cultivation to waste places, old fields, and along roadsides. It grows to be from one to three feet in height. The leaves are alternate on the stem, are arrow-shaped, and *narrow above the middle* of the leaf blade. The stem is often reddish and is strongly grooved. Upper leaves may be clasping the stem. The flowers are greenish-white and have no petals, but the five sepals are petal-like. There are eight honey-bearing yellow glands which alternate with the stamens. The pointed *seed is smooth and shining*. Note the sheath at the leaf axils.

INDIA WHEAT or TARTARY BUCKWHEAT

Fagopyrum tataricum

Buckwheat Family

This plant is very similar to the one above, but the leaves are not as narrow. The long-stemmed leaves are usually *broader than long*. The flowers grow on a long-stemmed flower stalk which grows from the sheath at the axils of the leaves. These flowers are similar to those of Buckwheat, but are greener and smaller. The *seed is very dull and rather rough*.

COAST JOINTWEED or SAND KNOTWEED

Polygonella articulata

Buckwheat Family

This plant grows in sandy places, on the sea coast, or in dunes between the beach and a salt marsh. It is from four to twenty-four inches tall and has wiry, erect or spreading stems. The plant is covered with a whitish powder, and does not bloom until mid September. The leaves are rather inconspicuous — hardly more than fleshy strings — with no stalks. The dainty flowers emerge from joints in the stem. The calyx has five pink parts (or white on some plants) with a conspicuous purplish midrib. There are no true petals. As the flowers fade, the sepals turn down in the shape of a bell and the outer surface turns bright pink.

POKEWEED, POKE or GARGET

Phytolacca americana

Pokeweed Family

Poke grows in damp thickets, in recent clearings, fields, or along roadsides where land is rich. It may reach a height of ten feet, but it is usually five or six feet tall. It is a tall, smooth, erect herb with large, long-stalked leaves and coarse reddish stems which are widely branching. It has a rather unpleasant odor and a very large, poisonous root. Young leafy sprouts may be cooked as greens, and the crimson juice has been used to color food, paint, and wines. The flowers are in clusters borne on separate stalks opposite the leaves. The flower has a green center and five, rounded, petal-like sepals but no true petals. The fruit is a purple-black, fleshy berry on a red stalk. The clusters drop to a hanging position after they ripen.

CARPETWEED or INDIAN CHICKWEED

Mollugo verticillata

Carpetweed Family

Carpetweed is a low, prostrate plant which forms mats sometimes twenty inches across. It grows along sandy river banks, in wasteplaces, cultivated grounds, and is widely distributed along railroad tracks. The spoon-shaped leaves are clustered in whorls of five or six at the joints. One-flowered flower stalks arise in the leaf axils. There are no true petals, but the five petal-like sepals are white on the inside. Usually there are only three stamens, but there may be five stamens alternating with the five sepals.

CORN SPURREY

Spergula arvensis

Pink Family

This plant is also called Poverty-weed, Pine Cheat, and Spurrey and is a weed of cultivated ground and fields. It varies in height from six to eighteen inches. Spurrey is a bright-green annual with numerous, thread-like leaves in whorls around the stem and tiny appendages at each fork. Numerous small flowers are in loose clusters at the top of the plant. Each has five white petals and five pointed sepals which are slightly longer than the petals. There may be five stamens in one flower and ten stamens in others growing on the same plant.

16

PROCUMBENT PEARLWORT or BIRD'S-EYE

Sagina procumbens

Chickweed Family

This pearlwort grows in moist places. It is a low, matted, spreading plant which is covered with minute, downy hairs and is usually not much taller than three inches. The linear leaves are in pairs. Numerous, tiny, whitish flowers are on slender stalks which are longer than the leaves. There are four green sepals which are usually longer than the four white petals. Sometimes there are no petals at all.

SPURRY or KNOTTED PEARLWORT

Sagina nodosa

Chickweed Family

Spurry grows in wet places to a height of from two to six inches. It is an erect, tufted perennial with sparingly-branched stems. The lower leaves are long and slender, but the upper leaves are shorter and have clusters of minute leaves in their axils. Each plant has only a few flowers and these are at the tips of the stems and branches. Each white flower has five petals, five sepals, and five styles. The petals are not much longer than the green sepals.

BLUNT-LEAVED SANDWORT or GROVE SANDWORT

Arenaria lateriflora

Pink Family

Grove Sandwort has five round white *unnotched petals* and five

smaller green sepals. The oval leaves
are from one-half to one inch long and
are arranged in uncrowded pairs along
the very slender stem. It grows in wet
spots and in woodlands to a height of
from two to eight inches tall.

THYME-LEAVED SANDWORT
Arenaria serpyllifolia
Pink Family

This tiny plant grows in sandy soil
and stony fields to a height of from
two to eight inches. It has tiny, oval,
pointed leaves about one-fourth of an
inch long. The leaves are arranged in
pairs on the wiry stem. The flower has
five tiny rounded, unnotched, white
petals which are shorter than the
sepals.

SEA CHICKWEED
Arenaria peploides
Pink Family

Sea Chickweed is a bushy, maritime
plant with stout, fleshy stems and
leaves. It grows in sand on sea beaches
to a height of nearly two feet. It may
be tufted or have only one stem with
many leafy branches. It may be
standing erect or be reclining on the
sand. The fleshy, paired, oblong leaves
are attached directly to the stem
(sessile) and may even clasp the stem.
Small flowers grow in clusters either at
the summit of the stem, singly in axils
of the leaves, or in the forks where
branches adjoin the main stem. Each
flower has five petals and sepals, but
flowers on some plants may have six
petals. There are either eight or ten
stamens in the center. Another name
for this plant is Sea-beach Sandwort.
Some botanists give *Honkenya
peploides* as the Latin name for this
plant.

MOUNTAIN SANDWORT

Arenaria groenlandica

Pink Family

This looks similar to a chickweed, but the petals are only slightly notched. The very narrow basal leaves form tufts on the ground. It has five white petals which are longer than the sepals. Mountain Sandwort grows on or near rocks, especially in higher elevations, to a height of from two to five inches.

COMMON CHICKWEED

Stellaria media

Pink Family

There are many kinds of chickweed but the one shown is most common. It grows as a weed in gardens, fields, and moist places to a height of from four to sixteen inches. The weak, reclining stems have pairs of small roundish leaves with pointed tips. The flowers (see enlargement) have five deeply notched white petals which are shorter than the sepals.

COMMON or LESSER STITCHWORT

Stellaria graminea

Pink Family

This weak, reclining or leaning plant grows in grassy places and along roadsides to a height of from twelve to twenty inches. The small, narrow leaves are in pairs and are widest just above the base. The small white flowers are in long-stalked, branching clusters at the top of the four-angled stem. The five spreading petals are deeply-notched, and are slightly longer than the sepals which are firm and ribbed.

19

MOUSE-EAR CHICKWEED

Cerastium vulgatum

Pink Family

This widely distributed chickweed grows in waste places to a height of from six to eighteen inches. It has hairy stalkless leaves about three-fourths of an inch long and the stems are covered with sticky hairs. The deeply notched petals are about the same length as the sepals.

FIELD CHICKWEED

Cerastium arvense

Pink Family

This plant grows close to the ground in dry, rocky places and reaches a height of from four to sixteen inches. The flowers are more than one-half inch broad and have five white petals with two lobes on each petal.

EVENING LYCHNIS
or WHITE CAMPION

Lychnis alba

Pink Family

This campion has fragrant white flowers which open at night, and their white forked petals are said to attract moths which spread the pollen from one flower to another. Five curved stamens protrude from the center. Lychnis grows in fields and waste places to a height of from one to three feet. It is a hairy, sticky plant.

BLADDER CAMPION

Silene cucubalus

Pink Family

This common flower grows in fields and along roadsides to a height of nearly three feet. It has many flowers in loose clusters at the ends of the many branches. The unique part of this wild flower is the cup-shaped calyx behind the white petals. It is tan or greenish and is inflated like a football. The veins are clearly visible on this calyx. Each flower has five petals, but each petal is so deeply notched that it looks like two. Many stamens hang out from the center of the blossom. The leaves are from three to four inches long and are rounded at the base and pointed at the tip. They are arranged in pairs along the hairy stem of the plant.

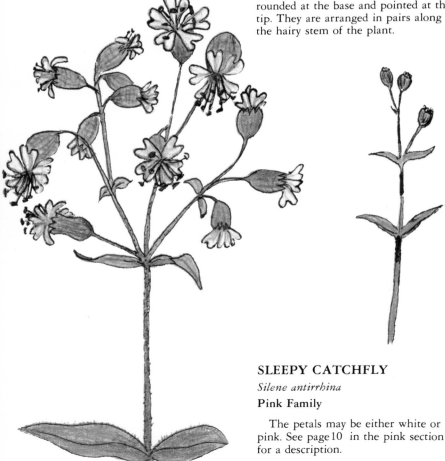

SLEEPY CATCHFLY

Silene antirrhina

Pink Family

The petals may be either white or pink. See page 10 in the pink section for a description.

21

NIGHT-FLOWERING CATCH-FLY

Silene noctiflora
Pink Family

Sticky Cockle is another name given to this plant which grows in cultivated ground and in waste places to a height of from one to three feet. It is a tall, erect plant with pointed leaves and fragrant white flowers which open at night. It is very sticky and fragrant, and should not be confused with Lychnis alba on page 20.   The leaves are united at the base. The barrel-shaped calyx has beautiful, very prominent, green markings and ribs on it and there are five pointed teeth at the top. The five petals are creamy-white with pink at the base. The petals are forked or deeply-notched, and there are three styles on the top of the pistil in the center.

FRAGRANT WATER-LILY

Nymphaea odorata
Water-Lily Family

This gold-centered white flower may be found floating on still ponds and quiet waters. The leaf is large and platter-like with a deep slit on one side. It is shiny green on top, but is often purple on the underside. The flowers are from three to five inches across and are very fragrant. The petals are pointed and tapering, but diminish in size towards the center of the plant.

22

TALL MEADOW RUE

Thalictrum polygamum

Buttercup Family

This tall plant with large, plumy clusters of white flowers is quite common in wet meadows, swamps, roadside ditches, and streambanks where it grows to a height of from three to ten feet. The stout stem is light green, but may be tinged with magenta at axils of branches. The compound leaves are divided and redivided into many roundish blue-green, three-lobed leaflets. The decorative, misty flower cluster may be up to a foot long on larger plants. It is made up of white *flowers with no petals.* The male (staminate) flowers are made up of numerous, showy, thread-like stamens. Usually the male and female flowers are on different plants, but some plants have flowers containing both pistils and stamens, making them perfect.

THIMBLEWEED

Anemone virginiana

Buttercup Family

There are several thimbleweeds in our area and they can be distinguished only by technical, botanical inspection. The one shown grows in open woods, thickets, and clearings and is less than three feet tall. It has hairy dark green leaves that are heavily veined. On the lower, larger leaves (not shown) the segments of the leaf blades curl towards the base. The flower is at the top of the stout stem and is from two-thirds to one and one-half inches broad. It has five greenish-white sepals that look like petals. The receptacle on which the flower rests grows larger after the flower fades and becomes thimble-shaped.

VIRGIN'S BOWER
Clematis virginiana
Buttercup Family

Virgin's Bower is a beautiful trailing vine which climbs over other plants and shrubs to a height of ten feet or more. Leaf stalks act as tendrils which coil around other plants as a means of support. Virgin's Bower is quite common in moist places along lanes, at edges of woods, or on stream banks. The dark green leaf blades are usually divided into three sharply-toothed segments. Small flowers with four greenish-white sepals and no real petals are arranged in flat clusters. Male flowers (staminate) are on one plant, and female flowers (pistillate) flowers are on others, and they are cross fertilized by bees. The fruits have a feathery tail or plume and are very conspicuous in the late summer. These feathery clusters give rise to another common name, Old Man's Beard.

GOLDTHREAD
Coptis groenlandica
Buttercup Family

Goldthread is a small plant from three to six inches tall which grows from a thin yellow underground stem which looks like a root. This "root" has been used for dyes and medicines and is said to be helpful in curing canker sores if chewed. Several leafless stalks grow on each plant and each bears a single flower at the tip. The flower is about three-fourths of an inch broad and has from five to seven showy white sepals and insignificant small, club-like petals. The showy sepals are white inside, but are often shaded with brown or gray on the back. The shiny evergreen leaves have three wedge-shaped parts and the underside is a paler color.

24

BLACK COHOSH
or BUGBANE
Cimcifuga racemosa
Buttercup Family

Bugbane grows in moist shady woods to a height of from three to eight feet. It has enormous, stalked leaves which are divided into sets of three, then are re-divided into sets of three toothed, cut, leaflets. One leaf is so large and has so many divided leaflets, that one might think it is a large branch with many leaves. A wand-like spike of white flowers towers high above the leaves. These flowers have a very unpleasant odor — even to insects which appear to avoid the plant. The four or five white petal-like sepals fall early and leave bushy tufts of numerous stamens centered by a single pistil. This pistil becomes a small seed pod which makes an odd rattling sound when it is dried.

RED BANEBERRY
Actaea rubra
Buttercup Family

The Red Baneberry grows to be between one and two feet in height. It can be found growing in shaded woodlands and thickets. If there is a woodland spring or stream nearby, one is likely to find a Red Baneberry growing in the shadows beside it.

The tiny white flowers are arranged in a dense cluster at the end of the stem. Each individual flower has from four to ten petals and numerous white stamens which tend to give it a feathery appearance when viewed from a distance.

After the flowers have gone by, a cluster of scarlet-red poisonous berries appears. Each berry has a black dot at the end, is on its own separate stem, and is about one-half inch long.

The leaves are pointed and sharply toothed with either rounded or pointed teeth. The leaves are arranged in groups of three and the veins on the leaves are very noticeable.

WHITE BANEBERRY

Actaea pachypoda or alba

Buttercup Family

What a delight to find White Baneberry in the fruiting stage growing in moist, rich woods and thickets! This fruit cluster is very conspicuous in mid or late summer. Each fruit is an oval, white berry with a dark spot at the tip. The central stem of the cluster is red and each berry is on a thick red stalk. The berries are poisonous and can cause serious illness or death.

White Baneberry is an erect, bushy plant with large leaves which are divided into many smaller toothed leaflets. It grows to a height of from one to two feet. The tiny white flowers are in a thick, oblong, feathery cluster which is above the leaves. Each flower has four or five tiny sepals which fall as the flowers open. There are from four to ten small, white, flat petals and numerous stamens. This tuft of white stamens gives the "feathery" look to the flower cluster.

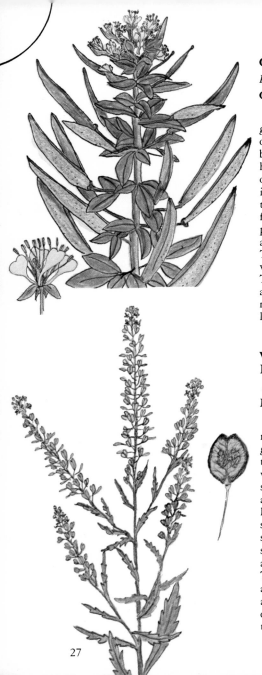

CLAMMY WEED

Polanisia graveolens

Caper Family

Clammy Weed grows on sandy or gravelly banks and shores to a height of from six to eighteen inches. It is a branching plant that is sticky and hairy, and has leaves similar to those on a clover plant. Each leaf is divided into three, oval segments with toothless margins. The yellowish-white flowers are in long, leafy clusters. The petals have long claws at their base and broad, notched tips. (See insert) There are from nine to twelve stamens which may be longer than the petals. The sepals are slightly unequal, and are purplish in color. The rough pod may be nearly two inches long on larger plants.

WILD PEPPERGRASS or POOR-MAN'S PEPPER

Lepidium virginicum   27

Mustard Family

Peppergrass is common along roadsides and in wasteplaces where it grows to a height of from six to twenty-four inches. It is a branching weed with peppery-tasting circular seed pods which are clustered thickly around the flower stems. Upper stem leaves are deeply toothed and have short stalks which do not embrace the stem. Basal leaves have stalks with small lobes on each side of the mid rib and a large, toothed, terminal lobe. The tiny, white, four-petaled flowers are in a long cluster which lengthens as the bottom flowers go to seed. The circular fruit has an indentation at the tip.

HOARY ALYSSUM

Berteroa incana

Mustard Family

Hoary Alyssum is a hairy plant with stiff branched stems. It grows as a weed in waste places to a height of from one to two feet. The leaves are alternate on the stem and are long and untoothed. The tiny white flowers have four deeply notched petals. Eliptical hairy seedpods with a point at the tip develop as the flowers fade.

FIELD PENNY-CRESS

Thlaspi arvense

Mustard Family

Field Penny-cress is a common weed. It has wide-toothed leaves on the stem and no basal leaves. The four-petaled white flowers line the top of the stem and open from the bottom upwards. As the flowers fade, a flat, round, deeply notched seed pod appears. The pod is nearly one-half inch broad when mature and is winged. Several seeds are in each of the two cells.

28

SHEPHERD'S PURSE
Capsella bursa-pastoris
Mustard Family

Shepherd's Purse is an insignificant weed of lawns and waste places. It grows to a height of from six to twenty inches. There is a circle of dandelion-like leaves at the bottom of the plant and toothed leaves on the stem. The flower stalk contains many flowers on short stems which branch off from the main stem. The bottom buds open first. Each tiny flower (1/12 inch broad) is white and has four petals. When the flowers fade, a triangular seed pod forms. The seed has a center seam and the two halves are puffed out like a purse.

TRUE WATER CRESS
Nasturtium officinale
Mustard Family

Water Cress is a smooth, floating or creeping plant which grows in brooks or in ditches. It is from four to ten inches high. The tiny white flowers have four petals and are from one-half to one and one-third inches long. The juicy oval leaves are divided into from three to nine parts, but most leaves have five parts. These oval leaves have a pungent refreshing taste and are used in salads, sandwiches, or as a garnish for foods.

HORSERADISH

Armoracia lapathifolia

Mustard Family

Horseradish is a plant which grows in moist wasteland to a height of from two to four feet. It has a thick root which may be ground up and used in food preparation and as a medicine. The large long-stalked basal leaves are from six to ten inches long. The flowers are in terminal racemes which arise from the upper leaf axils. They are small and have four white petals. The tiny seed pods are egg-shaped, but fall early, often before the seeds inside are perfected.

LAKE CRESS

Armoracia aquatica

Mustard Family

Lake Cress is a rather uncommon — but native — perennial which grows in the quiet water of lakes and streams. It is a weak plant which grows from a submerged, slender root. It has simple or branching stems whose tips show above the water. The submerged leaves are divided into numerous hair-like segments, but the stem leaves above the water are lance-shaped or elliptical and have toothed margins. The white flowers have four white petals. Each flower is about one-half to three-fourths inch wide. Flowers are in clusters above the surface of the water. Each flower is on its own pedicel (flower stem) which lengthens as the flower opens.

30

ALPINE CRESS
Cardamine bellidifolia
Mustard Family

Alpine Cress is a smooth, tufted, dwarf perennial only two to five inches high. It grows on alpine summits of New England mountains by brooks, in cold ravines, or on wet, mossy rocks. The lower leaves have long petioles (leaf stalks) and egg-shaped blades. The margins may have a few rounded teeth or have no teeth at all. Upper leaves have shorter petioles. From one to five white flowers are in terminal clusters. Each has four white petals about twice as long as the calyx. The erect linear pods may be from three-fourths to one and a fourth inches long.

SLENDER-LEAVED SUNDEW
Drosera linearis
Sundew Family

The leaves of this Sundew are very narrow and are usually longer than the flower-bearing stalk. There are from one to four white flowers on each plant, often solitary on individual flower stalks. It grows in bogs and wet sand to a height of from two to five inches.

ROUND-LEAVED SUNDEW
Drosera rotundifolia
Sundew Family

This plant grows in acid or peaty soil of bogs and swamps to a height of from four to twelve inches. Usually Sundew plants grow close together in mat-like clusters. The small, round

leaves are at the base of the plant on long slender stalks. Each leaf is covered with reddish glandular hairs which give off moisture like tiny dew drops. The leafless flower stalk bears from three to fifteen flowers which have five white petals and a greenish "eye."

SPATULATE-LEAVED SUNDEW

Drosera intermedia

Sundew Family

This Sundew has longer, more oval shaped leaves. The blades are up to an inch long and are broader towards the tip. The leaf stems are smooth and erect and up to two inches long. This Sundew grows in acid bogs — especially near the coast — to a height of from two to eight inches. The leaves are in a circle at the base of the flower stem and have glandular hairs only on the upper surface. The flowers are white and are born on leafless flower stalks.

THREAD-LEAVED SUNDEW

Drosera filiformis

Sundew Family

This sundew has sticky glandular hairs on erect string-like leaves. The small purplish-white flowers are on a long, curved stalk. They begin to open at the bottom and open a few at a time. The plant is from eight to ten inches tall and grows in damp sand on coastal plains.

LIVELONG SAXIFRAGE

Saxigraga aizoon

Saxifrage Family

This saxifrage lives on dry rocks or in limy gravel or rocks and is seldom more than a foot tall. It spreads by stolens, so that several plants may be joined together. There is a lime-encrusted pore on the upper surface at the base of each tooth on the margin of the leaf. There are small leaves on the stem, but larger, leathery, basal leaves are in a dense rosette at the base of the stem. These leaves are broadest near the round tip, and have toothed margins. There are several flowers with broad white petals in a flatish flower cluster at the top of the erect stem. The petals are sometimes spotted with red. Each flower has five sepals, five petals, ten stamens, and two pistils which are joined together at their base and produce a joined seed pod. The base of the flower is cuplike.

GRASS-OF-PARNASSUS

Parnassia glauca

Saxifrage Family

This plant grows in wet meadows — especially those with limy soil — to a height of from eight inches to two feet. It is not a grass, and can be easily identified by the lined-flowers at the tips of the stems. Each stem has one stalkless leaf which embraces the stem. The broad, basal leaves are on long stalks and may be blue-green in color. The flowers have five spreading, white petals with conspicuous green veins running lengthwise. There are five yellow stamens alternating with the petals.

MEADOWSWEET

Spiraea latifolia

Rose Family

Meadowsweet — also called Quaker Lady — grows in sparse woods, openings, or at edges of fields to a height of three or four feet. It is a branching shrub which is a close relative to Steeplebush on page 111 but has a smooth, reddish stem and *white flowers* instead of deep pink. The small, oval leaves are on short stalks, have toothed margins, and are a paler color on the under side. The dainty five-petaled white (or pink tinged) flowers are in a dense, terminal cluster. Each tiny flower is about one-fourth of an inch broad, has five spreading petals, and a tuft of numerous stamens in the center.

WOOD STRAWBERRY

Fragaria vesca

Rose Family

Wood Strawberry is a tufted plant less than a foot tall which grows in rocky woods or open places. It is also called Sow-Teat and Hedge Strawberry. It differs from Wild Strawberry because the achenes (seeds) are on the surface of the fruit and not embedded in it. It may be found blooming into August. The leaf and flower stalks have spreading hairs. The leaves are divided into three firm, dark-green leaflets which are strongly veined on the top and are deeply toothed at the margins. There are from one to nine white flowers in the cluster which often rise above the leaves. The strawberry is more cone-shaped than round, and does not have the rich deep red color of the earlier wild strawberry. It is good to eat.

34

THREE-TOOTHED CINQUEFOIL

Potentilla tridentata

Rose Family

The Three-Toothed Cinquefoil is a tiny plant which grows in great patches at high elevations and on dry, rocky slopes. It has white blossoms with many long yellow stamens. The leaves are mostly near the base. Each is divided into three segments which are three-toothed at the end. These leaves turn deep red in the fall.

QUEEN-OF-THE-MEADOWS

Filipendula ulmaria

Rose Family

Queen-of-the-meadows is similar to Queen-of-the-prairie on page 112, but it has white flowers. It is an escape from cultivation and is said to have been used for medicinal purposes and for a fermented beverage called mead. It grows along roads and in thickets to a height of from two to four feet. The branching stem bears divided leaves which are covered with a white down on the underside. The end leaf segment has from three to five toothed lobes and is larger than the side leaf segments. Numerous five-petaled white flowers are in a spreading cluster at the summit of the stem. Twenty or more stamens form a tuft in the center of each fragrant flower and give a feathery appearance to the cluster. Other common names for this flower are Sweet Hay, Meadow Queen, and Honey Sweet.

WHITE AVENS

Geum canadense

Rose Family

White Avens is a straggling, branching plant which is up to four feet tall. It can be either smooth or hairy. The principal leaves have three pointed segments, but the upper ones may be simple and the lower ones may have five parts. The flowers are replaced by bristly seed-like fruits, each section of which has a tiny "tail" which is formed by the styles. This plant grows at edges of woods and in thickets.

BAKED-APPLE BERRY or CLOUDBERRY

Rubus chamaemorus

Rose Family

This plant grows in bogs and on wet mountain slopes. It has creeping underground stems from which erect stalks grow to a height of from three to eight inches. The solitary flower has white petals and a tuft of numerous yellow-tipped stamens in the center. It commonly has two or three broad five-lobed leaves with toothed margins. The fruit is a peach-colored, red-orange, or yellow berry which is edible, and has the flavor of baked apples.

36

SWAMP BLACKBERRY

Rubus hispidus

Rose Family

There are many blackberry or
dewberry plants in our area, but this
Hispid Swamp Blackberry or Running
Swamp Blackberry blooms later than
many of the others. It rarely grows in
dry soil, and is usually found in swales,
swamps, and in low ground. The stems
are slender, slightly woody, and are
creeping. There are erect branches
rising from the creeping stem which
may be from four to twelve inches tall.
There are weak bristles on the
creeping stems, and the upright
branches may or may not have
prickles. The leaves are lustrous, dark
green on top, and may be bronze or
purple-tinged on the under surface.
They are mostly evergreen. Each leaf is
on a long stalk, and is divided into
three oblong-pointed leaflets with
toothed margins. There are bristles
along the midrib on the underside of
the leaf. The white flowers are in lax
clusters on long flower stalks which
rise from the top of the branch or
from the leaf axils. The five petals are
longer than the sepals which are very
hairy. The fruit which forms later is a
small reddish berry resembling the
common blackberry. When it is ripe it
is nearly black, and it is very sweet.

DEWDROP

Dalibarda repens

Rose Family

False Violet, Robin-Run-Away,
Dalibarda are other names given to
this low, spreading plant. It grows in
rich woods to a height of from two to
five inches. The downy leaves are
nearly round and have finely scalloped

edges. They are on long petioles (leaf stalks). The flowers are on separate reddish stalks. Each flower is about one-half inch broad, has five petals, and a tuft of bushy stamens in the center.

CANADIAN GREAT BURNET
Sanguisorba canadensis
Rose Family

Burnet grows in wet soil of swamps, bogs, and ditches to a height of from one to six feet. It is a tall, showy plant with compound, rose-like foliage and long-stalked spikes of feathery, white flowers. The lower flowers on the spike open first while the upper part is still tightly budded. The leaves are divided into many oval leaflets with short stalks and small-toothed margins. The small flowers are crowded on dense spikes which may be as long as eight inches. Four white sepals take the place of the petals, and there are four long, club-shaped, white stamens which protrude from the center of each small flower. This gives the spike its feathery appearance.

WHITE CLOVER
Trifolium repens
Pea Family

This is the common clover found on lawns and in fields. The flowers and leaves are on separate stalks arising from creeping runners. The leaf-segments are broad, toothed, and usually have a pale triangular-shaped mark on each leaflet. The flowers are tiny and pea-like, but are arranged in roundish heads. They turn from white to pinkish to brown as they age and turn downward.

ALSIKE CLOVER

Trifolium hybridum

Pea Family

This clover has smooth stems from one to three feet tall. It grows along roads and in fields. The leaf segments are in sets of three, are elliptical in shape, and do not have the light-colored triangle on them that the white clover does. The flowers are creamy white tinged with peach color, but very quickly fade and turn brown.

WHITE SWEET-CLOVER

Melilotus alba

Pea Family

This sweet clover grows along roadsides and in waste lands to a height of from two to eight feet. The leaves are divided into three narrow clover-like leaflets which are rarely longer than one inch. These are toothed on the outer half and are very fragrant when crushed. The small white flowers are arranged in numerous slender, tapering clusters which grow from leaf axils. Each individual flower is not more than one-fourth of an inch in length.

HAIRY BUSH CLOVER

Lespedeza hirta

Pea Family

This bush clover grows in dry or sandy places in open woods and along roadsides to a height of from two to five feet. It has stiff, stout stems which are erect and branching. It is densely

hairy. The leaves are divided into three oval or roundish leaflets which are blunt at each end. There is sometimes a notch at the tip of each leaflet and the petioles are shorter than the leaflets are. The clover-like flowers are in dense, cylindric heads on long stalks. The flowers are creamy or yellowish-white and there is usually a purple spot near the base of the upper petal. The calyx is pointed and hairy, and the fruit pod which forms later is oval, pointed, and hairy.

COMMON WOOD-SORREL

Oxalis montana

Wood-Sorrel Family

Wood-sorrel grows in rich, cool woods to a height of three or four inches and usually spreads to cover large areas. Each leaf is divided into three heart-shaped leaflets and looks like a shamrock. Each flower has five white or pale pink petals which are strongly veined with pink. Sometimes the tips of the petals are deeply notched.

SENECA SNAKEROOT

Polygala senega

Milkwort Family

Seneca Snakeroot grows in dry or moist woods and rocky places to a height of from six to eighteen inches. There are usually several upright stems originating from the same base. The tiny white flowers are pea-like with broad white wings. They are arranged in a slender, dense terminal cluster. Narrow lance-shaped leaves are attached singly to the stem.

40

WHORLED MILKWORT

Polygala verticillata

Milkwort Family

This milkwort grows in fields or along roadsides in dry, sterile, open habitats. It is seldom more than a foot tall. This milkwort is distinguished from others because most of its leaves are in whorls of from three to seven at each level. The long, slender leaves have a slight bristle at the tip. There are no basal leaves. The greenish, white, or magenta-tipped flowers are clustered in dense, conical spikes which are nearly an inch long. Each tiny flower is on a tiny stalk. There are five sepals; three are small and greenish and two are larger and look like petals. There are three petals which are united with each other and with the stamen tube.

FLOWERING SPURGE

Euphorbia corollata

Spurge Family

Flowering Spurge is an erect, smooth plant with one or more branching stems with oval, alternate leaves. The stem is often spotted, and will emit a milky juice when it is broken. It grows to a height of from ten inches to three feet in dry soil of open woods, clearings, fields, or roadsides. The smooth oval leaves are bright green in color. There is a whorl of leaves just below the flower cluster. The rather showy flowers are in a flat cluster rising from the center of the top whorl of leaves. Each cluster is make up of five or six smaller clusters. Five cup-shaped bracts which look like five white petals surround a tiny cluster of real flowers. One female

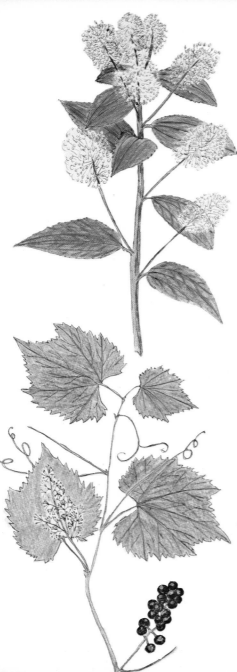

flower is in the center, and it is surrounded by numerous male flowers. The two other common names for this plant are Tramp's Spurge and Wild Hippo.

NEW JERSEY TEA OR REDROOT

Ceanothus americanus

Buckthorn Family

New Jersey Tea is a low shrub with several or many erect stems rising from a deep-reddish root. The woody stem is brownish-green or bronze-colored. It grows in sandy or dry soil in open woods and fields or on rocky banks. It is usually from one to four feet tall. During Revolutionary times, American soldiers brewed tea from the dried leaves of this plant. The dull green leaves are alternate on the stem. They have a pointed tip, rounded base, and finely-toothed margins. The leaf has three conspicuous nerves and is hairy on the underside.

Tiny creamy-white flowers with five petals are in dense, cone-shaped clusters on long stalks which rise from axils of the leaves or from the ends of the branches. The plumy flower cluster has a pleasant odor, and the three-lobed fruit which forms later is nearly black when it is mature.

RIVER GRAPE

Vitus vulpina

Vine Family

Other names for this vine are Winter Grape, Frost Grape, and Chicken Grape. It grows on banks of rivers, in rich thickets, or near water. It is a high-climbing vine with shining, light-green leaves, and tendrils at irregular places along the stem. The

42

leaves usually have three sharply-toothed, pointed lobes. The leaves are alternate and are on long stalks. The tiny fragrant flowers are in a long compound cluster on a stalk arising from the leaf axil. The fruits are black grapes with bluish powder on them. They are about one half inch in diameter, and are rather sweet further west. Here in the northeast, they ripen later and are more apt to be sour until the frost hits them to sweeten them.

MARSHMALLOW
MARSH MALLOW

Althaea officinalis

Mallow Family

Marshmallow is a tall, many-flowered plant which was formerly cultivated for a substance in the roots from which medicine and marshmallow were made. It now grows wild at edges of salt or fresh marshes to a height of from two to four feet. The heart-shaped leaves are downy and are gray-green in color. They have coarsely-toothed or shallowly-lobed margins. Lower leaves may be either heart shaped or be cut into three distinct lobes. The showy pink or pale rose-colored flowers are clustered in axils of leaves. They have five petals and are from one to one-and-a-half inches broad.

BIENNIAL GAURA

Gaura biennis

Evening Primrose Family

Gaura is a rather straggling, downy plant with long branches bearing small leaves and ending in wand-like clusters of small white flowers. It grows in

meadows, prairies and open woodlands and shores to a height of from two to five feet, though occasionally it may be taller. The leaves are attached singly on the stem. They taper at both ends and have outward-pointing teeth on the margins. The long-tubed flowers bloom two or three at a time. Each has four white petals and eight stamens which are on the end of a tube which extends beyond the ovary. The pistil in the center has a cross-shaped tip (stigma) which is typical to many other flowers in this family.

43

SMALLER ENCHANTER'S NIGHTSHADE

Circaea alpina

Evening Primrose Family

Smaller Enchanter's Nightshade is a fragile plant found in openings in cool, moist woods where it often grows in large patches. Elongated clusters of white flowers rise above the leaves and give a "lacy" appearance to the patch of green. The whole plant is usually less than a foot tall. The thin, fragile leaves are opposite, and have coarsely-toothed margins. They come to an abrupt rather than tapering point. The very unique flowers have only *two* sepals, *two* petals and *two* stamens. The white petals may be so deeply cut that there seems to be four petals.

LARGER ENCHANTER'S NIGHTSHADE

Circaea quadrisulcata

Evening Primrose Family

This larger species is very similar to the one at the left, but grows to be from one to two feet tall. The paired leaves are irregularly toothed, are rather firm, and are dark green on the top. The ripe fruit (see insert) has from three to five corrugations on each face and contains strong hooked bristles.

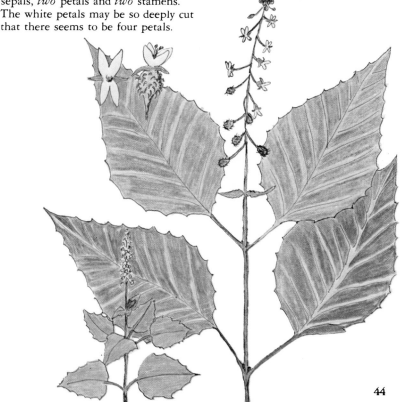

AMERICAN SPIKENARD

Aralia racemosa

Ginseng Family

The first time I saw American Spikenard growing, I told my companion that "it looks like an overgrown sarsaparilla." He laughed and said, "That's just what it is!" Indeed, it is a close relative of Aralia nudicaulis on page 46.

This large prickless-plant is very branching and grows to a height of from two to ten feet. It grows in rich woods and thickets and is known for its large, spicy, aromatic root. The slightly downy leaves are divided into three (rarely five) compound divisions. These divisions are sub-divided into thin heart-shaped leaf segments with sharply-toothed margins and a pointed tip. The greenish-white flowers are in compound clusters along the main stem. The fruit is purple. Other names given to this plant are Petty Morrel, Life-of-Man, Spice Bush, and Old Maid's Root.

BRISTLY SARSAPARILLA
Aralia hispida
Ginseng Family

This Sarsaparilla is easily distinguished from the one below by the bristles on the woody stem. The plant is larger and more branching. The stem bears several leaves which are divided into segments. The umbels *are not* on separate stalks, but attached right to the leaf-bearing stems. This plant grows in dry woods and along roadsides and railroad beds to a height of from one to three feet.

WILD SARSAPARILLA
Aralia nudicaulis
Ginseng Family

This plant has one large umbrella-like leaf which is divided into three segments and then divided again to give the appearance of a leafy branch. The single leafless flowering stalk is shorter than the leaf stem and is also divided — usually into threes but up to seven parts. Each part bears a round, ball-like cluster (umbel) at the tip. The individual flowers' in this umbel are greenish white with five turned-back petals in a cup-shaped calyx. Five white stamens protrude from each flower and give the umbels a fuzzy appearance. Wild Sarsparilla grows in open woods to a height of from eight to sixteen inches.

46

GINSENG
Panax quinquefolius
Ginseng Family

Ginseng is also called Sang and Red-Berry. It grows in rich, cool woods to a height of from eight to sixteen inches, but it is now very rare. This species with the tuberous root shaped like a human body is prized by Chinese for medicine. Our ginsengs are now very rare because roots were dug extensively and sold. *DO NOT PICK* Ginseng if you are lucky enough to know where it grows. The erect, simple stem has a solitary whorl of three, long-stalked leaves. Each leaf is then divided into five smaller, oval leaflets with toothed margins. The small, rounded, flower cluster on a slender stalk is made up of from six to twenty white or yellow-green flowers. Each plant usually has only one flower umbel. The fruit is a cluster of red berries.

WATER PENNYWORT or MARSH PENNYWORT
Hydrocotyl americana
Parsley Family

This small fragile plant grows in wet places in meadows and woods. It is a branching and creeping plant with thread-like stems and tiny white or greenish flowers growing in clusters at the leaf axils. There are also runners which originate in the axils of the leaves. The very thin, shiny leaves are rather round and have a delicately scalloped or shallowly lobed margin. They are deeply notched at the base and are on long petioles (leaf stalks). The weak, pale green, smooth stem frequently takes root at the joints.

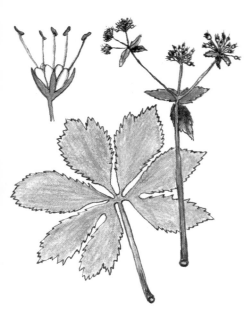

BLACK SNAKEROOT

Sanicula marilandica

Parsley Family

This plant grows in thickets and rich woods to a height of from one to four feet. It has a hollow stem and long-stalked blue-green leaves. They are divided into five parts, but the two lower leaflets are so deeply lobed that it has the appearance of seven parts. The tiny flowers are greenish-white and are arranged in small uneven umbels. There are leafy bracts at the base of these umbels. The fruit is an oval-shaped bur with many hooked bristles on it. The green sepals are nearly the same length as the white petals, but the stamens protrude far out.

POISON HEMLOCK

Conium maculatum

Parsley Family

This is a large branching plant found in wastelands growing to a height of from two to six feet. It has dark green fern-like leaves which are broadly triangular in general outline but are deeply cut. The stems are hollow, grooved and are spotted with purple, and have a very unpleasant odor when crushed. The juice is poisonous.

BULB-BEARING WATER HEMLOCK

Circuta bulbifera

Parsley Family

This is an erect, slender, branching plant which grows in swamps and wet thickets to a height of from one to nearly four feet. It rises from a fleshy, tuberous root. The leaves are divided and then divided again into long, linear, toothed segments. The upper leaves are more threadlike, and there are numerous *bulblets in the axils of upper* leaves. This is the identifying characteristic to look for. The tiny, white flowers are in umbels like other plants in this family. The fruit is a broad-oval, ribbed capsule.

WATER HEMLOCK or SPOTTED COWBANE

Cicuta maculata

Parsley Family

This poisonous plant grows in wet meadows, ditches, and swamps to a height of from three to six feet. It has a smooth, stout, much-branched stem that is streaked with purple. The leaves are divided into two or three sections and each section is re-divided into many coarsely toothed, pointed leaflets which are often tinged with red. The illustration shows one entire leaf with its many leaflets. A distinctive characteristic to help in identifying this plant is the veins in the leaflets. They run from the midrib to the notches *between* the teeth — not to the tips of the teeth as on most leaves. The flowers are tiny and have five tiny petals. They are arranged in numerous umbels above the leafy portion of the plant. The umbels are sometimes as large as four inches across.

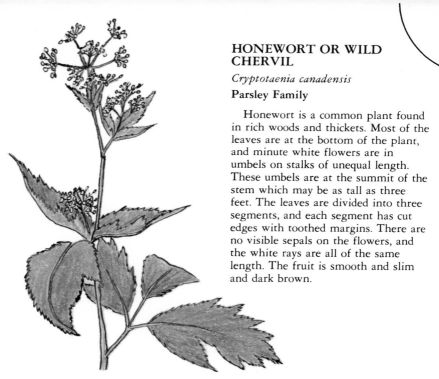

HONEWORT OR WILD CHERVIL
Cryptotaenia canadensis
Parsley Family

Honewort is a common plant found in rich woods and thickets. Most of the leaves are at the bottom of the plant, and minute white flowers are in umbels on stalks of unequal length. These umbels are at the summit of the stem which may be as tall as three feet. The leaves are divided into three segments, and each segment has cut edges with toothed margins. There are no visible sepals on the flowers, and the white rays are all of the same length. The fruit is smooth and slim and dark brown.

CARAWAY
Carum carvi
Parsley Family

Caraway grows in waste places and neglected fields to a height of from one to two feet. It has umbels of small white flowers both at the top of the plant and arising from the leaf axils. The leaves are very narrowly cut into thread-like division. The stems are hollow and hairless. There are two distinctive characteristics helpful in identification. The slightly curved, ribbed seeds which are aromatic and are used in cooking is one. The other is the fact that the flower cluster usually does not have leaf bracts under it as do other members in this family.

50

BURNET SAXIFRAGE

Pimpinella saxifraga

Parsley Family

Burnet Saxifrage is a smooth, erect perennial which is very branching. It grows along roadsides, in fields and wasteplaces, and on shores to a height of one or two feet. Most of the leaves are near the base of the plant. The lowest leaves have from four to ten pairs of coarsely-toothed leaflets along a central stalk. Each leaflet is round in general outline and does not have a pointed tip. The upper stem leaves are shorter stalked and have fewer pairs of narrower segments. The tiny white flowers are in flat-topped umbels with from seven to twenty smaller clusters within the umbel. A distinctive characteristic is the lack of a circle of bracts at the base of the umbel.

WATER PARSNIP

Sium suave

Parsley Family

This fragrant plant grows in swamps, or on muddy shores where its base is partly submerged in water. It may vary in height from two to six feet. The erect stem has furrows and strong ridges and the stem branches above the middle of the plant. It is easily distinguished from deadly poisonous Cicuta maculata (See page 49) by this corrugated stem and the leaves. The basal leaves are finely-dissected and may be submerged in water, but upper leaves are divided into very narrow, pointed segments with evenly-toothed margins. Tiny, white flowers are in large flat umbels at the top of the plant. Below each flower umbel is a circle of small, narrow, green bracts.

51

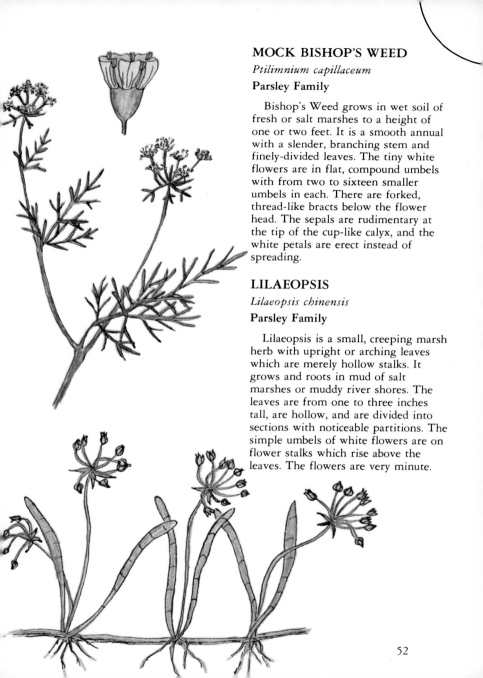

MOCK BISHOP'S WEED

Ptilimnium capillaceum

Parsley Family

Bishop's Weed grows in wet soil of fresh or salt marshes to a height of one or two feet. It is a smooth annual with a slender, branching stem and finely-divided leaves. The tiny white flowers are in flat, compound umbels with from two to sixteen smaller umbels in each. There are forked, thread-like bracts below the flower head. The sepals are rudimentary at the tip of the cup-like calyx, and the white petals are erect instead of spreading.

LILAEOPSIS

Lilaeopsis chinensis

Parsley Family

Lilaeopsis is a small, creeping marsh herb with upright or arching leaves which are merely hollow stalks. It grows and roots in mud of salt marshes or muddy river shores. The leaves are from one to three inches tall, are hollow, and are divided into sections with noticeable partitions. The simple umbels of white flowers are on flower stalks which rise above the leaves. The flowers are very minute.

SCOTCH LOVAGE

Ligusticum scothicum

Parsley Family

This plant has stout purple stems
which are more or less branched. It
grows along rocky and sandy seashores
to a height of twelve to twenty-four
inches. The shiny, thick leaves are
nine-parted and are grouped in sets of
three pointed, sharply-toothed leaflets.
The white flowers are tiny and are
grouped in umbels at the top of the
plant and at the end of the branches.
Each umbel is in turn divided into
smaller umbels.

SEA COAST ANGELICA

Coelopleurum lucidum

Parsley Family

This is a stout maritime perennial
which grows along rocky or gravelly
coasts in cooler regions. The plant may
be from one to four feet tall. It is
usually smooth, except for the hairs
under the flower umbel. The stem may
have gummy spots on it. The leaves
are divided into three parts which are
then re-divided into three, thin,
irregularly-cut leaflets. There is a very
large, inflated sheath at the base of the
leaf stalk. This sheath is heart shaped.
The tiny greenish-white flowers are in
a compound umbel which may have
from twenty to fifty smaller umbels in
it. The central umbel on the plant is
the largest, and may be from three to
five inches broad. The oval fruits have
prominent, nearly equal, corky ribs
which are not winged.

HEMLOCK-PARSLEY

Conioselinum chinense

Parsley Family

Hemlock-Parsley resembles Poison Hemlock on page 48. It is harmless, but because of its similarity to Poison Hemlock and the possibility of mistaking one for the other, the amateur would be wisest to leave *both* of them alone.

Hemlock-Parsley grows to a height of two to five feet in thickets, meadows, woods, or in cold swamps. The leaves are divided into leaflets and re-divided into finely cut segments. The leaf stalk forms a wide sheath with translucent margins. The small white flowers have five petals with incurved tips and are arranged in flat umbels which may be six inches across on larger plants. The thick, oval, flattened fruit has side ribs which extend into broad wings.

ANGELICA

Angelica venenosa

Parsley Family

Angelica is a tall plant which is said to be very poisonous. It grows in dry woods, thickets, and openings to a height up to six feet. This member of the Parsley family may be distinguished from others by the fine down on the stem. The basal and lower leaves are divided and re-divided into thick oblong leaflets with toothed margins. The upper leaves are merely linear or lance-shaped sheaths which may or may not have small leaf blades. The sheaths are very broad and showy. Tiny whitish-green flowers are in a broad umbel which has no more than

54

thirty-five smaller umbels in it. The fruits are downy and have three ribs at the center of each face and two "wings" at each margin.

PURPLE ANGELICA

Angelica atropurpurea

Parsley Family

Purple Angelica is a very large plant — sometimes as tall as nine feet. It grows along streams and in swamps or wet woods. It has a dark purple stem and the stalks of the upper leaves have a papery swollen sheath which almost encircles the stem. The leaf branch is *attached to this sheath,* not to the main stem itself. This branch has three smaller branches, and then each is redivided into five sharply-toothed, uneven leaflets of differing shapes and sizes. The tiny white flowers are in umbels from four to eight inches across. The umbels are also re-divided into from twenty to forty-five smaller umbels. This is called a compound umbel.

COW-PARSNIP or MASTERWORT

Heracleum maximum

Parsley Family

Cow-Parsnip grows in moist ground to a height of from four to ten feet. It is a huge, stout, plant with compound leaves and a wooly, grooved stem. The stem is hollow, and may be two inches thick at the base. The rank-smelling plant has a distinctive inflated sheath at the base of the leaf stalk. The huge leaves are often over a foot broad.

They are divided into three sections, and each section is shaped like a maple leaf with toothed margins. The white flowers are arranged in spreading, flat-topped clusters which may be from six to twelve inches broad. The cluster is a compound umbel, because it has from eight to thirty smaller clusters within the giant umbel. The petals are wedge-shaped or clawed with a notch at the tip. They are white, but may be purple-tinged on some plants. The outer flowers on the flat cluster are often larger than the inner ones.

QUEEN ANNE'S LACE

Daucus carota

Parsley Family

This plant has many names. Wild Carrot, Bird's Nest, and Queen Anne's Lace are only a few. It grows in fields and dry waste places to a height of from one to four feet. It has flat-topped clusters of tiny white five-petaled flowers. Usually there are one or two tiny sterile purple flowers in the center of the flat head. This plant is hated by dairy farmers, because it gives an unpleasant flavor to milk produced by cows who eat it. Note the three stiff green bracts below the flower head. These curve upwards and the outer edges of the cluster curl to form a cup-shaped bunch of brown wool resembling a bird's nest when the flower goes to seed.

BUNCHBERRY
Cornus canadensis
Dogwood Family

The Bunchberry is a beautiful little herb which grows in large patches in cool woodlands all across the northern United States and Canada. A first glance would tell us that the flower has four white petals, but this is not true.

From the center of a circle of leaves grows a tiny stem which supports four white bracts and a tiny insignificant cluster of greenish-white blossoms in the center.

The whole plant seldom reaches a height of more than six or eight inches. When the flowers fade, a cluster of brilliant red berries forms. The berries are edible, though many consider them tasteless. They are quite seedy, and not good for pies.

ONE-FLOWERED WINTERGREEN
Moneses uniflora
Wintergreen Family

This lovely little wildflower is found in the deep woods — usually under pine trees. It is seldom more than four or five inches tall and usually even shorter than that. The thin, roundish leaves are veiny and have toothed margins. The solitary flower is usually in a nodding or side position. There are five rounded petals with uneven edges, ten stamens in a circle around the protruding pistil in the center. There are five green sepals on the back of the flower. The petals are usually white, but may be a delicate rose color.

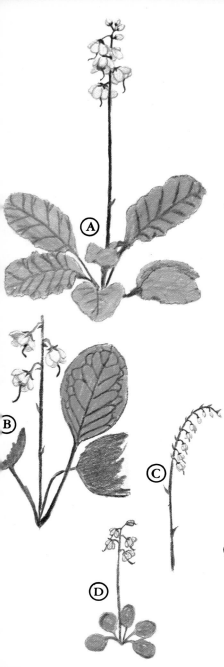

PYROLA
Wintergreen Family

The flower at the top of the page shows the typical shape of all Pyrolas. They all have a circle of basal leaves and a single leafless stalk. They vary in height from six to twelve inches. Distinctive characteristics which help in identification are given for four different pyrolas.

(A) SHINLEAF PYROLA

Pyrola elliptica is the most common pyrola. It has large dull green elliptical leaves which are rounded at the ends. The blade of the leaf is longer than the leaf stem. Note the long curving pistils protruding from the centers of the greenish-veined white flowers.

(B) ROUND-LEAVED PYROLA

Pyrola rotundifolia is similar to Shinleaf but is larger and has leaves which are shinier and rounder. The petioles (leaf stems) are often as long as the leaf blade itself. It has white petals and grows in woods and bogs.

(C) ONE-SIDED PYROLA

Pyrola secunda. Notice how the greenish-yellow flowers are arranged on only one side of the drooping stem. The leaf blades are shining, ovate, and toothed.

(D) GREENISH-FLOWERED PYROLA

Pyrola virens is a smaller pyrola and has thick broad leaf-blades with round ends and long stalks. The flowers are greenish and the style points downward, then turns up at the end.

58

INDIAN PIPE

Monotropa uniflora

Wintergreen Family

Indian Pipe is a parasitic plant which is usually waxy white but turns black as the fruit ripens. It is from two to twelve inches high and grows in rich, shady woods. The leaves are like white scales along the thick, fleshy stem. The single, odorless flower hangs with its tip towards the ground.

GIANT BIRD'S-NEST or PINEDROPS

Pterosporo andromedea

Wintergreen Family

This very rare plant is a parasite which grows under pine trees and other conifers to a height up to three feet. The tall leafless stalk is grooved and is covered with sticky hairs. The stalk is brown or purplish and has numerous brown scales at the base. The flowers vary from red to white, and the petals are joined together to form an inverted, bell-shaped vase.

SWAMP HONEYSUCKLE

Rhododendron viscosum

Heath Family

This is a much-branched shrub found in wet woods, swamps, and thickets. It is often as tall as six feet. The leaves are longer than wide, and the biggest part of the leaf is usually nearest to the tip of the leaf. The leaf tips can be either rounded or pointed. The trumpet-shaped white flowers have a long tube which is covered with fine, sticky, red hairs. The five long, curving stamens and the end of the pistil protrude about a half inch from the throat of the flower.

MOSS PLANT; CASSIOPE
Cassiope hypnoides
Heath Family

Cassiope is a low heath-like shrub which is much-branched, tufted, or moss-like. It grows to a height of from one to five inches in mossy alpine areas on mountain summits. It is an evergreen plant with needle-like leaves which overlap each other on the stem. Solitary bell or cup-shaped flowers nod from the tips of the branches. The flowers are white or tinged with rose. The corolla is five-cleft and has eight or ten stamens in the center.

WINTERGREEN or CHECKERBERRY
Gaultheria procumbens
Heath Family

Wintergreen is a low, spicy, semi-woody plant with creeping roots and underground stems. The branches are erect and upright and stand from two to six inches tall. Each stem bears several thick oblong evergreen leaves that are shiny on top and pale underneath. The flowers are white or sometimes touched with pink. They are bell-shaped and hang down from the curved stalk. They are found in woods and open places in sandy soil — especially near evergreen trees. The fruit is a bright red berry and often lasts throughout the winter until the new blossoms appear in spring.

BEARBERRY

Arctostaphylos uva-ursi

Heath Family

Bearberry is a trailing shrub with paddle-shaped leaves. This plant forms dense carpets several yards across and only a few inches tall. It grows in sandy or rocky places and is often used as a ground-cover by highway departments. The waxy white flowers hang in clusters from the tips of the plant. The flowers are urn-shaped with a small lobed mouth which is often tinged with pink. The fruit is a dull red berry which lasts into November. It is dry and mealy with a single stone inside. Other names for this plant are Kinnikinick, Mealberry, Hog-Cranberry, and Bousserole.

DIAPENSIA

Diapensia lapponica

Diapensia Family

Diapensia forms low, leafy, evergreen mats on rocks of high elevations. The mat is usually less than four inches tall. The stems are woody and are crowded with opposite, flat, blunt, unlobed leaves less than one-half inch long. The pretty white flowers rise above the leafy mats on short stalks. The corolla is a white, erect bell with a margin of five roundish lobes. The five yellow-tipped stamens are fastened between the five lobes of the flower.

61

STAR FLOWER
Trientalis borealis
Primrose Family

This is a dainty, fragile woodland plant with one whorl of pointed green leaves at the summit. There are from five to ten leaves in the whorl, and the plant grows to be from three to nine inches tall. From the center of the whorl, two tiny stemmed flowers arise. These flowers are white and have pointed petals. The flowers are about one-half inch wide and have about seven petals, though the number varies somewhat. There is one stamen for each petal, and the golden anthers at the tip of each stamen are clearly visible against the white petals.

BROOKWEED or WATER PIMPERNEL
Samolus parviflorus
Primrose Family

Brookweed grows in wet places in shallow water, mud, or sand to a height of from six inches to two feet. It is a smooth, leafy plant with tiny white flowers growing in spreading clusters at the top of the stem. The alternate, spoon-shaped leaves have the widest part of the blade towards the tip, and they taper to stalks. The basal leaves are in a circle around the stem of the plant. The flower has a five-parted, cup-shaped calyx and a bell-shaped, five-petaled corolla. There are five true stamens, five false ones, and one globe-shaped pistil.

FEATHERFOIL

Hottonia inflata

Primrose Family

Water Violet and Water Feather are other names given to this plant. It is an equatic herb with erect hollow flower stems which are almost leafless. The main stem is submerged and spongy. It grows in the late autumn and winter, and sometimes reaches the surface and flowers in the spring. It grows in pools and ditches or shallow, stagnant ponds. There are from three to eight inches showing above the water, but more of the plant is submerged. The leaves are dissected into thread-like divisions which are crowded at the base of the plant. The corolla is a short, five-part tube with five stamens. It is shorter than the five-part green caylx. (See the insert) The whitish flowers are whorled in clusters of from two to ten flowers at the joints of the hollow stem.

MARSH FELWORT

Lomatogonium rotatum

Gentian Family

This flower may be either blue or white. See page 277 in the blue section for details.

BUCKBEAN or MARSH TREFOIL

Menyanthes trifoliata

Gentian Family

This plant grows in shallow water
of ponds, marshes, and bogs to a
height of from four to twelve inches. It
has a stout stem with alternate leaves
near the base. Each leaf has three oval
leaflets. The white, funnel-shaped
flower has five recurved petals which
are fringed on the inner surface with
long white hairs. The flowers are in a
tight terminal cluster at the end of the
stem.

FLOATING HEARTS

Nymphoides cordata

Gentian Family

This plant has floating water-lily-
like leaves and an umbel of small
white flowers. It grows in quiet water
of ponds on very long, slender,
submerged stems. The leaf is broadly
oval with a heart-shaped base. If the
plant is sterile, there is only one
floating leaf, but if the plant is in
bloom, there are two or more leaves.
The corolla is white or cream-colored
with a short tube and five petals. The
calyx is parted nearly to the base and
has five oblong lobes.

CLASPING-LEAVED DOGBANE

Apocynum sibiricum

Dogbane Family

This dogbane is similar to Spreading Dogbane on page 137 in the pink section. The oblong leaves, however, *have no leaf stem,* and the wide rounding or heart-shaped base of the leaf spread wide and nearly clasp the stem of the plant. The veins of the leaves go almost straight out from the midvein and form wide angles. The small flowers are in branching clusters. The corolla lobes are nearly erect — not spreading as on Spreading Dogbane. The five petals are milky white. The plant is nearly hairless, and the seed pods are very long and slender and hang down in pairs. This dogbane grows in rocky or gravelly soil — often along streams. It may be erect and branching, or it may recline and form large, prostrate mats.

POKE MILKWEED

Asclepias exaltata

Milkweed Family

Poke Milkweed is from three to six feet tall and grows in the moist upland woods. It has thin leaves which have broad middles but are pointed at each end. The leaves are often in a drooping position. The flower is white to dull-purple and the hoods are white to pink. They are arranged in several loosely-flowered umbels which are in a drooping position from the upper leaf axils.

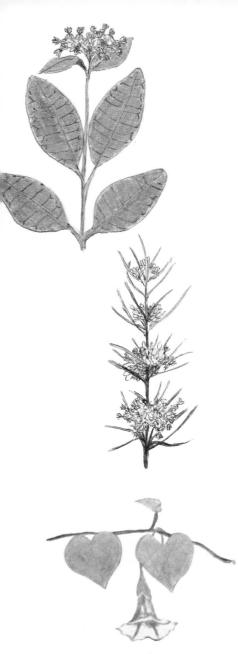

WHITE MILKWEED

Asclepias variegata

Milkweed Family

White Milkweed grows in moist or dry upland woods and thickets to a height of from two to three feet. The stout stem has several pairs of oblong, blunt-tipped leaves. The flowers are white with purplish centers and are in a terminal cluster. The flower is similar to that of most milkweeds (see page 311 for enlargement), but the five cups above the five turned-back petals are rounded outward on this milkweed.

WHORLED MILKWEED

Asclepias verticillata

Milkweed Family

This milkweed grows in dry or moist fields, along roads, and in upland woods. It generally has an unbranched stem which is from one to two feet tall. The leaves are very slender and the edges are rolled underneath. There are from three to six leaves in circles around the stem at regular intervals. The flowers are like typical milkweed flowers, but are smaller. They are greenish-white and are in clusters at the leaf axils.

WILD POTATO-VINE

Ipomoea pandurata

Morning-Glory Family

Wild Potato-Vine is a long trailing and twining plant similar to the garden-grown Morning Glories. It has a large funnel-shaped white flower with pink stripes reaching out from the center. The leaves are very heart-shaped and each leaf is attached to the main stem individually. It is found in dry fields and roadsides.

ERECT or LOW BINDWEED
Convolvulus spithamaeus
Morning-Glory Family

This bindweed is generally downy. It is either trailing or erect, but it *does not twine*. It grows in sandy or rocky soil to a height of from three to twenty inches. The leaves are oval and are on short stalks. The base of the blade may be either indented or tapering. The lowest leaves are very small. The funnel-shaped corolla is white and from two to three inches long. The flowers grow from axils of lower leaves, and the leaves usually extend above the flowers. Plants usually bear from one to four flowers.

HEDGE BINDWEED
Convolvulus sepium
Morning-Glory Family

This is a white flower, but see the pink section, page 140 for a detailed description of Bindweed.

FIELD BINDWEED
Convolvulus arvensis
Morning-Glory Family

Field Bindweed is very similar to Hedge Bindweed, but the leaves are much smaller and less pointed at the tips. The flowers are less than an inch wide and vary from white to pink, but are usually white. This wild flower is widespread throughout New England and grows prostrate along the ground or climbs over shrubs, stonewalls, compost heaps, and decaying boxes and buildings.

DODDER or LOVE VINE

Cuscuta gronovii

Morning-Glory Family

Dodders are parasitic vines with no leaves or green color. The thread-like yellow or orange stems twine closely around the stems of host plants and exhaust their juices by means of tiny suckers. There are about twelve species in our area and all are quite similar. They grow in low ground and thickets and often become troublesome plants in gardens. Dodders begin their life as a ground plant, but when they become established on the host plant, the ground root of the Dodder dies and the Dodder becomes completely dependent upon its host for its nourishment. The waxy-white, five-lobed flowers have greenish-white sepals. Flowers are arranged in many clusters along the twining stem.

VIRGINIA WATERLEAF

Hydrophyllum virginianum

Waterleaf Family

The flowers on this plant vary from white to pale violet. Look on page 313 in the violet section for details about this plant.

BROAD-LEAVED WATERLEAF

Hydrophyllum canadense

Waterleaf Family

Broad-Leaved Waterleaf grows in rich, moist woods or in open wet places to a height of from twelve to twenty inches. The leaves and stems are sparsely hairy. The maple-like leaves have from five to nine lobes and each lobe is coarsely toothed. The flower has five sepals, five petals, and five stamens which protrude from the center of the flower. The white to pale purple flower is barrel-shaped because the petals do not spread open.

COMMON HOARHOUND
Marrubium vulgare
Mint Family

This hoarhound grows in waste places to a height of from one to three feet. It is an aromatic, erect plant with a stout, square, white stem with white hairs on the stems and leaves. The oval leaves have round-toothed margins and narrow to a stalk at the base. They are rough and whitish on the top, but woolly on the underside. The white, two-lipped flowers are in dense clusters in the leaf axils. The upper lip of the corolla is erect and notched. The lower lip is spreading and is divided into three lobes — the middle lobe being the widest. The woolly, cup-shaped calyx has ten spiny, pointed teeth which curve backwards.

CATNIP
Nepeta cataria
Mint Family

Catnip grows in fields and waste places to a height of from six to thirty-six inches. Catnip has paired leaves, square stems, and tubular, two-lipped flowers which are all characteristic of members of this family. The leaves are pointed and have toothed margins and long stalks. The flower cluster may be a continuous, cylindrical shape, or it may be interrupted by bare places on the stalk. The flowers are dull white or pale purple and the lower lip is dotted with purple. The tube of the corolla is curved, and the throat is open, exposing the two pair of stamens.

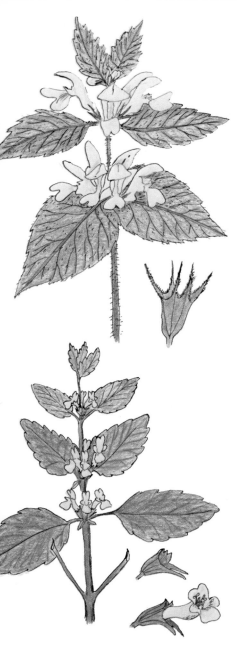

WHITE DEAD-NETTLE or SNOWFLAKE

Lamium album

Mint Family

White Dead-Nettle grows in wasteplaces, along roadsides, and in old lawns to a height of from six to twelve inches. It has square, stout, hairy stems which may be reclining with only the tip pointing upward. The heart-shaped leaves have toothed margins and are on petioles. The stem, leaves, and calyx are all hairy. Many white flowers are in a whorl in leaf axils. The flowers are about an inch long and have a wide-open mouth. The two-lipped corolla is creamy white and is about the same length as the calyx. The upper lip is arched and has two ridges. The lower lip is lobed and each of the side lobes has a slender tooth at the tip. The calyx is cup-shaped with sharp, spreading teeth.

GARDEN or LEMON BALM

Melissa officinalis

Mint Family

Balm is an Old World herb which was brought to America by colonists and has now become naturalized in thickets, woods, and waste places. It varies in height from one to three feet. It is a rather bushy plant with a stout, erect stem. The oval, long-stalked leaves have scalloped edges and give off a lemony odor when they are crushed. The flowers are in small clusters at the axils of the leaves. The tubular, almost-white corolla curves upward and is about one-half of an inch long. The calyx is a two-lipped cup. The upper lip has three short, triangular teeth and the lower lip is deeply cut into two longer, spine-tipped teeth.

70

VIRGINIA MOUNTAIN MINT

Pycnanthemum virginianum

Mint Family

There are about fifteen mountain mints in our area, but only two are given here as sample flowers. For further identification, consult more technical books by looking under the Latin name of Pycnanthemum. The white mountain mint shown here grows in dry to wet thickets, gravelly shores, and dry fields and pastures to a height of from one to three feet. It has a stout, stiff, square stem and a slight fragrance of mint. The stem has smooth sides, but has fine down at the angles of the stem and on the veins of the leaves. The stem is very leafy. The narrow, tapering leaves have broad bases and rough edges. They have no stalks and may be smooth or minutely hairy on the underside. The tiny white to pale lilac flowers are in crowded, flat-topped clusters, but only a few flowers from each cluster bloom at one time. The flower is two-lipped with a straight, rather flat, upper lip and a three-cleft spreading lower lip which may be dotted with purple. The lower pair of stamens is longer than the upper pair.

HOARY MOUNTAIN MINT

Pycnanthemum incanum

Mint Family

This mountain mint grows in woods and thickets. It is similar to the one above, but the hairy stem is intermixed with short curving hairs and long straight ones. The toothed, oval pointed leaves are hairy on the under side. The calyx is very hairy with sharp, slender teeth. The tubular flower is white or pale lilac. The upper lip is upright, but the three lobes of the lower lip are nearly parallel and are purple spotted.

WILD THYME
Thymus serpyllum
Mint Family

These flowers may be either pinkish, lavender, or white. See page 320 in the lavender section for a description.

(A) BUGLE WEED
Lycopus virginicus
Mint Family

This flower may be either lavender or white. See page 320 in the lavender section for details.

(B) CUT-LEAVED WATER HOREHOUND
Lycopus americanus
Mint Family

This flower is very similar to Bugle Weed, but the leaves are deeply cut. See page 320 in the lavender section for details.

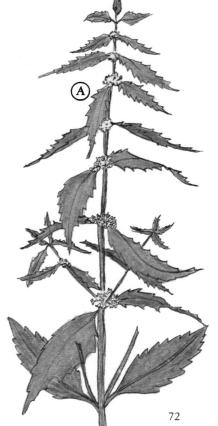

72

AMERICAN WILD MINT

Mentha arvensis var. villosa

Mint Family

Most mints vary in color from white to lavender. If your specimen looks similar to the one pictured here, turn to page 321 in the lavender section.

The one shown here grows in marshes, swamps, and moist soil to a height of from six inches to two feet. The erect, slender, four-sided stem may be branched or simple. A distinctive characteristic used to identify this plant is the amount of hair on the stem near the lowest flower cluster. The angles of the stem are obviously more hairy than the sides are. The leaves have soft hairs on both surfaces and will emit an odor of pennyroyal when crushed. The whorls of flowers in the axils of the leaves are shown here as white, but they may also be lavender or pink. The oblong calyx is hairy and has five nerves and five short, pointed teeth.

BEEF-STEAK PLANT or PERILLA

Perilla frutescens

Mint Family

The flowers on this plant may be dull white or purplish. See page 322 in the purple section for plant description.

73

BLACK NIGHTSHADE

Solanum americanum

Nightshade Family

Black Nightshade grows in rocky or dry, open woods, thickets, shores, or clearings to a height up to three feet. It is a slender branching plant with undivided and unlobed leaves. It is thought by many to be the Deadly Nightshade (Solanum nigrum), but it is not. The leaves and unripe berries do contain poison, but it disappears from the berries as they ripen. Many people do eat ripe berries — cooked or uncooked — with no apparant harm; but because some people might be poisoned by these berries, it would be wise to leave them alone. The pale green, oval-pointed leaves are on slender leaf stalks and may have toothed or untoothed margins. The small flowers are in small clusters at leaf axils. Each flower has five white petals — possibly tinged with purple — which are turned backwards. The calyx has five, unequal, spreading lobes which may be either pointed or blunt. The berry is shiny and black, but quickly falls when it is ripe.

WHITE-FLOWERED GROUND CHERRY

Chamaesoracha grandiflora

Potato Family

White-flowered Ground Cherry resembles Ground Cherry on page 202. It is an erect annual with long, sticky hairs on the stem. It grows in sandy or rocky soil, in recent clearings, and along roadsides to a height of from six to thirty-six inches. The long pointed leaves usually do not have teeth on their margins. Several flowers — up to two inches broad — are borne at the same level on the plant. The large cup-shaped corolla is usually white with a yellow center, but on some plants the flower may be tinged with violet. The calyx is not angled or ribbed and is open at the mouth. It *is not an inflated bladder-like enclosure* for the berry as is the calyx of the Clammy Ground Cherry.

JIMSONWEED
Datura stramonium
Nightshade Family

Jimsonweed is a coarse upright weed of fields, barnyards, and waste places. The plant is poisonous. The flowers are white to lavender and are trumpet-shaped. They are usually from three to five inches long. The green cup-like calyx is half as long as the flower itself. The leaves are very thin, pointed at the tip, and are deeply cut with uneven, triangular teeth. Each leaf is singly attached to the main stem. On some species of Jimsonweed, the stem is green and the flowers are white; another species has a purple stem and pale violet blossoms.

MOTH MULLEIN
Verbascum blattaria
Figwort Family

This plant grows as a weed along roadsides, in vacant lots and other waste places to a height of from one to three feet. The stem is slender and fuzzy and the leaves vary in size and shape. They are lance-shaped in general outline and are coarsely toothed and covered with whitish wool. The flat, five-lobed flowers may be either white or yellow and are on separate pedicels (flower stems) at the top of the plant. The buds are roundish and button-like.

WHITE MULLEIN
Verbascum lychnitis
Figwort Family

This mullein grows along roads and in sandy fields and waste lands to a height up to four feet. The stem is branched and the plant is covered with

white wool. The flowers are smaller than those on Moth Mullein, and may be either white or yellow. The flowers have five lobes and are arranged in a branching pyramid-shaped cluster at the top of the plant.

TURTLEHEAD
SNAKEHEAD

Chelone glabra

Figwort Family

Turtlehead has a four-sided stem and tight clusters of flowers at the summit. It grows in moist ground along streams and in thickets or swamps to a height of from one to three feet. The bright, deep green leaves are lance or egg-shaped and have toothed margins. The leaves are on short stalks and are arranged in pairs on the stem. Usually the leaves are not hairy.

The flowers are usually a creamy white color, but may be tinged with pale purple or yellow as they age. Each one is about an inch long. The upper lip of the egg-shaped corolla is arched above the lower lip. The two lips are partly open, and very nearly resemble the head of a turtle — thus giving the plant its common name.

FOXGLOVE BEARDTONGUE
or WHITE PENSTEMON

Penstemon digitalis

Figwort Family

This beardtongue grows in fields, woodlands, or along roadsides to a height of from two to five feet. It is a smooth and shining plant with purplish stems and a spreading cluster of flowers at the top of the stem. The leaves are long and pointed, are

76

opposite, and clasp the stem at their base. The tubular corolla has a narrow base, but is abruptly inflated in the middle of the tube. The corolla is whitish and sometimes has purple lines on the inside. The two-lipped flower is wide open at the throat. The upper lip is erect and two-lobed while the bottom lip is spreading and has three lobes. The anthers are usually hairy, and though there are five stamens as the Latin names suggests, the fifth one is sterile. See page 325 in Lavender section for another Beardtongue.

CULVER'S ROOT

Veronicastrum virginicum

Figwort Family

Culver's Root grows in moist or dry upland woods and thickets to a height of from three to seven feet. It has slender, pointed leaves in whorls of three or six. The white flowers are tubular with four or five lobes. Two stamens and the style protrude from the throat of the flower giving the crowded flower-spike a fuzzy appearance.

EYEBRIGHT

Euphrasia americana

Figwort Family

Eyebright grows in fields and roadsides to a height of less than a foot. It has tiny paired leaves with from three to five sharp points on each side margin. The flowers grow from the axils of the leaves and have practically no stem. They have a four-lobed calyx and a two-lipped corolla. The bottom lip is lobed. The upper lip is pale blue or lavender and the bottom lip is white with violet lines.

WATER-WILLOW

Justicia americana

Acanthus Family

This bicolored flower varies in color from white to pale violet. See page 329 in the lavender section for more details.

NORTHERN BEDSTRAW

Galium boreale

Madder Family

Northern Bedstraw grows in rocky meadows, on shores, or along streams to a height of from twelve to forty inches. It has linear leaves in whorls of four around the stem. Each leaf has three nerves on it. Numerous tiny, white, four-petaled flowers are in tight compound clusters. The stems are smooth and sparsely branched below the flower clusters.

FRAGRANT BEDSTRAW or SWEET-SCENTED BEDSTRAW

Galium triflorum

Madder Family

This bedstraw grows in woods and thickets and reclines on nearby plants. It has narrow lance-shaped leaves in whorls of six at regular intervals on the stem. The upper leaves have a minute spine at the tip, and the leaf margins are rough or scratchy to touch. The greenish flowers (or burs which follow the flowers) are in sets of threes at the end of the branches and from axils of leaves.

78

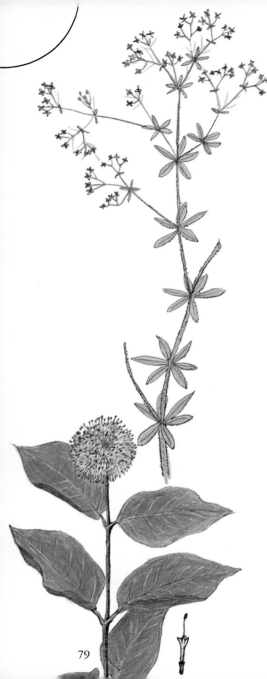

ROUGH BEDSTRAW
Galium asprellum
Madder Family

This is similar to the other Bedstraws on page 78. It is a much-branching plant which leans on near-by plants and bushes. Square stems have backward-hooked prickles on them. The light green leaves are in whorls of four, five, or six, but most often in sixes. The leaflets have prickles at the margins and the mid-rib, and they have a sharp point at the tip. The tiny white flowers are in many clusters at the ends of the numerous branches and from the axils of the upper leaves. The flowers have a rather unpleasant odor.

BUTTON BUSH; BUTTON TREE; GLOBE FLOWER; HONEY BALLS
Cephalanthus occidentalis
Madder Family

This pretty shrub grows in swamps and bogs or at the borders of streams to a height of from three to eight feet. It usually has smooth branches with leaves on leaf stems. Leaves are usually opposite each other on the stem, but may be in whorls of three. Each leaf is rounded at the base, has untoothed margins, and a pointed tip. Small white tubular flowers are arranged in a dense round head which is about one inch in diameter. The enlargement of a single flower shows the four sepals, four petals, and one thread-like pistil which protrudes from the throat of the funnel-shaped flower. The flowers have a jasmine-like fragrance. When flowers fade, a hard, brown, ball-shaped seed pod forms.

79

SWAMP VALERIAN

Valeriana uliginosa

Valerian Family

This smooth, upright herb with
opposite leaves grows in limy swamps
and wet woods to a height of from ten
to thirty inches. There is a rosette of
deep-green, stalked leaves which may
or may not be deeply cut. The stem
leaves are usually divided into long,
narrow leaflets with the end one being
the longest. The dull magenta, pink, or
white flowers are only about one-third
of an inch long and are in clusters at
the tip of the stem. The corolla is
flaring, tubular, and is *constricted
towards the base.* There are three very
prominent stamens, and instead of
a calyx there are feathery whitish or
pinkish-green bristles.

WILD CUCUMBER or WILD
BALSAM APPLE

Echinocystis lobata

Gourd Family

The wild cucumber is a large, showy,
annual climbing vine. It grows in
sunny areas where the soil is rich,
especially along rivers or near rotting
stumps. It sometimes completely
covers old stumps or shrubs and the
blossoms make a "fuzzy" covering.
Wild Cucumber is sometimes cultivated
as an arbor or fence vine. The yellow-
green stem is sharply angular, but is
nearly smooth. It has three-forked
tendrils appearing regularly at the leaf
axils. The deeply-veined leaves are
very thin and will wilt quickly when
picked. The leaves are rough on both

80

sides and are arranged singly along the stem at intervals of from six to eight inches. They usually have five sharply-pointed lobes with toothed margins, but the number of lobes varies from three to seven.

The small flowers are greenish white and each has six twisted petals. The numerous staminate flowers (male) are arranged in long, loose narrow racemes which stand above the leaf. The pistillate flowers (female) are alone or in smaller clusters below the leaf axil where falling pollen can fertilize them easily. After pollenization, new male flowers will continue to open and bloom, but the female flower will produce a fleshy, oval, green fruit about two inches long. This soft pod has two cavities with two flat seeds in each. It is covered on the outside with soft, slender spines. As the fruit matures, it dries and opens at the bottom.

MARSH BELLFLOWER
BEDSTRAW BELLFLOWER

Campanula aparinoides

Bluebell Family

This flower is also blue. Look for details on page 289 in the blue section

BONESET or THROUGHWORT

Eupatorium perfoliatum

Composite Family

Boneset is a stout, rough, woolly plant with tough, veiny leaves and a white, flat-topped flower cluster. It grows to a height of from two to five feet in wet meadows and low grounds or in marshes and swamps. The leaves have been brewed for a bitter tea or tonic. The pointed leaves are light green in color. They are in pairs and are united at their bases around the stem. The pair of leaves look like a single leaf with the stem piercing it. The pairs of leaves on the upper stems are long and pointed, but might not be united around the stem. The leaves are deeply veined and have a wrinkled appearance.

LATE-FLOWERING THROUGHWORT

Eupatorium serotinum

Composite Family

This plant grows in low thickets, clearings, or in moist woods to a height of from three to eight feet. It is much-branched and very hairy. The long-stalked leaves are longer than they are wide and usually have three main nerves. They are finely hairy and have sharply-toothed margins. Larger, lower leaves may be five-nerved from the base to the tip. Numerous white flower heads are in a flat cluster at the top of the plant. Each flower head has from seven to fifteen tiny white flowers. The bracts under the flower heads have white margins.

WHITE SNAKEROOT

Eupatorium rugosum

Composite Family

White Snakeroot is a fairly common woodland perennial which is poisonous to cattle; and milk from them may then transmit this poison to people who drink it. It grows in woodlands, rich woods, and thickets to a height of from one to five feet. The broad, rather heart-shaped leaves have sharp points and toothed margins. The larger leaves are on stalks which are an inch or more long. Numerous small flower heads containing from ten to thirty flowers in each are arranged in a flat-topped cluster at the tip of the plant. The flowers are a brilliant white color.

PALE or WHITE GOLDENROD

Solidago bicolor

Composite Family

Silverrod — another common name — grows in dry or sandy soil to a height of from one to four feet. The stout stem is usually hairy, but may be smooth on some plants. The stem is usually not branching. The lower leaves are oblong, blunt at the tips, hairy, narrow into a margined leaf stem, and have round-toothed margins. The upper leaves are smaller, narrower, have more pointed tips, and may not have teeth or a leaf stalk. The flower heads are one-fourth of an inch or less high and are in small clusters amongst the upper leaves. The rays of flowers are white and may turn backwards. The bracts under each flower head may be light green or whitish.

WHORLED WOOD ASTER

Aster acuminatus

Composite Family

The Whorled Wood Aster is easily identified from other asters by its thin leaves and downy, reddish stem which often appears to be zig-zag instead of straight. This aster grows in dry woods and clearings to a height of from eight to thirty-six inches.

The thin leaves are generally elliptic or lance-shaped. They have sharply-toothed margins and taper to a narrow, stalkless base. The leaves are uniformly scattered along the stem — thus giving the appearance of being in whorls, though they *are not*. The lower leaves are slightly smaller than the middle or upper stem leaves. Veins on the underside of the leaves are hairy. The typical aster heads are quite large — about one or one and a half inches broad. They are in a loose cluster at the top of the plant. The rays on the flower heads are white or purple-tinged and each head has from ten to eighteen petal-like rays.

FLAT-TOPPED WHITE ASTER

Aster umbellatus

Composite Family

There are several species of white asters in our area, but this one is easily identified by its rather flat-topped cluster of white flower heads with yellow centers which may turn purple with age. It grows to a height of from two to seven feet at edges of thickets or in moist soil at boarders of woods. It is a tall bushy plant with rather long narrow leaves and many erect branches with flowers at the tips. The leaves have rough margins, but are toothless.

84

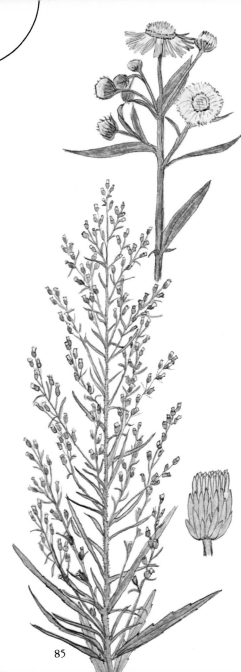

DAISY FLEABANE
Erigeron strigosus
Composite Family

Daisy Fleabane grows in dry open soil in fields, along roadsides, and on rocky slopes to a height of from one to four feet. It has a slender stem which is branched at the top, and a flat-topped flower cluster. A distinctive characteristic of this fleabane is the fact that the *hairs lie close* to the stem and do not spread as on other fleabanes. The stem leaves are narrow and pointed. The margins are usually untoothed. The lower leaves are spatulate-shaped with a long, slender stalk and toothed margins. The yellow disk of the flower head is usually less than two-fifths of an inch across and there are many white rays which are the same length as the width of this disk.

HORSE-WEED OR CANADA FLEABANE
Erigeron canadensis
Composite Family

Other names for this plant are Mule Tail, Hog-Weed, and Butter-Weed. It is a tall, erect, hairy weed with numerous, narrow, bristly leaves. It grows in waste lands and fields to a height of from one to six feet. The lower leaves have the broadest part of the blade nearest the tip of the leaf, and they may have toothed margins. Upper stem leaves are more linear in shape. The flower arrangement at the summit of the stem consists of many small flower-heads in branching clusters. Each is about one-fifth of an inch broad, contains numerous white ray flowers and has green bracts of unequal length at its base.

WHITE-TOPPED ASTER
Sericocarpus asteroides
Composite Family

White-Topped Aster grows in dry
woods and clearings to a height of six
inches to two feet. It is an aster-like
plant which is placed in the aster
genus by some botanists and in a
separate genus by others. The stem is
usually hairy. The leaves are of various
shapes and sizes; have toothed edges;
and are sometimes stalked and veiny.
The spatulate leaves have a very
narrow base and are broadest near the
outer half. The flower heads are in
dense, flat-topped clusters at the top of
the plant. Each flower head has a
creamy-yellow center disk and four or
five white or cream-colored rays.
Below each flower head is a barrel-
shaped formation of green, hairy
bracts. The tips of the outer bracts are
tipped downwards.

FIELD PUSSYTOES
Antennaria neglecta
Composite Family

This smaller Pussytoes spreads by
long slender runners and often forms
dense mats in dry fields and open
slopes. The basal leaves have only one
main rib and they are spoon-shaped.
They taper as they near the stem. The
flower stem is from four to twelve
inches tall, has several very narrow
stem leaves, and several crowded
flower heads at the top. The crowded
heads pressed closely together form a
rounded, knobbed cluster like a kitten's
paw.

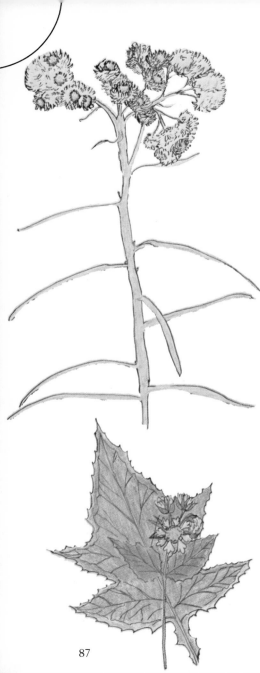

PEARLY EVERLASTING

Anaphalis margaritacea

Composite Family

Pearly Everlasting is an erect, non-branching plant with grayish, cottony stems, usually from one to two feet tall. It grows singly, or in great patches in dry soil — especially sand or gravel — in pastures, dry open wasteland and along roads. It is often picked before the flowers are more than half open, hung in an upside-down position to dry, and used in dried-flower arrangements. The leaves are long and narrow, gray-green on the top, and woolly-white on the underside. The globular flower heads are on short stalks in a flat, branching cluster at the top of the plant. Dry petal-like white bracts are arranged around the yellow staminate (male) center. Pistillate (female) flowers are on separate plants.

LEAF CUP

Polymnia canadensis

Composite Family

Leaf Cup grows in moist, limy woods or ravines or at the bases of cliffs to a height of from two to five feet. It is a coarse plant which is often hairy and sticky on the upper part of the plant. The lower leaves are broad and thin, have stalks, and lobed and toothed margins. They are generally in pairs. The upper leaves are triangular shaped, may be unlobed, and may not be in pairs. The flowers are in small heads with yellow centers. Most heads have five toothed, white rays, but some heads may have fewer — or none at all.

GALENGALE or GALLANT SOLDIERS
Galinsoga parviflora
Composite Family

This weed grows in waste places and around old dwellings to a height of from six to eighteen inches. There are hairs lying flat on the surface of the stem. The tiny inconspicuous flower heads are about one-fourth of an inch across. The conical center is orange-yellow and there are four or five white rays — each of which has three lobes at the tip. The broad leaves are coarsely toothed and the lower leaves are on petioles (leaf stalks). The plant and flowers are so tiny an enlargement has been made to show detail.

YARROW
Achillea millefolium
Composite Family

Yarrow is a woody plant with soft aromatic, fern-like leaves and a flat-topped, or rounded flower cluster. Close inspection seems to reveal single five-petaled flowers — but this is not true. These are really flower heads and the five "petals" are five ray flowers, each of which is a complete flower in itself. The flower-cluster is usually white but is rarely pink. Yarrow grows along roadsides and in fields to a height of from one to three feet.

STINKING MAYWEED

Anthemis cotula

Composite Family

This daisy-like plant grows abundantly in waste places and in barnyards to a height of from eight to twenty-four inches. The foliage is thrice-cut and has a very strong unpleasant odor. The leaves also cause blisters on hands of farm workers who harvest this along with the hay crop. Other names are Stinking Chamomile and Dog-Fennel.

SCENTLESS or WILD CHAMOMILE

Matricaria maritima

Composite Family

This chamomile grows in waste places and is similar to the one below, but the flowers are larger, rays are longer, and there is *no odor*. It grows in waste places near sea ports and is quite localized. It is usually from six to eighteen inches tall, but the branches are usually in a reclining and horizontally-spreading position. The leaves on this plant are divided into segments which are then divided again into fleshy linear segments.

WILD CHAMOMILE

Matricaria chamomilla

Composite Family

Wild Chamomile is a branching pineapple-scented weed which grows in waste places and along roadsides to a height of eight to thirty-two inches. The leaves are finely cut into linear segments. The numerous daisy-like heads have yellow centers and white rays which have five teeth at the tips.

OX-EYE DAISY

Chrysanthemum leucanthemum

Composite Family

This familiar plant grows abundantly in fields and along roadsides. It has dark narrow, much-lobed leaves and is from one to three feet tall. What appears to be a single flower with white petals is really a group of very tiny flowers of two types. The disk flowers are yellow and in the center, but are too numerous and too small to be seen without a magnifying glass. The ray flowers are the white petal-shaped rays that grow outward around the yellow center.

FEVERFEW

Chrysanthemum parthenium

Composite Family

Corn-Marigold is another name for this flower. It grows in waste places to a height of from twelve to thirty-two inches. It is a bushy plant with a pungent aroma and deeply-lobed gray-green leaves. It has many daisy-like flower heads with large yellow centers and short, stubby white rays.

PILEWORT or FIREWEED

Erechtites hieracifolia

Composite Family

Pilewort is a course, erect, weedy plant which varies greatly in size. It may be only a few inches tall or as high as eight feet if conditions are favorable to its growth. The stem is grooved and is usually hairy. It grows in damp thickets, woods, and waste places. The narrow leaves are alternate each other on the stem. They may have short stalks or none at all. The margins of the leaves are usually deeply cut. Tiny, tubular white flowers are arranged in many small flower heads. Each head is surrounded by a ring of pointed bracts of equal length.

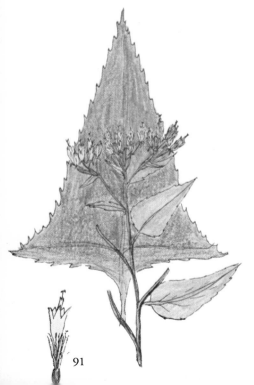

SWEET-SCENTED INDIAN PLANTAIN

Cacalia suaveolens

Composite Family

This is a smooth, leafy plant with a striped stem. It grows in moist woods and clearings in shaded places. It is from three to five feet tall. The leaves are triangular in general outline, but the basal lobes on the leaf point outward at wide angles. Each leaf has a petiole (leaf stalk), but the lower leaves have margined petioles. The margins of the leaves are toothed. The flowerheads are in flat-topped clusters. Each head will have from twenty to thirty tiny funnel-shaped flowers with five lobes at the tip.

91

RATTLESNAKE-ROOT OR WHITE LETTUCE

Prenanthes alba

Composite Family

White Lettuce grows in thin, rich woods and thickets to a height of from two to five feet. It has a smooth, stiff, round stem which is usually tinged with magenta and has a whitish powder on it. The smooth, deep-green leaves are varied in shape. The lower ones are usually three-sided with a few teeth at the margins. The upper leaves are merely deeply cut, and the uppermost ones may have two small side lobes or none at all. The drooping, dull cream-colored flowers are occasionally tinged with purple. The green floral envelope has eight magenta-tipped sections. Between the floral envelope and the white petals, there are cinnamon-colored or crimson brown hairs called the pappus. (see insert) The stamens are quite prominent and hang from the center of the drooping flower.

GALL-OF-THE-EARTH

Prenanthes trifoliata

Composite Family

This plant grows on dry slopes, in clearings and thickets to a height of from one to five feet. It is a smooth plant with waxy, reddish stem. The leaves are nearly all on long stalks which may also be tinged with red. The lower leaves are lobed or divided into three irregularly-toothed lobes. The creamy-white, drooping, flower heads have from six to eight pale-green or pinkish bracts and the pappus is white or creamy.

92

TALL WHITE LETTUCE

Prenanthes altissima

Composite Family

This lettuce grows in moist woodlands and thickets to a height of from three to seven feet. It is a tall, smooth species with a green or magenta-tinged stem and long-stalked leaves of various shapes and sizes. Though the leaves vary greatly, they are triangular in general outline. They may be deeply lobed or have no lobes at all. All of the leaves have long stalks. There are only about five greenish bracts to the flower head and the pappus is creamy white — not cinnamon colored as on Prenanthes alba. The numerous, dull cream-colored flowers are in a hanging position in a narrow terminal cluster or in smaller clusters rising from the leaf axils.

MEADOW GARLIC
Allium canadense
Lily Family

This plant has a strong onion-like odor. It grows in moist meadows or open woods to a height of from ten to twenty-four inches. The stem is erect and is leafy only on the lower third of the plant. The leaves are flat and narrow like grass. They are not hollow as in the field species. The umbel at the top of the stem differs from plant to plant. There are many bulblets in the group. Usually there are two or three pink or white flowers, but this is not always the case. There is a spathe under the umbel which has three parts — unlike the one-part spathe in the field species.

Another common name for this plant is Wild Garlic.

FIELD GARLIC
Allium vineale
Lily Family

Field Garlic grows in fields and meadows to a height of from one to three feet. The "head" contains pink or white flowers mixed with bulblets with tails. These tails are really a long fragile leaf. There is a single papery bract below the umbel of flowers. This plant has very slender rounded leaves which ascend part way up the stem. The leaves are not flat like grass, but are rounded. They are usually hollow towards the base of the leaf.

94

WILD CHIVES

Allium schoenoprasum
var. sibricium

Lily Family

This tall plant emits a very strong onion-like odor. At the base of the stout stem is a whitish bulb which is often narrower than the stem itself. The leaves are erect and hollow, often turning brown and hanging down as the flower head matures. The numerous flowers are arranged in a compact head at the top. Each flower is bell-shaped and points upward on its own tiny pedicel. There are six pointed, pink or lavender petals with a whitish base and a fine purple line at the midrib of each petal. Below the flower cluster are two wide, papery bracts which look very much like the outside skin on an onion.

SHOWY LADY'S SLIPPER

Cypripedium reginae

Orchid Family

See page 7 in white section for details.

ROSE POGONIA or SNAKE-MOUTH

Pogonia ophioglossoides

Orchid Family

Rose Pogonia grows in acid soil of wet meadows and sphagnum bogs to a height of from eight to sixteen inches. Each plant has perfumed flowers which are borne singly — or rarely in a pair — at the summit of the stem. There is a single broad leaf sheathing the stem at mid-point. The color range is from pale lavender to bright rose and rarely white. The petals and sepals are about the same size and have a silky texture. The showy, fringed lower lip is crested with yellow hairs.

NODDING POGONIA or THREE BIRDS ORCHIS

Triphora trianthophora

Orchid Family

This small orchid is usually from three to ten inches tall and grows in hardwood forests — especially under beech trees — where there is rich, humus soil and leaf mold. This rare species is the only one of its genus to be found in our area. It is not showy, and the plant is often hidden among the fallen leaves. The plant dies down after blooming, but produce tubers which often lie dormant under the leaves for several years at a time.

From two to eight tiny, oval leaves alternately clasp the fragile stem. Each plant has three flowers (occasionally only one or two) at the top. The buds

are in a nodding position, but usually become more erect as the bud opens. Most plants will have one in bud, one flower open fully, and one flower gone by, and it is rare to find all three flowers on one plant in bloom at the same time. The flowers are in a pendulous position and vary from pink to almost white. The slender sepals are longer than the three-lobed lip. The upper sepal arches and the lip has three greenish ridges running lengthwise and a crinkled edge.

GRASS-PINK or CALOPOGON

Calopogon puchellus

Orchid Family

This orchid appears to be "upside down" as the yellow, crested lip is upright at the top whereas in most other orchids the crested, hairy lip is at the bottom. This orchid grows in wet acid soil of bogs, peat meadows, and swamps to a height of from four to eighteen inches. The slender grass-like stem has from two to ten orchids at the top and a single, slender leaf which sheaths the stem at the base. Both the stalk and the leaf grow from a very small white bulb. The flowers are rose-purple to pink and are from one to one and three-fourths inches long.

DRAGON'S MOUTH
or ARETHUSA

Arethusa bulbosa

Orchid Family

This is a short-stemmed orchid which grows to a height of from five to ten inches. It usually grows in groups of several in sphagnum bogs, swamps, or mossy depressions in moist woods. The single flower at the top is from one to two inches high. The three erect sepals and the two hood-like petals are above the drooping lip. The lip is variegated with purplish blotches and is crested down the face with three hairy ridges. There are from one to three loose bracts toward the base. After the flower dies, a single grass-like leaf will grow from within the upper bract.

flower greatly enlarged

FAIRY SLIPPER
or CALYPSO

Calypso bulbosa

Orchid Family

This lovely little orchid grows in deep, mossy, coniferous woods to a height of from four to eight inches. The Fairy Slipper produces a single round-oval basal leaf in the fall which lasts through to flowering time. In the spring, the underground bulb sends up a leafless scape (flowering stem directly from the ground), which bears a solitary flower at the top. The flower is similar in shape to a lady slipper and is about three-fourths of an inch long. The sepals and side petals are similar in shape and are pale purple. The boat-shaped lip is whitish and shades to yellow toward the tip. It has reddish-brown or purple-brown marks on the inside. The lip is spotted with purple and is crested with three rows of yellow hairs. There are two tiny horns at the toe of the slipper.

WATER SMARTWEED or AMPHIBIOUS KNOTWEED

Polygonum amphibium

Buckwheat Family

Water Smartweed grows in water or mud, but as the name implies, there is a land form which grows on land. More often than not, however, the plant found will be the aquatic form. They are similar, but the land form is much more hairy. If the plant is in water, the stem and leaves may be floating but on the land plants, the leaves stand erect. The leaves are thick, smooth, and shiny on the top. The small, bright pink, thickly-clustered flowers are in a stubby, oblong spike usually *less than an inch* long. These spikes are straight and erect — *not nodding* as on other smartweeds. The calyx has five rose-colored sepals which look like petals, but there are no true petals. There are five stamens in the center.

SWAMP SMARTWEED

Polygonum coccineum

Buckwheat Family

Swamp Smartweed is a variable plant with both land and aquatic forms, and intermediate forms between the two. It differs from Polygonum amphibium because the flower cluster is longer — usually much more than an inch. The aquatic form has thin floating leaves with rounded bases and swollen, cup-like sheaths at the leaf joints. The swollen sheath is not as prominent on the land forms; the leaves taper at the base; and the leaves stand upright on the land form. The handsome, slender spikes of deep pink flowers are at the tips of the branches.

SMARTWEED or PINKWEED

Polygonum pensylvanicum

Buckwheat Family

This smartweed is a branched weed with spikes of variegated pink and white flowers. It grows in fields, waste places, and along roadsides to a height of from one to three feet. The sheaths around the leaf axils are *not fringed.* The joints of the stem are reddish and the long pointed leaves are shiny, but do not have the prominent darker V-shaped mark that Lady's Thumb does. A hand lens will show the tiny hairlike glands on the upper stems and branches. The cylindrical "spikes" of tiny flowers are dense, blunt at the tip, and *are not drooping.* They are generally bright pink, but are occasionally white, or are mixed with both pink and white flowers in the same cluster.

PALE SMARTWEED or WATER SMARTWEED

Polygonum lapathifolium

Buckwheat Family

This smartweed is similar to Lady's Thumb on page 101, but the stems are usually green and there is *no fringe on the sheath* around the stem at the leaf axils. The stem is either simple or branched, and is swollen at the nodes. The lance-shaped leaves are on short petioles, and there may be hairs on the stalks and the bottom side of the midrib. The flowers are in slender clusters with *bent or drooping tips.* The tiny flowers are pink or purplish, but may be greenish-white. The base of each flower is usually green. There is no

100

corolla, but the calyx is comprised
of five petal-like sepals. This
smartweed grows in fields, waste
ground, and especially wet places
to a height of from one to three
feet.

LADY'S THUMB or REDLEG
Polygonum persicaria
Buckwheat Family

This plant is similar to Smartweed
on page 100, but the papery sheaths at
the base of the leaves are *fringed with
bristles*. This papery sheath formed by
the stipules at the base of each leaf is
an important character among the
members of the buckwheat family;
often used to distinguish one plant
from another. The pink flower spike is
dense and cylindrical, and rarely more
than an inch long. The leaves often
have a dark, triangular-shaped blotch
in the center, and the stems are
reddish.

ARROW-LEAVED
TEARTHUMB
Polygonum sagittatum
Buckwheat Family

This slender-stemmed plant grows
in marshes and in wet meadows. It is a
loosely, branching plant which may
grow to a length of several feet,
crawling over the ground or — most
often — reclining on other plants. Its
height is usually limited to from one to
three feet. The slender, weak, square
stems usually rest on other plants with
the aid of hooked, sharp prickles on

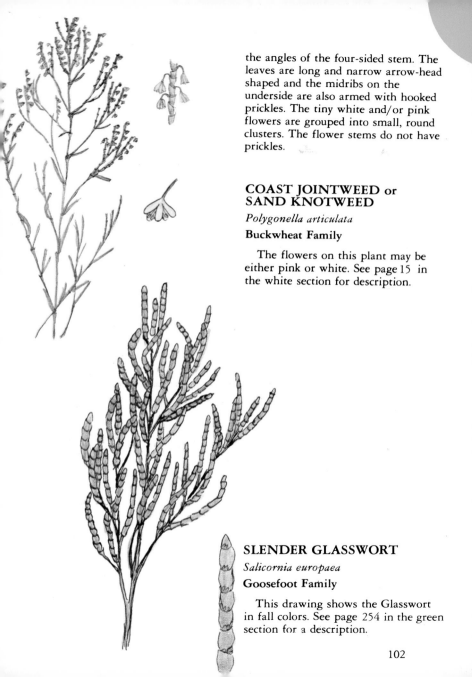

the angles of the four-sided stem. The leaves are long and narrow arrow-head shaped and the midribs on the underside are also armed with hooked prickles. The tiny white and/or pink flowers are grouped into small, round clusters. The flower stems do not have prickles.

COAST JOINTWEED or SAND KNOTWEED

Polygonella articulata

Buckwheat Family

The flowers on this plant may be either pink or white. See page 15 in the white section for description.

SLENDER GLASSWORT

Salicornia europaea

Goosefoot Family

This drawing shows the Glasswort in fall colors. See page 254 in the green section for a description.

FOUR-O'CLOCK or UMBRELLA-WORT

Mirabilis nyctaginea

Four-o'clock Family

Four-o'clock grows in prairies and waste places where there is rich soil. It is usually about three feet tall, but varies in height to from one to six feet. The stem is repeatedly forked. It is a rather weedy plant with broad, paired leaves with stalks and heart-shaped bases. The flower cluster is unique! From one to five small pink flowers are clustered together in a broad, veiny, five-lobed green cup-like structure. Each flower is short, funnel-shaped, and has five spreading petals. The calyx is also five lobed.

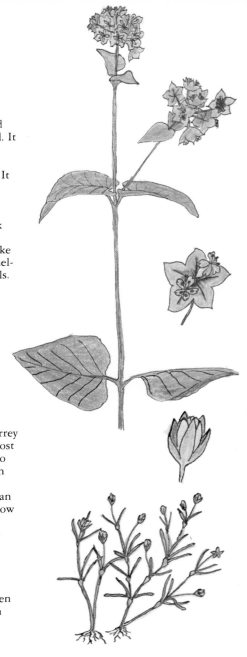

SAND SPURREY

Spergularia marina

Pink Family

This plant is also called Red Spurrey or Salt-marsh Sand Spurrey. It is most common on sea shores, but may also be found growing in salt or brackish marshes and wet soil. It is a short, prostrate plant usually not taller than six inches. The leaves are very narrow and fleshy and grow in pairs from pointed stipules at the joints in the stem. There are numerous pink flowers growing on short stalks — usually only one from each pair of leaves. There are five pink petals which are shorter than the five green sepals, and there are not more than five stamens in the center.

103

CORN COCKLE

Agrostemma githago

Pink Family

Corn Cockle is a tall, silky annual which grows in grainfields or waste places to a height of from one to three feet. The opposite leaves are long and narrow, pale green in color, and are covered with silky hairs. The large flowers are on long stalks. Each flower has five wide, veined, purple-pink petals which are paler toward the center. The petals are sometimes spotted with black. The oval calyx is strongly ribbed and the five, slender teeth are longer than the petals. There are ten stamens and one pistil in the center of the flower.

RED CAMPION or RED BIRD'S EYE

Lychnis dioica

Pink Family

Red Campion grows in waste places and along roadsides to a height of one or two feet. It is a hairy plant with loosely-forking stems and hairy basal leaves on long stalks. The hairy stem leaves are attached directly to the stem opposite each other. Numerous showy pink or red flowers are in a cluster at the top of the plant. There are five petals, but each is deeply cut into two lobes. Though showy, the flower is almost odorless. The calyx is hairy and cup-shaped.

104

RAGGED-ROBIN

Lychnis flos-cuculi

Pink Family

This member of the pink family is quickly identified by its five deeply cleft rose or white petals. The plant is from one to three feet tall and grows in fields and wet meadows where it often covers large areas.

MOSS CAMPION

Silene acaulis

Pink Family

Moss Campion is restricted to alpine areas at higher elevations where it is a delight to find growing where little else will. It is a dwarf plant — from one to three inches tall — which forms dense mats or tuft. The widely-branching stems are covered with crowded, needle-like leaves and there are numerous flowers above the leaves. Each flower is at the tip of the leafy stem. It has five pink to lilac petals which may be forked, notched, or round-tipped. The calyx is slender and tubular. There are ten stamens.

SLEEPY CATCHFLY

Silene antirrhina

Pink Family

This plant is easily recognized by the dark sticky places mid-way between each pair of leaves. The stem is from eight to thirty inches tall and the pairs of narrow leaves are spaced wide apart. Below the tiny pink or white flowers there is an inflated bladder. On some plants, the petals are not present.

SWEET-WILLIAM CATCHFLY

Silene armeria

Pink Family

Garden Catchfly, Lobel's Catchfly, or None-so-Pretty are other common names given to this plant. It has escaped to roadsides and fields where it is seldom more than a foot tall. It is a smooth annual with an erect stem and branches. The slender, pointed leaves are in pairs, have no leaf stems, and have a whitish powder on them. The small, long-tubed, pink flowers are in a rather flat-topped cluster. Each calyx is slender and ribbed. The five spreading petals are usually notched.

FIRE PINK

Silene virginica

Pink Family

The Fire Pink, one of our most vivid wild flowers, may be found in dry, open woods from May to August.

It grows to a height of one to two feet. The dark green leaves around the base of the plant are long and thin and are narrowed from the tip to the base.

The stems and leaves are covered with little hairs that give off a fluid which makes the plant sticky to touch. Insects often have difficulty climbing on this plant and get their feet so gummed up they die. For this reason, it is often called Catchfly.

Each flower has five deep crimson oblong petals which are notched at the tip. Its ten stamens may be seen protruding from the throat of the flower. The flowers are about one inch in diameter and are loosely clustered together at the end of the flower stalk.

106

SOAPWORT or BOUNCING BET

Saponaria officinalis

Pink Family

Soapwort grows along roadsides, on railroad banks and in waste places, but it is seldom found far from civilization. It may be from one to two feet tall, and is a rather stout-stemmed plant with clusters of ragged-looking pink or white flowers with reflexed, notched petals. It is a common species which has been naturalized from Europe, but .now grows along roads in great abundance. The name of soapwort refers to the lather which forms when juice is mixed with water, and older books say that this lather was used as a soap substitute. The smooth leaves are oval; have from three to five ribs; and are opposite on the stem. The flowers have a spicy odor and five long-clawed petals with notched tips which vary in color from a delicate magenta, to pink, to white. Plants are frequently found on which the flowers are double.

COWHERB or COW COCKLE

Saponaria vaccaria

Pink Family

Cowherb grows in wasteplaces and in cultivated ground to a height of from one to three feet. It is a smooth annual which is branching towards the top of the plant; and is similar to, but less common than, Bouncing Bet. The oval-pointed to lanceolate-shaped leaves are in pairs. The flowers are in loose clusters at the top of the plant. Each flower has five pale red or pink petals which have rounded teeth. The calyx is oblong and rather cup-shaped, has five ribs, and becomes rather inflated when in the fruiting stage.

LOW GYPSOPHYLL

Gypsophila muralis

Pink Family

This low, branching plant — related to the commercially-grown Baby's Breath — is a frail green plant with hair-like stems. Gypsophyll has established itself as a weed in waste places where it reaches a height of from four to seven inches. The top of the plant is smooth, but the base is slightly rough. Numerous tiny pink or purplish flowers are at the tips of the thread-like stalks which rise from the leaf axils. Paired leaves are long and narrow. The calyx is cup-shaped and is shorter than the petals.

MAIDEN PINK or MEADOW PINK

Dianthus deltoides

Pink Family

Maiden Pink has a slender creeping stem from which erect, wiry stems grow. Maiden Pink may be found growing in sandy fields, along roadsides, or in open woods. It is usually less than one foot tall. From five to eight pairs of very narrow, erect leaves are on the stem. Crimson pink or rose-purple flowers — resembling those of Sweet William — are on stalks at the top of the plant. The flowers bloom singly, though there may be several buds in a cluster. Each flower has five broad, spreading petals which are "pinked" at the outer edge. A short, broad bract with a narrow point is at the base of each flower.

108

WILD COLUMBINE
Aquilegia canadensis
Buttercup Family

This wild flower is one of the most beautiful, delicate, and odd-shaped of our New England wild flowers. The name columbine comes from a Latin word "columba" which means dove. Some people think the petals resemble doves. The flower on the Wild Columbine looks like a ballet skirt of gold and scarlet. Each flower has five petals which seem to grow backwards from the stems. The flowers hang downward from the stem instead of facing up. The stamens of this flower hang down below the petals and give a jewel-like effect. There are other species of columbine which may be white, purple, or blue, but those which are most common in New England are red with yellow centers. The plant itself grows to a height of one to two feet. It grows in rocky woods and slopes and amid boulders on shady wooded banks. For this reason, some call this wild flower Rock Bells. The leaves of the columbine seem to grow at the bottom of the plant and the flowers tower above them. Each leaf is divided into three parts and each part is re-divided into sets of three-scalloped leaflets.

ALLEGHENY-VINE or CLIMBING FUMITORY
Adlumia fungosa
Poppy Family

This vine is found on moist wooded slopes or rocky, shaded cliffs. It climbs over bushes and supports itself by its coiling leafstalks. The leaves are divided into many small, round,

toothed segments usually in sets of three. The main stalk may climb to a height of from ten to twelve feet. The flowers hang in drooping clusters from leaf axils and are whitish or pale pink. Each flower has four petals which are united into a hollow corolla about one-half of an inch long.

PALE CORYDALIS
Corydalis sempervirens
Poppy Family

This slender-stemmed, erect plant is found in dry rocky woods and grows to a height of from one to two feet. The leaves are deeply cut and are grayish green in color. The leaves are often covered with a white powdery substance. The lower leaves have leaf stems (petioles) but the upper leaves are attached directly to the main stem. The flowers are arranged in branching groups and each one has a pale pink single bulbous spur with yellow lips.

FUMITORY or EARTH-SMOKE
Fumaria officinalis
Poppy Family

Fumitory is a gray-green climbing plant with finely cut leaflets in sets of three or five. The stem is very lax and much branched and is from eight to forty inches long. The finely pronged leaflets are a gray-green color and give the appearance of smoke from a distance. The flowers are in racemes and are pinkish purple and tipped with maroon. The summit is sometimes dark red. Each flower has a single spur and is about one and one-half inches long.

ROSEROOT SEDUM

Sedum rosea

Orpine Family

This is an arctic plant which is found growing in large clumps in depressions of rock ledges on off-shore islands of Maine, and in higher elevations further south. It has a thick, juicy, light-colored stem which emits the odor of roses when crushed. The pale-green leaves are usually tipped with red, are about an inch long, and have teeth at the tips. The leaves are crowded, arranged in circles, and overlap each other spirally. The flowers are at the summit of the stem in a flat-topped, circular cluster. The flowers are staminate or pistillate (rarely perfect) and occur on separate plants. The male flowers are yellowish and the female flowers are reddish or purplish. After fertilization, the female flower develops into a four-beaked, dry cluster. The top of each looks like a four-pointed, orange star and this changes the flat-topped flower cluster from red to bright orange.

STEEPLEBUSH or HARDHACK

Spiraea tomentosa

Rose Family

This erect shrub has woody stems which form clumps in abandoned pastures and fields. It is seldom taller than three feet. The oval leaves have unequally-toothed margins; are smooth and dark green on the upper surface, but are darker and covered with a rusty wool on the under side. The rose-pink or purple flowers grow in elongated spires at the top

of the plant. Each small flower has five delicate, spreading petals and a tuft of stamens in the center. This tuft gives a feathery appearance to the pointed flower spire. When the petals fall, the stiff, brownish flower spike may be dried to be used in dried-flower arrangements where it is very effective and lasts for years.

(A) MARSH CINQUEFOIL
Potentilla palustris
Rose Family

This cinquefoil has reclining or erect reddish-green stems that rise from a long underground stem. The large leaves are on long petioles and have from five to seven toothed leaflets. The three leaflets at the end of the petiole are united. There are only a few flowers at the top of the leafy, hairy stem. The flowers are a deep red-purple and the five petals are shorter and narrower than the wide, purple sepals. The plant is from eight to twenty-four inches tall.

(B) QUEEN-OF-THE-PRAIRIE
Filipendula rubra
Rose Family

Queen-of-the-prairie is a tall plant with deep-green, divided leaf blades and a full divergent cluster of small pink flowers at the top of the stem. It grows in meadows and moist prairies to a height of from two to eight feet. The end segment of the leaf is large and has several lobes with uneven, jagged teeth. The side segments of the leaf are much smaller, but are also deeply lobed or cut. The fragrant, deep-pink flowers

112

have five petals, five sepals, and numerous stamens and pistils forming a tuft in the center. Flowers are in a feathery cluster which spreads out at the top rather than coming to a peak or a point as does the Steeplebush which is a close relative.

PURPLE-FLOWERING RASPBERRY

Rubus odoratus

Rose Family

This shrub grows in shady rocky woods or moist ravines. It has maple-shaped leaves which are from five to ten inches broad. The leaves and the stem are both hairy. The stem does not have prickles as do other raspberries. On older, larger stems the bark sheds. The five-petaled flower is similar to that of a rose. It is purplish red in color and about two inches across. It has broad, long, brown sepals. After the flower fades, a dry acid berry develops.

SWEETBRIER

Rosa eglanteria

Rose Family

A distinguishing feature of this plant is the stout prickles which curve downward. The long arching stems have many pink flowers which are smaller than most other roses. The leaflets are more round than most roses and are double toothed — a smaller tooth between each two larger teeth.

113

NORTHEASTERN ROSE
Rosa nitida
Rose Family

This low slender shrub is found in swamps, bogs, or in moist soil. It grows to a height of from one to three feet. The stem has many slender, straight, dark purple prickles which are all about the same length. The flower is pink and about two inches broad. The leaf has many small crowded leaflets.

LOW or PASTURE ROSE
Rosa virginiana
Rose Family

This rose is a low or bushy rose with either dull or shiny green leaves divided into from three to seven (but usually five) thin, toothed leaflets. The appendages at the base of the leaf stem (stipules) are narrow and flaring. **Identifying features of this rose are the glandular hairs which are on the** round fruit, the stems, and the lobed sepals. This hairy condition is especially noticeable on younger plants. The stem is armed with slender curved or straight prickles which are wide at the base. The stems are a ruddy-brown color, and the canes are bristly — especially at the lower part of the plant. The pale or deep crimson flowers are two or three inches broad and usually fade in color after opening. The roses are grouped in small clusters. The long, pointed sepals are reflexed when the flower is blooming, but spread wide as the fruit matures. The globular berry-like fruit is covered with glandular hairs. This rose is usually from one to five feet in height and grows in dry or rocky soil or in moist to dry thickets, clearings, and swamps.

PASTURE ROSE

Rosa carolina

Rose Family

This rose is found in dry rocky ground and upland pastures and grows to a height of from six inches to three feet. It is a much-branched shrub. The flowers are two inches broad and have a delightful aroma. A distinctive characteristic is the sharp slender straight prickles which grow only where the leaves branch off from the stems.

RUGOSA ROSE
or WRINKLED ROSE

Rosa rugosa

Rose Family

This rose has very large, deep rose blossoms which fade to white as they age. (There is also a white-flowered variety.) It is a large shrub of sand dunes, seasides, and roadsides and grows to a height of from two to six feet. It is much larger than the other roses shown, and the distinctive characteristic is the heavily-wrinkled leaves and the prickly stems. The stem and the prickles themselves are hairy. The large orange fruit is good to eat and is excellent for jelly.

RABBIT'S FOOT CLOVER
Trifolium arvense
Pea Family

This clover is easy to identify by its fuzzy, grayish-pink, cylindrical heads. The leaves are parted into three narrow segments. Rabbit's Foot Clover grows in waste places and along roadsides to a height of from four to sixteen inches.

RED CLOVER
Trifolium pratense
Pea Family

The magenta and white round head of the Red Clover is familiar to all. Red Clover grows from six to thirty inches tall in fields and along paths and roads. The stem is covered with soft white hairs. The leaf has three parts, and each leaflet has a lighter green triangular shape in the middle. There is a light green, papery sheath on the stem from which new leaves grow. A close look at a freshly-opened head is a great reward. The points on the round head are actually perfect sweet-pea-like flowers with a magenta upper hood and a white three-lobed bottom lip.

116

ALSIKE CLOVER
Trifolium hybridum
Pea Family

This clover is both pink and white. Look on page 39 in the white section for details.

CROWN VETCH
Coronilla varia
Pea Family

Crown Vetch is very similar to the other vetches on pages 301-302 except that it has a *circle* or crown of flowers instead of a long raceme of them. The flowers are bi-colored, with the top lip being pink and the bottom whitish. The leaves have from eleven to twenty-five small paired leaflets — each with an abrupt small tip at the end. Crown Vetch grows in waste places and along roadsides and is now sold commercially as a groundcover for dry slopes.

SHOWY TICK-TREFOIL or CANADA TICK-TREFOIL

Desmodium canadense

Pea Family

Showy Tick-Trefoil is our most showy species. It is a bushy, hairy plant which grows in dry open woods, at the edges of fields, or on river banks to a height of from two to six feet. The clover-like leaves have three long-oval leaflets and are *nearly stalkless* where they are attached to the stem. The magenta or pink pea-like blossoms are about one-half of an inch long, and are in crowded clusters at the top of the stout *leafy stem*. The fruit is a hairy pod which has from three to five joints. Each segment of the pod is up to one-half inch long. The pod is more deeply and sharply *curved at the bottom* than at the top. See page 300 in lavender section for two other tick-trefoils.

BEACH PEA

Lathyrus japonicus
Pea Family

Beach Pea is a stout, reclining plant with branching stems as long as four and five feet. It grows along sea beaches and lake shores. The main stems and the leaf-bearing stems are sharply angled with four flat sides, but the part of the stem which bears the flowers is round. The leaflets are pea-green in color and are usually in pairs. There is a sharp point at the tip of the otherwise toothless leaflet. There are large arrowhead-shaped stipules which embrace the stalk at the point where new branches occur. The flowers are in long-stalked clusters of from three to ten. They vary in color from pink to purple and are about three-fourths of an inch long. They are shaped like sweet peas and the lower lip is lighter in color than the turned-back upper lip. See page 302 in lavender section for Marsh Pea.

WILD BEAN

Strophostyles helvola
Pea Family

Wild Bean is a twining or trailing vine with hairy, branching stems. It grows in sandy fields, thickets, and especially near the coast. It may be from two to eight feet long. The leaves are divided into three leaflets with rounded bases and pointed tips. These leaflets have a thick texture, and may be bluntly lobed at the base with two unequal lobes. The pink or purple flowers are pea-like and are about one-half of an inch long. From three to twelve of these flowers are

together in a cluster at the end of a long stalk which originates in the leaf axil. The slender keel of the corolla is strongly curved. The slender seed pods are from one to three inches long and are covered with fine hairs.

MEADOW CRANESBILL

Geranium pratense

Geranium Family

This variety of Geranium is similar to Wild Geranium but has more deeply cleft leaves with seven narrow segments. The beak of the fruit is densely hairy. The flowers are a more blue-purple and the stalks are wooly. It grows to a height of from one to two feet and is more prevalent in Northern New England than the Wild Geranium is. (Also see p. 305)

BICKNELL'S GERANIUM or CRANESBILL

Geranium bicknellii

Geranium Family

This native geranium is very similar to Herb Robert on page 121 but the leaves are less intricately cut and each toothed segment *does not have* its own stalk as those on Herb Robert do. The stems and branches are hairy, and the small purplish or magenta flowers are less than one-half inch broad and *are in pairs*. Each flower has five notched petals which are only slightly longer than the five sepals. The beak of the fruit is long and pointed, but it splits and curls when ripe. This geranium grows in open woods, clearings, and in disturbed soil to a height of from eight to sixteen inches.

120

CAROLINA CRANESBILL

Geranium carolinianum

Geranium Family

In this geranium, the flowers form a dense cluster. It is a bushy plant which grows in dry sandy soil and waste lands to be nearly two feet tall. The leaves are deeply cut into from five to nine narrow lobes.

HERB-ROBERT

Geranium robertianum

Geranium Family

This flower grows in rocky woods, shady areas, and on shores to a height of nearly two feet. It has hairy, reddish stems, and fern-like leaves that are divided into three or five finely cut sections. The end segment of each has its own stalk. The flowers are one-half inch broad, pink or reddish purple, and have unnotched petals. The leaves have a disagreeable odor when crushed.

STORKSBILL
or ALFILARIA

Erodium cicutarium

Geranium Family

The leaves of this plant are fern-like and usually last through the winter as a rosette on the ground. The flowering stems rise from the midst of these and at first are only a few inches tall. The flowers are rose-colored and are less than one-half of an inch broad. Later the plant grows taller and is more branching. Storksbill grows along roadsides in sandy soil and is from three to twelve inches tall. Dried seed pods form twisted corkscrews.

121

FRINGED POLYGALA
or GAY WINGS
Polygala paucifolia
Milkwort Family

   Bird-On-The-Wing and Flowering
Wintergreen are two other common
names given to this little flower. It
grows in sunny spots in the woods, at
the bases of trees, and along stone
walls. The plant is only about four
inches tall, but has a root that is
sometimes over a foot in length. The
stem bends sharply as it enters the
soil. Both leaves and flowers are
clustered together at the top of the
stem. The pink or magenta tube-like
flower is made up of two pink sepals
which are wing-shaped and three small
petals which join together to form a
hollow tube. Part of the third petal is
fringed. The leaves and flower are
both about an inch long, and the shiny
leaves are sharply pointed.

RACEMED MILKWORT
Polygala polygama
Milkwort Family

   This milkwort grows from four to
twenty inches high in dry sandy soil or
open sandy woods. The leaves are
attached singly and the stem is very
leafy. The showy rose-colored flowers
are in a loose slender raceme at the
top of the stalk. Each flower is about
one-third inch long.

122

FIELD MILKWORT
or POLYGALA
Polygala sanguinea
Milkwort Family

This polygala, though usually bright rose-purple, may also be greenish or even white. It grows in moist sunny meadows to a height of from two to twelve inches. The flower head is oblong and sometimes there are several flower heads on one plant. The leaves are alternately attached on the stem and the stem is sometimes branched. All three of the Milkworts mentioned have concealed fertile fruit beneath the ground surface.

HIGH MALLOW
Malva sylvestris
Mallow Family

This mallow is quite often an escape from cultivation, though it grows wild along roadsides and in waste places to a height of from one to three feet. It is a fairly common plant with an erect, hairy, branching stem. The broad leaves are crinkly, have five or seven lobes, and toothed margins. They are light green and have long leaf stalks. The delicate flowers are large and have five heart-shaped pink or rose-purple petals which are veined with a deeper color. The flowers are in small clusters at leaf axils. The stamens are united in a central column around the pistils.

123

COMMON MALLOW

Malva neglecta

Mallow Family

This common creeping weed grows abundantly in farmyards, gardens, and in waste places. It has round or heart-shaped leaves that are from one to three inches broad. Each leaf is on its own leaf stem (petiole) and has from five to seven shallow lobes. The pink, lavender, or bluish-white blossoms are about one-half inch broad and have five heart-shaped petals. The flowers grow from the leaf axils. The stamens are united in a column around the pistil as in the Musk mallow. The fruit that forms after the flower fades resembles a flat round cheese. Perhaps this is why many people call this plant by another name — Cheeses.

MUSK MALLOW

Malva moschata

Mallow Family

The Musk Mallow is a tall branching plant which grows in fields, along roadsides, and in waste places throughout the eastern states. The plant is often over two feet tall. The leaves are from one to four inches broad and are intricately cut into deep-toothed narrow segments. The flowers are one and one-half to two inches broad and have five notched petals. The flower gives off a light musk-scented odor. The flowers are usually clustered together at leafy ends of the stems or branches. The pink or white petals are several times larger than the green pointed triangular-shaped sepals beneath. The numerous stamens surround the pistil and form a column which rises from the center of the flower.

124

SWAMP ROSE MALLOW

Hibiscus palustris
Mallow Family

Marsh Mallow, Mallow Rose, or Sea Hollyhock are other names given to this plant. It grows in fresh or salt marshes — especially near the coast — to a height of from five to seven feet. It is a tall plant with numerous cane-like stems. The large hollyhock-like blossom has a long style tipped with five round stigmas — typical of many members of this family. The leaves have pointed tips and rounded bases and are toothed at the margin. Lower leaves may be lobed, but upper ones are usually simple. The upper surface of the leaves is dark green, but there is a white powder on the underside. Leaves have long petioles (leaf stems). The pink flowers are from four to seven inches across and are usually in a cluster. Each flower is on its own stout pedicel (flower stalk). The drawing shows the distinctive circle of green bracts below the calyx.

Hibiscus palustris forma peckii
Another form of this plant (not shown) is very similar, but the flowers are a creamy white with a red center.

MARSH ST. JOHN'S-WORT

Hypericum virginicum
St. John's-wort Family

Marsh St. John's-wort is an erect, simple or bushy plant with paired leaves. It grows in wet sands, bogs, and swamps to a height of one or two feet. The stems are usually pinkish-brown, but may turn to a darker red later in the season. Close inspection will reveal the glands that dot the leaves. The pale leaves are

125

round-tipped and have a clasping or
heart-shaped base. There is a slight
bloom on the underside of the leaves.
Leaves may become a brighter color
as the seed capsules form. The pink
or flesh-colored flowers are in small
clusters at the tips of the stems.
Three groups with three stamens in
each group alternate with three
orange glands in the center of the
flower. The five sepals may be
pinkish in color. The seed capsule is
long and pointed and is red-purple in
color.

MEADOW BEAUTY or DEER GRASS

Rhexia virginica

Meadow Beauty Family

Meadow Beauty grows in sandy
soil or in low wet meadows, in
marshes, or at the edges of shallow
lakes and streams. It usually grows in
clusters and varies in height from ten
to eighteen inches. It is the only
species in our area of a member of a
larger tropical family. Deer Grass is a
beautiful perennial with a squarish
stem which may be simple or
branching. The paired leaves are
smooth, oval, light green and have
no stalk. There are three ribs on each
leaf, and the margins have very sharp
teeth or bristles. This plant is said to
be a favorite food for deer farther
west. The fragile, red-purple flowers
are clustered at the top of the plant.
There are four broad petals with
beautiful, curved anthers at the tips
of the eight stamens. The gracefully
curving pistil extends far out of the
flower to insure good cross
pollination. The calyx tube is urn-
shaped with four curving teeth at the
tip. In the fall, the leaves and stem
become scarlet in color.

126

FIREWEED or
GREAT WILLOW-HERB

Epilobium angustifolium

Evening-Primrose Family

Fireweed is a tall leafy plant with spikes of rose-magenta flowers at the top of the plant. It grows in clearings, thickets, along woodland roads and beside railroads — especially where the land has been burned over. It may be from four inches to six feet in height. American Indians called it Wickiup or Wickopy — perhaps because they used it to make their shelters which they called wigwarms or wickiups.

The alternate lance-shaped leaves are green above, but paler and veiny on the underside. The flowers are magenta or pink and have four spreading petals which may be as long as one-half inch. Unopened buds at the tip of the spike point downward, but rise as they expand and open. The fruit is a slender pod with silky-tufted seeds inside.

HAIRY WILLOW-HERB

Epilobium hirsutum

Evening-Primrose Family

This willow-herb is a bushy, much-branched plant with a stout, densely-hairy stem. It grows in waste places, roadside thickets, and meadows to a height of from two to six feet. The leaves are mostly opposite on the stem, are hairy, and have finely-toothed margins. The small pink or purplish flowers are in long clusters in the axils of the upper leaves or at the top of the plant. There are four petals, each of which is notched at the tip. The cross-shaped tip of the pistil (stigma) is noticeable in the center of the flower.

PURPLE-LEAVED WILLOW-HERB

Epilobium coloratum

Evening-Primrose Family

This hairy willow-herb is erect and freely branched. It grows in wet places to a height of from one to three feet. The leaves are narrow and lance-shaped with numerous teeth. Sometimes the leaves are marked with purple. The numerous minute flowers are less than one-fourth of an inch long and have four white or pink petals. The flowers are sometimes in a nodding position. The numerous seed pods are as long as two inches and stand erect. They split open when mature to expose the many seeds with white hairs.

NORTHERN WILLOW-HERB

Epilobium glandulosum

Evening-Primrose Family

This stout, leafy willow-herb grows in wet places to a height of from one to three feet. It sends out stolons similar to those on strawberry plants to start new plants for the next year. The toothed leaves are attached to the stem without long petioles and the leaves are not marked with purple. The numerous pink flowers have four petals and are erect. The seed pod splits lengthwise to expose the seeds with whitish hairs.

PIPSISSEWA or PRINCE'S PINE

Chimaphila umbellata var. cisatlantica

Wintergreen Family

This fragrant wild flower grows in great patches on the floor of forests where there is an underlying sandy soil and a carpet of decaying leaves or pine needles. The plant grows to a height of from four to twelve inches. Numerous shiny evergreen leaves are arranged in whorls or scattered along the stem. The leaves vary in length from one to two and one-half inches, are sharply toothed at the edges, and may have either blunt or pointed tips. The flowers — arranged in a loose cluster at the top of the leaf-bearing stalk — are about one-half inch broad and vary in color from white to dark pink. The five petals are noticeably cup-shaped, rounded at the tips, and widely spread. Ten violet anthers are evenly arranged like beads around the flat-topped central pistil.

SPOTTED WINTERGREEN

Chimaphila maculata

Wintergreen Family

This woodland plant is also called Spotted Pipsissewa, and indeed it is very similar to Pipsissewa above.

It grows from an underground stem and has erect branches from four to ten inches tall. The nodding waxy flowers are fragrant and can be either white or pink. They have five recurved petals and ten stamens which form a crown in the center. The round tip of the pistil (stigma) forms the central point of the crown. The long evergreen leaves are arranged in whorls of four. They are toothed, sharply pointed, and have a whitish pattern at the midvein.

ONE-FLOWERED WINTERGREEN

Moneses uniflora

Wintergreen Family

This tiny flower is seldom taller than five inches. It grows in mossy, sheltered woods. The leaves are tiny, round, and finely toothed. A solitary pink or white flower hangs face down from the tip of the stem. It is fragrant and very similar to that on Pipsissewa. (See p. 57)

AMERICAN RHODODENDRON GREAT LAUREL ROSE BAY

Rhododendron maximum

Heath Family

This beautiful native shrub grows in low, dense woods, usually near a lake or swamp, or stream. Where it flourishes, it forms Rhododendron jungles because the branches interlace in such a way as to make passage impossible. It is a woody shrub which may be from six to thirty feet tall. The thick, leathery leaves are evergreen, and they droop downwards during winter. They are oblong and have a point at the tip. The lovely flowers are in large clusters. Each flower is somewhat cup-shaped, has five waxy petals and may be nearly two inches across. The petals are white, or tinged with pink. The throat of the flower may be greenish and have pink, orange, or green spots in it. There are usually ten stamens and only one pistil. The flower cluster turns pinker with age. This plant is protected by Maine state law.

MOUNTAIN LAUREL

Kalmia latifolia

Heath Family

Mountain Laurel is an evergreen shrub usually about three feet tall. Where it is abundant, however, it grows to be as tall as ten feet and forms dense thickets. The leaves are alternate on the woody stem and are shiny and leathery. The cluster of blossoms is made up of cup-shaped pink flowers with five petals joined together. There are ten stamens which form arching spokes from the center of the flower to tiny pits on the side of the flower. These are released when insects light on the flowers. Mountain Laurel is protected by Maine law.

SHEEP LAUREL or LAMBKILL

Kalmia angustifolia

Heath Family

This branching shrub grows up to 3 ft. tall but is usually about fifteen or twenty inches tall. It grows in pastures, rocky slopes, and in swamps. The cuplike flowers form in a cluster at the end of last year's growth of leaves, and the new leaves seem to grow upwards from the middle of this cluster of flowers. The leaves occur in 3's along the stem. The older leaves below are narrow and are in a drooping position. Sometimes the underside of the leaf is hairy.

BOG LAUREL
Kalmia polifolia
Heath Family

Bog Laurel is a smaller shrub found in bogs — usually less than three feet tall. It is sparingly branched and has leaves which are arranged in pairs. The edges of the leaves are rolled backwards and the under sides of the leaves are covered with white hairs. The flowers are similar to the Mountain Laurel but are smaller and paler in color.

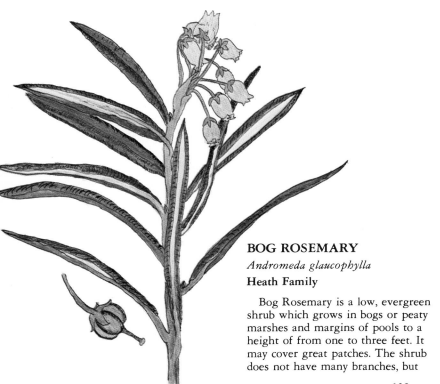

BOG ROSEMARY
Andromeda glaucophylla
Heath Family

Bog Rosemary is a low, evergreen shrub which grows in bogs or peaty marshes and margins of pools to a height of from one to three feet. It may cover great patches. The shrub does not have many branches, but

many shrubs will grow together. New growth has leaves which are larger and wider than the older shrubs. Firm, narrow leaves are alternate on the woody stem. They are blue-green on the top and covered with white wool on the underside. The sides of the leaves roll under. The flowers are in small umbels, but each barrel-shaped flower is on its own curved pedicel (flower stalk). The fruits which form later last all winter.

HEATHER
SCOTCH HEATHER
Calluna vulgaris
Heath Family

Heather is a low fern-like evergreen shrub with tiny, sharp needles in four rows along the branches. It was introduced from Europe, but has now naturalized in peaty or damp sandy soils. This shrub is from five to fifteen inches tall. Minute opposite leaves are crowded and overlapping each other on the branches. Pink flowers are in long — sometimes one-sided — clusters. The corolla is much shorter and less showy than the calyx of four colored sepals. (see enlargement)

LARGE CRANBERRY
Vaccinium macrocarpon
Heath Family

This creeping shrub grows in bogs and wet places to a height up to twelve inches. It has alternate, blunt, oval leaves. The flower stems rise from the axils of the reduced leaves midway on the stem. The nodding flowers are solitary on each flower stem (pedicel), but there may be three or four pedicels on each plant. Flowers are pink and have four petals that turn back so far they often overlap at the top. The red and yellow stamens protrude from the center to form a "beak". The fruit is a juicy, seedy berry which matures in late fall and is used in making cranberry sauce.

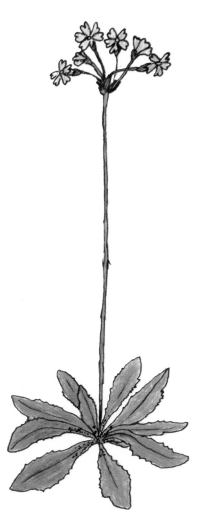

BIRD'S-EYE PRIMROSE

Primula mistassinica

Primrose Family

This dwarf primrose grows on wet banks, gravelly shores, or on rocks to a height of from six to twelve inches. The leaves are arranged in a ring at the bottom of the flower stalk. The base of the leaf is tapering and the margins are toothed. The leaves are smooth, but the lower sides are often covered with a white or yellow powder. The flowers are funnel-shaped and may be either pink or pale purple. Usually there is a yellow eye. The flowers are in a loose cluster of from two to eight at the top of the single flower stalk. Each flower has a five-lobed corolla and is from one-half to three-fourths of an inch broad.

134

SCARLET PIMPERNEL

Anagallis arvensis

Primrose Family

Scarlet Pimpernel is an erect, branching plant which grows on lawns, in gardens, and along roadsides to a height of four to twelve inches. The paired, oval leaves are pointed and have no leaf stem. They are attached directly to the main stem. The star-like scarlet flowers have five petals and only open in fair weather. Each flower is on its own slender pedicel which rises from the axil of the leaf.

SEA MILKWORT

Glaux maritima

Primrose Family

Sea Milkwort is a pale fleshy plant which often rests on the ground. It grows on beaches and at the edges of salt marshes to a height of from two to six inches. It is a branching plant with narrow, oblong, or linear leaves which end in a blunt point. A tiny flower with five petal-like sepals is tucked into the axil of each leaf. The flower usually is pink, but may vary from white to pink.

SALT MARSH PINK or SEA PINK

Sabatia stellaris

Gentian Family

Marsh Pink grows in salt meadows and marshes to a height of six to twenty inches. It is a slender, loosely-branched plant with narrow, opposite leaves and large, crimson-pink flowers at the tips of the branches. The light green leaves are oblong to lance-shaped and narrow to a point at the base and at the tip. The large flowers vary in color from deep pink to almost white. Each flower usually has five petals, each of which is marked with a yellow base outlined in crimson. The calyx has five linear parts which are almost as long as the petals. The upper half of the style in the center is divided into two spreading parts.

PLYMOUTH GENTIAN or LARGE SABATIA

Sabatia kennedyana

Gentain Family

This rare wildflower grows in Canada and in a few places in Southern New England, especially near Plymouth, Massachusetts where it is called Rose of Plymouth. It grows at margins of fresh water ponds in an area of peaty or sandy soil which is bared as the water level lowers. The stem leaves are in pairs and are not stalked. Each exquisite flower has from nine to eleven rose-pink petals with a yellow base outlined in crimson. Each flower may be up to two inches across, and a plant may have from one to twenty-four flowers on it.

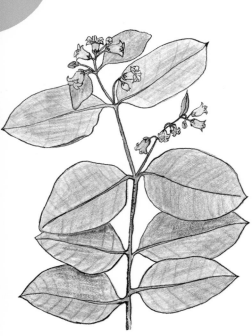

SPREADING DOGBANE
or INDIAN HEMP

Apocynum androsaemifolium

Dogbane Family

Spreading Dogbane is a shrubby plant with ruddy-colored stems that are so branching there is little evidence of one main stem. The stems are not woody and will bend easily. A milky juice comes from the stem if it is broken. Along the ruddy stem are pairs of large, oval leaves. This plant grows in thickets and along paths and roadsides to a height of from one to three feet. Numerous flowers are in loose clusters at the ends of the branches. Each fragrant, bell-shaped flower hangs on its own curved stem. They are pale pink and are striped inside with deep rose. The five teeth on the bell curve outwards.

FOUR-LEAVED MILKWEED

Asclepias quadrifolia

Milkweed Family

This milkweed has whorls of four pointed, oval leaves, but at the top of the plant the leaves may only be in pairs. The leaves have long stalks (petioles). The plant grows in dry woods to a height of from one to two and one-half feet. There are several loose clusters of flowers at the top, and the flowers are pale pink or lavender and often have whitish hoods.

COMMON MILKWEED
Asclepias syriaca
Milkweed Family

This stout, downy plant grows along roads and in dry fields to a height of from three to six feet. The broad oval leaves are thick and are covered with a grayish down on the underside. The flowers are in numerous round umbels at the top of the plant and in upper leaf axils. The umbels are sometimes so heavy that they are in a drooping position. The flowers are in soft shades of rose, lavender, pink, and dull, brownish purple. The erect pointed seed pods are gray-green and have a warty appearance. The pods are up to four inches long.

SWAMP MILKWEED
Asclepias incarnata
Milkweed Family

Swamp Milkweed (not shown) is similar to the one above, but grows in swamps and thickets to a height of from two to four feet. The stem has less milky juice and is very leafy. The leaves are much narrower than those on the Common Milkweed. The pink flowers are in smaller umbels and there are several of these together at the *top of each plant,* giving the appearance of a rather flat-topped cluster.

BLUNT-LEAVED MILKWEED
Asclepias amplexicaulis
Milkweed Family

This milkweed is a small plant which grows in dry soil to a height of from two to three feet. It can be identified by its wavy-edged leaves which clasp the stem at the base. The flowers are greenish-purple with pink hoods. Usually there is only one flower umbel on each plant. The seed pods are more slender than those of the Common Milkweed, and they are practically smooth.

138

SMALL RED MORNING-GLORY

Ipomoea coccinea

Morning-Glory Family

This morning glory grows in waste places, thickets, and along roadsides. It has a twining stem which climbs to a height of several feet or trails along the ground. The thin, heart-shaped leaves are on slender leaf stems. The red face of the flower is slightly five-lobed. The small scarlet, trumpet-shaped flowers are on long flower stalks which are usually not longer than the leaves. The green sepals have bristle-shaped appendages.

COMMON MORNING-GLORY

Ipomea purpurea

Morning-Glory Family

This familiar, twining vine grows in wasteplaces — especially where it has escaped from gardens. It is from four to ten feet long and may be trailing on the ground or climbing on near-by shrubs. The broad heart-shaped leaves are on slender leaf stalks. The funnel-shaped corolla may be purple, pink, blue, or white. Usually from one to five flowers are on the same stalk. The sepals, flower stalk, and stem are all hairy.

139

HEDGE BINDWEED

Convolvulus sepium

Morning-Glory Family

This member of the morning-glory family grows in a trailing or twining manner and is often several feet long. It grows in fields, on beaches, in thickets, along roadsides, and climbs over fences, stonewalls, hedgerows, and old compost heaps. The leaves are arrowhead-shaped with blunt basal lobes which point away from the center vein. The leaves vary in size from two to five inches long. Each leaf has its own leaf stem which is attached to the main twining stem. The flowers are shaped like a funnel and are usually pink with white stripes. They vary from pale pink to white, however, and often fade with age. There are five lobes on the spreading mouth of the trumpet-shaped flower. The five stamens are attached at the base of the tube, but the tips or anthers often protrude from center.

MOSS PINK or GROUND PHLOX

Phlox subulata

Phlox Family

Moss Pink is a low creeping plant that spreads over rocky or sandy land. It carpets hillsides and is commonly found in cemeteries or along lanes. The stem of this plant is much branched, and crowded with stiff-pointed leaves, but only grows a few inches high. The tips of the branches turn upwards and end in clusters of five-petaled tube-like flowers. The flowers bloom simultaneously and hide the moss-type foliage from view. This mass of flowers can be breath-takingly beautiful when viewed from a distance. The colors range from white to bright pink, to orchid, but pink is the most common.

140

WILD SWEET WILLIAM

Phlox maculata

Phlox Family

This wild flower is similar to the garden variety, but has a slender purple-spotted stem and the flowers are arranged in a long cylindrical cluster. The flowers have five pink petals which are joined to make a long corolla tube. There are five pointed green sepals at the base of the long tube. This plant is from one and one-half to three feet tall and grows in low woods and near river banks. It has opposite unnotched leaves which are smooth and firm.

FALL or GARDEN PHLOX

Phlox paniculata

Phlox Family

This tall garden escape grows near old dwellings, along borders of woodlands, or in thickets and is usually from two to six feet in height. The stout, smooth stem soon forms clumps which will come up year after year. The opposite, long, dark-green pointed leaves are very veiny and they have short leaf stalks or no stalks at all. The long-tubed flowers are in clusters at the top of the stem. The broad, dense cluster has many green bracts among the flowers. The flowers vary in color from pink, to purplish, to white. Each one is about an inch in length and has five spreading petals. The anthers are pale yellow or white.

COMFREY
Symphytum officinale
Borage Family

This erect, hairy plant has branching stems and is from two to three feet tall. It grows along roadsides and in waste places. The leaves do not have a petiole (leaf stem), but rather extend downward on the main stem to form long wings on either side. The leaves have very noticeable veins which stand out on the under side. They are lighter in color than the leaf, and form an odd pattern on the leaf. The tubular flowers are in curled clusters which are characteristic of flowers in the Borage Family. The flowers may be white, cream, pale pink, or dull purple and are about one third of an inch across.

142

AMERICAN GERMANDER or WOOD SAGE

Teucrium canadense

Mint Family

Germander grows in rich woods, thickets, and along shores to a height of from eight to thirty-six inches. It is a downy perennial with stiff stems and light-green leaves which have unevenly-toothed margins. The leaves have pointed tips, are paired on the stem, and are covered with fine hair on the under side. The light purple or magenta to pinkish-white flowers are in a long, wand-like flower spike at the top of the plant. Each flower is nearly three-fourths of an inch long and is arranged in whorls of about six flowers each. The flower is very unique, (see insert) because the stamens do not protrude from the center of the throat as they do on most mints, but through a *slit in the upper lip*. The broad, lower lip is spreading and has curvy margins and is mottled with darker spots.

MOTHERWORT

Leonurus cardiaca

Mint Family

Motherwort grows in waste places around dwellings to a height of from two to four feet. It is a familiar herb which has been naturalized from Europe and is now quite common. It has deeply-cut paired leaves and tiny pink flowers encircling the stem at the leaf axils. It has been cultivated in Europe for supposed medicinal value. The stem leaves are wedge-shaped toward the stem, but are

divided into three pointed segments at the tip. The lower leaves are more rounded, are slashed, and have a long petiole. The irregular flower is two-lipped. The upper lip is bearded and hooded over the lower lip which is smooth and extends downward. The green calyx has five thorn-like points.

FALSE DRAGONHEAD

Physostegia virginiana

Mint Family

This plant is also called Lion's Heart or Dragonhead or Obedient Flower. It grows in damp woods, along streams, or in wet meadows to a height of from one to four feet. The slender, erect, square stem is not hairy and may be branching at the top. The narrow, opposite leaves are not stalked. They are narrow and pointed and have sharply-toothed margins. The showy flowers are in a spire-like cluster at the top of the plant. Each flower is about an inch long and is rose-pink with purplish veins. The tube gradually enlarges upwards to an inflated throat. The round upper lip is concave and the lower lip is larger and is divided into three spreading lobes. The middle lobe is the largest, and it is notched. The calyx is also bell-shaped and has five pointed teeth. If you press the flower down, or up, or to one side, it will stay there — hence the reason for the name of Obedient Flower.

HEMP-NETTLE

Galeopsis tetrahit

Mint Family

Hemp-Nettle has either simple or branched, hairy, square stems with an enlarged place below each pair of leaves. The leaves are lance-shaped, toothed, and have hairs on both sides. The flowers are small but are massed together at the leaf axils. The tubular flower (see enlargement) is white, or pink, or variegated — with stiff, white hairs on the top of the upper lip. The flower is strongly two-lipped with the upper lip forming a hood over the three-lobed lower lip. The calyx at the base of the tubular flower has five sharp spines on it.

HENBIT

Lamium amplexicaule

Mint Family

Henbit has several branching, square stems which spring from one root. It is from four to sixteen inches tall and grows in wastelands and along roadsides. There are a few long-stemmed basal leaves with scalloped edges. The wide, stem leaves are roundish with scalloped edges, and surround the stem in pairs. The flowers are clustered in the axils of the upper leaves. The tubed flower (see enlargement) is opened wide at the top and the upper lip forms a hood over the lower, lobed lip. The flower varies from white to pinkish purple and has darker spots on it. The upper lip is crowned with a tuft of magenta hairs.

BEE-BALM or OSWEGO TEA
Monarda didyma
Mint Family

Bee-balm grows along stream banks and in moist meadows to a height of from two to four feet. It is a flower the humming birds seek. The stout, square stem has paired leaves and tubular, scarlet, flowers in a terminal head above red and green bracts. The stem is usually not hairy, but the leaves may be downy on the underside. Each vermillion to scarlet flower is an inch or more long. The corolla has an erect, arching upper lip and a spreading, three-lobed lower lip. The calyx is tubular with five teeth with hair-like tips. Only two of the stamens project from the throat of the flower.

MOUNTAIN MINTS
Pycnanthemum virginianum

There are about fifteen mountain mints in our area and they may be white or pale lilac in color. See page 71 in the white section for descriptions.

146

RED TURTLEHEAD

Chelone lyoni

Figwort Family

Red Turtlehead is a cultivated plant which has escaped and now grows wild in moist ground of shores and thickets. It grows to a height of from one to two-and-a-half feet. It is very similar to Turtlehead on page 76, but has broad, round-based leaf blades on distinct stalks. The leaf blades have coarsely-toothed margins. The turtle-head-shaped corolla is crimson or deep pink. The top lip is sharply ridged and the lower lip has a deep yellow beard and bright purple lines.

MUDWORT or MUDWEED

Limosella aquatica

Figwort Family

Mudwort is a small, closely matted or creeping annual with tufted leaves. It grows in sand and mud of shores and brooks to a height of one to five inches. the reclining branches often take root at the tip and produce new rosettes of long-petioled, oval leaves. The flowers are on the tips of leafless flower stalks. The corolla is pink, and is not much longer than the cup-like caylx. There is another mudwort which is very similar but has white blossoms and more thread-like leaves. It, too, is a tufted plant which grows in the mud.

PAINTED-CUP or INDIAN PAINT-BRUSH

Castilleja coccinea

Figwort Family

Painted-Cup is a hairy plant which grows in fields and meadows or in damp sandy soil. It grows to a height of from one to two feet. The leaves vary greatly, but all have several long narrow parts — with the middle segment being the longest. The leaf bracts at the top of the stem have three lobes and are tipped with scarlet. These nearly hide the small two-lipped greenish-yellow flowers, but the pistils protrude from among the scarlet-tipped leaves.

RED BARTSIA

Odontites serotina

Figwort Family

This hairy weed is common in fields and waste places. It grows to a height of from four to sixteen inches. It can be either branched or not branched. The leaves are narrow and have two or three blunt teeth on each leaf margin. The flowers are in a leafy spike at the top. Pairs of leaves are mixed right in with the reddish-purple flowers. Each flower is about a half-inch long and has two lips. The bottom lip has three lobes and the top lip is hood-like and does not fold backwards. The top lip is often covered with light red hairs.

LOPSEED

Phryma leptostachya

Lopseed Family

Lopseed grows in woods and
thickets to a height of from one to
three feet. There is no other species
in this family. Lopseed is a rather
slender, erect, perennial herb with a
branching four-angled stem. The
slender branches are opposite each
other. The broad, thin, opposite
leaves are pointed at the tips and
have coarsely-toothed margins. Lower
leaves have long stalks, but the upper
ones are shorter, or are lacking
entirely. The snapdragon-like flowers
are about one-fourth of an inch long
and are in narrow spikes at the top
of the stem and branches. The
flowers are usually opposite one
another on the stem. The corolla is
rose-pink or purplish and has two
lips. The upper lip is erect, notched
and concave, while the larger, lower
lip is divided into three, blunt,
spreading lobes. There are four
stamens. The cylindrical calyx is also
two-lipped with three, long, bristly
teeth on the upper lip and two
shorter, slender teeth on the lower
lip. The flowers are erect at first, but
when in full bloom, are at right
angles to the stem. The mature fruit
is pressed downward against the
stem in pairs.

BUTTONWEED

Diodia teres

Madder Family

Buttonweed is a small, hairy plant
with weak stems and short stalkless
leaves arranged in pairs. The two
opposite leaves are joined around the
stem by small membranes which

have bristles projecting. The leaves are long and slender, and usually not more than one and a half inches in length. The plant grows in dry places and is often growing as a weed in sandy lanes. Buttonweed is often reclining, but sometimes stands erect to a height of from six to twenty-four inches. There are from one to three funnel-shaped flowers in the leaf axils. They may be white, pink, or purplish. They have four petals and four sepals, and do not have a flower stalk.

PARTRIDGE-BERRY or RUNNING BOX

Mitchella repens
Madder Family

This low creeping plant grows in rich woods. The pink or white four-petaled flowers are joined together in pairs at the end of the trailing branches. The petals are hairy on the inside. The shiny evergreen leaves are small and nearly round with lighter colored veins. They are arranged in pairs along the stem. The fruit is a single red berry which develops from the bottom parts of both flowers. The berry has two blossom ends instead of only one as do most other berries.

TWINFLOWER

Linnaea borealis
Honeysuckle Family

This delicate plant of the cold woods, bogs, and peaty places has a creeping stem from which short erect branches rise. Nodding trumpet-shaped flowers hang in pairs from the tip of the branched stem. Each flower is about one-half inch long and has five small teeth. It is very fragrant. The stalk is very slender and from three to six inches tall. The leaves are very small and round and are arranged in pairs.

SWAMP VALERIAN

Valeriana uliginosa

Valerian Family

The flowers on this plant may be either pink or white. See page 80 in the white section for description.

CARDINAL FLOWER

Lobelia cardinalis

Bluebell Family

This brilliant red flower grows in wet meadows, marshes, and shady places at the water's edge — sometimes growing right in slow-moving water of a shady stream. It varies in height to from two to four feet. It is becoming quite rare and *should not be picked.* If you are fortunate, you might find a rare albino white form. The stem on this plant is coarse and has numerous, alternate, pointed leaves with toothed margins. The showy flowers grow in an elongated cluster along a central stem. The flower is somewhat two-lipped with the upper lip standing erect and the lower lip spreading and three-cleft. The five stamens are united into a tube around the fringed stigma. Each flower is quite large — up to two inches in length on larger plants.

151

NEW ENGLAND ASTER

Aster novae-angliae forma roseus

Composite Family

This is the pink or rose type of New England Aster which is explained more fully on page 335 in the purple section.

BURDOCK

Arctium minus

Composite Family

Burdock is a common biennial found in waste places. The first year, only large, rough, basal leaves are produced. These are heartshaped and are on long, thick petioles (leaf stems). This cluster of basal leaves has been called Wild Rhubarb by the un-knowing. The second year of growth, a large bushy, branching stem grows to a height up to five feet, but is more commonly shorter than that. Numerous flower heads are on short stalks or are attached directly to the stem (sessile). Individual flowers in each head are tubular and vary in color from pink to purple. The bracts holding the flower heads are bristly. They later form hard, round, brown burs which stick to clothes and animals.

152

DAY LILY

Hemerocallis fulva

Lily Family

This tawny-orange lily faces upward also, but may be distinguished from the Wood Lily because it has *no spots* and has a *leafless stem.* The long sword-like leaves grow in a clump at the base of the plant. There are clusters of long buds at the top of the stem, and each opens for one day only and then fades as another bud opens. Six long stamens and the pistil protrude from the throat of the funnel-shaped flower. The plant is from three to six feet tall and is not a native wild flower, but has escaped from cultivation.

WOOD LILY

Lilium philadelphicum

Lily Family

This lily grows from a bulb on an erect stem from one to three feet tall in dry woods or thickets. There are from one to five flowers at the summit which face upward. The leaves are in whorls around the stem. The six petals are usually a brilliant orange, but vary from yellow-orange to nearly red. There are purple spots on the inside of the petals near the base.

153

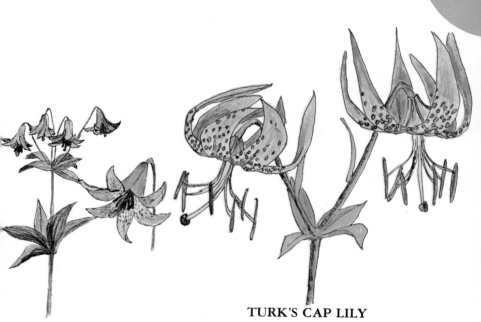

CANADA LILY

Lilium canadense
Lily Family

   Other names for this lily are Field Lily or Wild Yellow Lily. It is more typically a yellow lily, but the color varies from yellow to orange to almost red. The plant is from two to five feet tall and grows in moist open places or wet meadows. Canada Lily has clusters of up to twenty bell-shaped flowers — each on its own pedicel (flower stem). The flowers are in a nodding position at the summit of the stem or from the axils of upper leaves. There are six "petals" which curve outwards, but not backwards. There are large dark spots on the inside of the petals. The long, pointed leaves are usually in whorls at intervals around the slender stem.

TURK'S CAP LILY

Lilium superbum
Lily Family

   This lily grows in wet meadows and in swampy woods to a height of from three to eight feet. It is one of the taller members of this genus. It has whorls of smooth leaves which are not rough on the margins or veins as in Lilium canadense.
   The lower leaves are whorled, but upper ones may sometimes be only paired. The nodding flowers are on erect stalks — usually in pairs. They are orange-red with purple spots. As many as fifty flowers may occur on a large plant. The flower segments are more recurved than in Lilium canadense, and there is a green, starlike marking on the face of the flower. Six stamens and the pistil project far from the flower throat.

154

TIGER LILY

Lilium tigrinum

Lily Family

Tiger Lily is an escape from cultivation and is now growing "wild" along dry roadsides or in dry thickets. It is a tall lily similar to Turk's Cap Lily but the *leaves are alternate* — not in whorls. The shiny dark bulblets in axils of the leaves are distinctive on this plant. The large, showy, nodding orange or pink-red are spotted with purple. There is no green starlike marking. The three petals and three sepals are just alike and curve backwards.

BLACKBERRY LILY

Belamcanda chinensis

Iris Family

This is not a lily, but an iris. It grows to a height of from one to two feet in open woods, along roadsides, and in dry places. It has escaped from cultivation and now grows wild in some places. The flower has six equal salmon-orange petals with crimson markings and is about two inches broad. The buds open one at a time and each flower lasts for only one day. The narrow leaves are similar to those of most iris plants.

The name Blackberry Lily was probably given to this plant because of the fruit. The oblong seed pod splits open when it is dry to reveal a blackberry-like cluster of shiny black seeds.

YELLOW FRINGED ORCHIS
Habenaria ciliaris
Orchid Family

Orange Plume and Orange Orchis are other names for this orchid. It grows in swales, boggy meadows or in wet peaty soil — usually in full sun. It is from one to two feet in height and blooms into early September. The stem is very leafy. Lower leaves are oblong with pointed tips, but the upper ones are hardly more than pointed bracts. The flowers are deep orange in color and have a long slender spur and a deeply-fringed lower lip. The tightly-flowered spike at the tip of the plant may be three or more inches long.

SPOTTED TOUCH-ME-NOT or JEWELWEED
Impatiens capensis
Touch-me-not Family

This touch-me-not grows in wet shady areas in ditches, along streams, and in moist woods. It grows in colonies and varies in height from two to five feet. The succulent stems give off an orange juice when bruised. The plant is used by some of offset the effects of poison ivy. Orange, spotted blossoms hang like jewels from long flower stalks arising from leaf axils. The blossoms are in a horizontal position. They are orange-yellow and are mottled with reddish-brown. One sepal is large and forms a cone-shaped sac which ends in a curved spur. There are three petals — two of them are cut into unequal lobes. The alternate, thin leaves with toothed margins are whitish on the under side.

156

BUTTERFLY-WEED
or PLEURISY-ROOT

Asclepias tuberosa

Milkweed Family

This milkweed can easily be distinguished from other milkweeds by the bright orange flowers. The stout, hairy stems are from one to two feet high and are not milky when broken. The long, narrow, pointed leaves are hairy and alternate on the stem — possibly opposite on smaller branches. The bright orange flowers are numerous and are in a terminal cluster. Look at the inset to see a typical milkweed-like blossom. The hoods on the flowers are erect and longer than the stamens. Inside of each hood is an odd-looking horn. The five petals drop down around the stem.

ORANGE HAWKWEED or
DEVIL'S PAINTBRUSH

Hieracium aurantiacum

Composite Family

This particular hawkweed is always bright red-orange. It is a very hairy plant with long, tapering, basal leaves. Sometimes there are one or two reduced leaves on the stem, but not usually. Orange Hawkweed grows to a height of from six to twenty-four inches along roads and paths, and often covers an entire field. The flower heads are in tight terminal clusters at the summit of the stem. Some flower heads open soon while others are still closed in round or oval black, hairy buds. Each open head is from one-half to one inch broad. What appear to be orange strap-shaped petals with five teeth at the ends are not petals at all. These are really complete individual ray flowers.

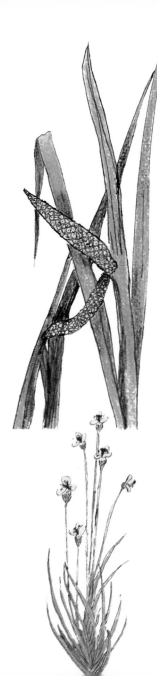

SWEET FLAG

Acorus calamus

Arum Family

Sweet Flag is a tall grass-like plant which grows in wet swampy places. It has long stiff, sword-like leaves which are as tall as four feet. There is a spadix of closely crowded tiny greenish-yellow flowers which jut out from the main stem at an angle. The stem is flat and very similar to the blade of the leaf. The rootstock of the Sweet Flag is very spicy-smelling and furnishes materials to make a drug called calamus.

YELLOW-EYED GRASS

Xyris caroliniana

Yellow-Eyed Grass Family

There are about twelve species of the Yellow-Eyed Grass and all are similar to the one pictured. They are classified according to small technicalities, so it would be unnecessary for the beginner to learn to distinguish one from another.

Yellow-Eyed Grass is a tufted grass-like plant which grows in wet meadows, bogs, or at the shore. The flower-bearing stalks are taller than the leaves. This stalk varies with the species, but may be as high as two or three feet in some cases. The flowers — held in a "cup" of overlapping scales — are bright yellow and have three petals. Three stamens and a three-branched style protrude from the center.

158

WATER STARGRASS

Heteranthera dubia

Pickerelweed Family

Water Stargrass is a submerged,
grass-like plant with a slender stem
and long, narrow, pointed leaves
which are almost translucent. The
leaves have parallel nerves. The plant
is submerged in shallow, quiet water
and may be two or three feet tall —
depending upon the depth of the
water. Solitary pale yellow flowers
are about one-half of an inch broad.
They have a long slender tube —
from one to one and a half inches —
which brings the flower to the
surface of the water. The flower has
five long, slender divisions and the
stamens in the center have arrow-
shaped tips. These stamens are
longer than the style on the pistil in
the center.

CANADA LILY
MEADOW LILY
WILD YELLOW LILY

Lilium canadense

Lily Family

This common lily is found growing
in low wet meadows or along
roadsides where it is wet. The
slender stem is hairless, light green,
and has whorls of light green,
pointed leaves at regular intervals. It
grows from two to five feet high.

At the top of the stem, several
flower stalks form and each has a
singular pendulous flower. The
flower is bell shaped with six petal-
like parts that curve backwards. The
outside color is a buff-yellow, but the
inside is a brighter color and is
spotted with reddish or purplish

brown. There are six long brown-tipped stamens in the center. This lily may also be orange. See p. 153 for further descriptive notes.

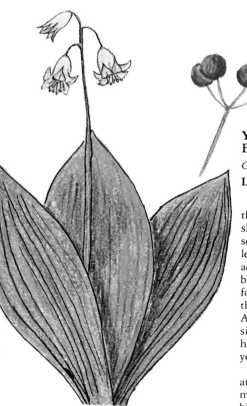

YELLOW CLINTONIA or BLUE BEAD LILY

Clintonia borealis

Lily Family

This lovely lily-like plant grows in the cool, moist woods and likes the shade. It is a member of the lily family so has the same type of vein-marked leaves. These large wide leaves are actually more striking than the small blossom. Each plant has from two to four shiny green leaves. From amidst these leaves, a single flower stalk rises. At the tip of the stalk, from three to six yellow bell-shaped flowers will hang. These are cream-colored or light yellow and look like miniature lilies.

Though the blossom itself is not too attractive, the berries which form later make up for this. The cluster of pure blue berries above the shiny wide leaves makes a distinctive picture. Blue is a rare color among wild flowers, but this uncommon color is striking on this Clintonia. For this reason, many call it the Blue Bead Lily.

The plant grows to be about a foot high, but varies more or less depending upon the habitat.

YELLOW STAR-GRASS
Hypoxis hirsuta
Amaryllis Family

Yellow Star-Grass is a common
flower which grows in the open woods
and meadows. It has a long blooming
season and is particularly attractive
when growing together with Blue-Eyed
Grass.

The flower has a clear yellow inside
and a green hairy outside. The leaves
are hairy and grass-like. Each plant
has several pointed star-like flowers on
separate flowering stalks which are
usually shorter than the leaves. The
entire plant grows from a corm to a
height of from three to seven inches.

YELLOW IRIS or
YELLOW SWORD FLAG
Iris pseudacorus
Iris Family

This is the only yellow iris likely
to be found growing in the wild. It is
a European escape from gardens, but
is now quite widely found as a "wild
flower". It grows in marshes, along
streams, and in wet meadows to a
height of from one to three feet. The
leaves are stiff, pale green and there
are several flowers on the flower
stem. Each blossom has bright yellow,
recurved sepals and erect spoon-shaped
petals. There is no crest as there is
on some in this family.

DOWNY or SMALL YELLOW LADY'S SLIPPER

Cypripedium parviflorum

Orchid Family

This lady's slipper grows in bogs, mossy swamps, wet woods, or near wet shores or damp rocks. It has a leafy, downy stem which may be from one to two and a half feet tall. There are three or four large, oval-pointed leaves with veins going lengthwise. The sepals on the flower are usually longer than the much-inflated lip. The top sepal may be greenish or madder-purple, or green striped with purple. The petals are very narrow and are usually twisted. The lip is pale yellow with purple lines. There is a tuft of white hairs inside of the opening in the lip. The flower is very fragrant.

BOG or LOESEL'S TWAY-BLADE

Liparis loeselii

Orchid Family

This twayblade grows in wet woods, bogs, or peaty meadows to a height of eight inches or so. It has two yellow-green leaves at the base of the flower stem. The leaves are strongly keeled. From two to twenty-five yellowish-green flowers are at the top of the stalk. The sepals and side petals are narrow, but the lower lip is broad.

162

PURSLANE or PUSSLEY
Portulaca oleracea
Purslane Family

Purslane grows in waste places and is commonly found in dooryards and gardens. It is hard to kill; will survive uprooting and exposure to the sun; and will take root again. It is from four to ten inches long and grows close to the ground, spreading in a mat or circle. The succulent, prostrate weed has thick, pink stems and rosettes of fleshy, paddle-shaped leaves with a tiny flower in center of each rosette. Each flower has five yellow petals and from seven to twelve stamens. They bloom only in morning sunshine.

BULLHEAD LILY
YELLOW POND LILY
Nuphar variegatum
Water-Lily Family

This species of yellow pond lily is the most common in the Northeast, though there are three other kinds which are very similar. Bullhead Lily grows at margins of ponds, in pools, in bogs, or in sluggish water. There are many broad flat leaves with rounded basal lobes with a closed or very narrow notch. The flattened leaf stem has a median rib running lengthwise. The leaves usually float on top of the water, but may stand erect on their stalks if water level lowers. The flowers are globular in general outline. What look like yellow petals are really thick, fleshy sepals. The true petals are scale-like. The base of the inner surface of the yellow sepals may be brownish or reddish. In the center of the flower is a yellow disk.

AMERICAN NELUMBO or LOTUS

Nelumbo lutea

Water-Lily Family

Lotus grows in rivers or lakes from a stout rootstock which is in the mud under the water. The leaf stems and flower stalks may be from three to seven feet long, depending upon the depth of the water in which it grows. The bowl-shaped leaves may be one or two feet broad. They sometimes rise a foot or more out of the water. The upper surface of the leaf is smooth and dark green, but the lower surface is veiny, hairy, or scaly. The fragrant, pale yellow flowers are on tough, rigid, flower stalks which have several air canals. Each flower is from four to ten inches broad and has concave petals. The petals are surrounded by four or five overlapping scales. The fruit is a green, flat-topped capsule with raised black dots on it.

CREEPING SPEARWORT

Ranunculus reptans

Buttercup Family

Creeping Spearwort grows in damp sandy or gravelly places or on muddy shores and is rarely taller than three to four inches. It has trailing, thread-like stems which are sometimes under water. The plant may take root at the nodes on the stem. The leaves on the trailing branches are very slender and from one to three occur together at each node. The flowers are usually solitary on a long flower stalk. Each has from four to seven (usually five) narrow yellow petals with a definite claw and from three to six nerves. There may be from ten to twenty yellow stamens in the center.

COMMON BUTTERCUP

Ranunculus acris

Buttercup Family

There are about thirty-six different species of buttercups in our area and all are quite similar to the one shown here as a sample plant. This is our most familiar one, and it grows in fields, meadows, and marshy places to a height of two or three feet. The flower is about an inch broad with five yellow, overlapping petals, five sepals, and many stiff yellow-green stamens in the center. The leaves are dark green and are very deeply cut or jagged. The flowers will fall soon after the plant is picked.

SWAMP BUTTERCUP

Ranunculus septentrionalis

Buttercup Family

This buttercup is confined to swamps and low wet ground of moist meadows and wet thickets. It is usually from one to three feet tall. The rather smooth stem is weak and hollow, and may be in a reclining position. The foliage is variable in size and shape. Most leaves are divided into three, toothed segments each of which has a short stalk. The deep green, uppermost leaves are narrower and toothless. The flowers are deep yellow, about an inch broad, but the petals are not usually overlapping as they are on the common buttercup.

CELANDINE
Chelidonium majus
Poppy Family

This tall branching plant has leaves which are actually more showy than the flowers. The tip of each branch usually has a loose cluster of buds which bloom one at a time. The flower usually has four bright yellow, rounded petals, but some may have five petals. When the petals fall, the pistil in the center grows to a long, slim seed capsule and begins to mature while other buds open and bloom. The thin, soft leaves are unevenly divided into from three to seven lobed leaflets. Both the stem and the leaves contain a yellow acrid juice that stains clothes and hands. The plant is abundant in moist places, at the edges of woods, and around dwellings and grows to a height of from one to two feet.

CREEPING BUTTERCUP
Ranunculus repens
Buttercup Family

Ranunculus repens has long creeping stems which send up erect, hairy branches. The leaves are divided into three long-stalked sections and the leaflets are very deeply cut and toothed. The yellow flowers have from five to nine petals. This buttercup grows in ditches, fields, and wet ground.

HORNED or SEA POPPY

Glaucium flavum

Poppy Family

Horned Poppy is abundant near
the coast, especially in waste places
where it is sandy. The stem grows to
be from two to three feet tall. Single
yellow flowers and several stem
leaves without stalks are very
distinctive. The deeply-cut, gray-
green leaves appear to surround the
stem. At the base of the plant, there
are more leaves which are lobed on
each side of the mid-rib. They are on
petioles (leaf stalks) and give forth a
yellowish juice when bruised. The
large four-petaled flower is at the
summit of the stem and has only two
sepals. The seed pod is very long (6-
12 in.) and is sickle-shaped.

GOLDEN CORYDALIS

Corydalis aurea

Poppy Family

Golden Corydalis is a golden-
yellow-flowered species which is
similar to the Corydalis on page 110.
It is more abundant in the west, but
is sometimes found on limy slopes or
in sandy or gravelly soil in open or
rocky woods. It is a branching plant
with slender stems and grows to be
from six to fourteen inches in height.
The compound, pale-green leaves are
beautifully cut into three-lobed
segments. The golden-yellow flowers
are in clusters which may or may not
rise above the foliage. Each flower is
longer than one-half inch and has a
flattened corolla which is closed at
the throat. The spur is slightly
curved and is one half or more as
long as the body of the flower. The
outer petals have a central ridge, but
do not have a crest on the back.

FALSE FLAX
DUTCH FLAX
GOLD-OF-PLEASURE
Camelina sativa
Mustard Family

False Flax is an erect herb with nearly smooth stems and ascending branches. The pods are about one-third of an inch long and each contains numerous seeds. This plant was formerly cultivated for its oily seeds which were used in soapmaking. It grows in waste places, along roadsides, or in cultivated fields to a height up to three feet.

The long, pointed leaves clasp the stem by their two basal lobes. The lower leaves have petioles (leaf stems) and may or may not have toothed margins. Numerous small yellow flowers with four sepals and petals are arranged in terminal clusters. The lower buds open first, and the cluster lengthens as flower go to seed. Each flower is on its own flower stalk (peduncle) from the central rib of the flower cluster.

WILD RADISH or
JOINTED CHARLOCK
Raphanus raphanistrum
Mustard Family

This member of the mustard family has a coarse, purple, bristly stem and deeply lobed leaves with a large rounded lobe at the end. The four-petaled flowers are pale yellow or whitish and are marked with showy lilac-colored veins.

The seed pod is noticeably beaded when it is mature. Jointed Charlock grows in waste places, sandy soil, and in vacant lots to a height of from one to two and one-half feet.

168

BLACK MUSTARD

Brassica nigra

Mustard Family

As on the other mustards, the flowers on the Black Mustard open first at the bottom of the spike. Small erect seed pods which closely hug the stem replace the flowers as new flowers farther up the spike start to open. The stem lengthens as new flowers open at the top. The basal leaves are shiny green and have a large end lobe with two pairs of smaller lobes. The top leaves on the stem are not lobed — only toothed.

ERUCASTRUM

Erucastrum gallicum

Mustard Family

This member of the mustard family has no common name. It is an annual herb with downy stem and leaves. It grows in waste places, in fields, and along roadsides to a height of from two to three feet. The long leaves are deeply-cut nearly to the midrib. The flowers have four pale, yellow petals. The flowers are in elongated clusters at the top of the plant or in the axils of the leaves. The seeds are long and slender.

169

WALL ROCKET or SAND ROCKET

Diplotaxis muralis

Mustard Family

Wall Rocket is another member of the mustard family, and is similar to others in this section. It grows in waste places and along roadsides, mostly near the coast. It is usually not more than twenty inches tall. The deeply-cut or toothed leaves are all near the base of the plant. The stem usually begins to branch from the base of the plant. The four yellow petals are about one-third of an inch long — about twice as long as the sepals. The seed pods that develop later grow to be one and one-half inches long.

HEDGE MUSTARD

Sisymbrium officinale

Mustard Family

This common weed blooms very early in the spring and grows larger as warmer weather comes. The flowers are very similar to those of Black Mustard, but they are much smaller — less than 1/5 inch wide. Seed pods about ½ inch in length form and are closely pressed to the stem. The leaves are much longer, are more angular and have deeper lobes and sharper teeth than the leaves on Black Mustard. On some plants there will be two or four long teeth at the base of the leaf.

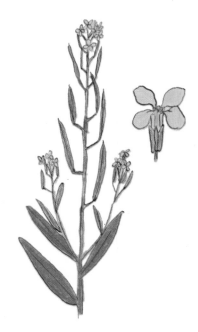

WORMSEED MUSTARD or TREACLE MUSTARD

Erysimum cheiranthoides

Mustard Family

Wormseed Mustard is an erect, simple or branching plant with minute hairs and many leaves. This plant is sometimes slightly grayish in color. It grows along streams and in fields to a height of from eight inches to two feet. The long, slender leaves have pointed tips and smooth or slightly-toothed margins. The lower leaves taper to a short petiole (leaf stem), but the upper ones are attached directly to the stem. The small yellow flowers have four petals. They are arranged in elongated clusters that lengthen as the bottom flowers bloom and go to seed. The seed pods *point upward* at an angle.

TANSY MUSTARD or FLIXWEED

Descurainia sophia

Mustard Family

Tansy Mustard is a slender, branching weed which grows along roadsides and in waste places to a height of from one to two and a half feet. The leaves are divided into numerous toothed segments. They are similar to leaves of Tansy on page 226. The small greenish-yellow or pale yellow blossoms have four petals and are similar to those on other mustards. The seed pods are very narrow and *have no beak* at the tip.

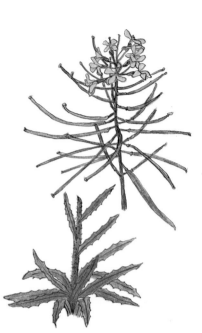

WESTERN WALLFLOWER

Erysimum asperum

Mustard Family

Western Wallflower is a stiff ash-colored perennial with simple or sparsely branching stems. It grows on prairies or bluffs and in open woods to a height up to three feet. It is only found in Southern New England. The narrow leaves are generally downy white. They are firm and thick. The stem leaves are more linear and may not have toothed margins. The flowers have four showy, yellow or orangish petals and are on a stalk-like base. The downy seed pods may be four inches long when mature. The seed pods *do not* point straight up.

CREEPING YELLOW CRESS

Rorippa sylvestris

Mustard Family

Creeping Yellow Cress grows in wet soil of meadows, shores, and damp roadsides where it rapidly spreads to become a troublesome weed. It is usually about twenty inches tall. This cress is similar to Water Cress on page 29 but has a yellow, four-petaled flower. The plant has creeping, underground stems and upright stalks which may be simple or branching. The thin leaves are deeply cut into divisions which are sharply toothed. The slender erect pods are slightly curved when mature.

YELLOW CRESS

Rorippa islandica

Mustard Family

There are several species of Yellow Cress but all are quite similar. Most grow in wet places. The four petals are yellow and very small. The plants are more easily identified by their seed pods which are short and rounded. The species shown grows to a height of up to four feet and can be either smooth or hairy. The leaves are very deeply lobed and each lobe is coarsely toothed.

YELLOW ROCKET or WINTER CRESS

Barbarea vulgaris

Mustard Family

This member of the mustard family can be easily recognized by its broad shiny upper leaves which are deeply cut and clasp the stem. The bottom leaves have a large end lobe and from two to four side lobes. The stem is very branching and from one to three feet tall. When the four-petaled yellow flowers fade, seed pods appear. These stand erect and close to the stem and are rarely longer than one inch. The beak on the tip of the seed pod is much shorter than that of other mustards. Yellow Rocket grows in wet meadows, fields, and along streams — sometimes making a whole field look yellow.

173

MOSSY STONECROP, LOVE-ENTANGLE or WALL PEPPER

Sedum acre

Orpine Family

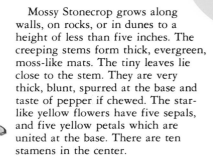

Mossy Stonecrop grows along walls, on rocks, or in dunes to a height of less than five inches. The creeping stems form thick, evergreen, moss-like mats. The tiny leaves lie close to the stem. They are very thick, blunt, spurred at the base and taste of pepper if chewed. The star-like yellow flowers have five sepals, and five yellow petals which are united at the base. There are ten stamens in the center.

YELLOW MOUNTAIN SAXIFRAGE

Saxifraga aizoides

Saxifrage Family

This plant is similar to Livelong Saxifrage on page 33 in the white section, so only a close-up of the flowers is shown. It is a small, matted or tufted plant with a leafy stem. It may be reclining or trailing. The alternate leaves are slender, thick, and rather fleshy. They are narrowed at the base and have a few hairs on their margins. Several flowers are in a branching cluster at the top of the stem. The yellow petals are oblong and are sometimes spotted with orange. The petals are not much longer than the sepals. The whole plant is rarely taller than six inches.

WITCH HAZEL

Hamamelis virginiana

Witch Hazel Family

Witch Hazel is a tall shrub which does not flower until the leaves are about ready to drop. It is perhaps the last flower one will see in the late autumn. It grows along streams or in moist woods and hillsides to a height of up to fifteen feet. Medicinal extract has long been obtained from its bark, and dowsers sometimes use the branches as divining rods for finding water.

The leaves are rough, rather oval, and have wavy-toothed margins. The base of the leaf is very different than other leaves, in that the leaf on one side of the midrib is much lower than the other side.

The pale yellow flowers are in clusters in axils where the leaves were attached. There are four sepals, four petals which are long, slender, and curving, and eight stamens. These flower clusters are often surrounded with brown three-parted scale-like bracts. Furry seed capsules enclosing the seeds do not mature until almost a year later, then the hard capsule bursts and sends seeds scattering.

INDIAN STRAWBERRY

Duchesnea indica

Rose Family

Indian Strawberry has a creeping stem from which leaves and flowerstalks arise. The leaf is three-parted and similar to those of a strawberry. The yellow flower has five bracts alternating with the five sepals on the back of the flower. The green bracts are three-toothed at the broad tip, and are longer than the petals and the sepals. The fruit is juicy and berry-like, but it is inedible.

SHRUBBY CINQUEFOIL
Potentilla fruticosa
Rose Family

This cinquefoil is also called Five Finger or Golden Hardhack, but the name given above is most common. It grows in wet or dry open ground in meadows or along shores to a height of from one to three feet. It is a shrubby plant with erect, branching stems, many divided leaves, and bright yellow flowers. The stems are woody — especially at the base — and have loose bark peeling off in shreds. The leaves are divided into from five to seven narrow leaflets with *toothless margins.* The olive, yellow-green leaves are silky or woolly with white hairs on the undersides, and the edges of the leaves sometimes curl backwards. The flowers are generally an inch or more broad and have five rounded, spreading petals.

SILVERY CINQUEFOIL
Potentilla argentea
Rose Family

This cinquefoil has branching stems and may be nearly two feet tall. It grows in dry soils in fields or openings in dry woods. The leaf has five narrow leaf segments with blunt, oak-like teeth. The edges often roll inward and the underside has silvery wool on it. The flowers are less than one-half inch across and are in clusters at the ends of the white, woolly branches. The five green sepals are prominent between the five wide petals.

176

ROUGH-FRUITED CINQUEFOIL

Potentilla recta

Rose Family

This cinquefoil grows in fields and along roads to a height of one or two feet. It is a very hairy, branching, leafy plant. The leaflets are in groups of five or seven and the flowers are larger than those of other cinquefoils. The flowers are in flat, terminal clusters, and each one may be as large as one inch across. Each petal is perfectly heart-shaped and it is a pleasure to walk along a path where these plants grow in abundance and find delightful, yellow hearts covering the ground about you.

ROUGH CINQUEFOIL or BARREN STRAWBERRY

Potentilla norvegica

Rose Family

This cinquefoil suggests a yellow-flowered strawberry plant, but it is much taller. It is a stout, bushy plant up to three feet tall. The leaves and stem are usually hairy. The leaves are in groups of three instead of five, and they have coarsely-toothed margins. The flowers are about one-half inch across and the petals are slightly shorter than the green sepals which can easily be seen between the petals.

SILVERWEED

Potentilla anserina

Rose Family

This cinquefoil spreads by reddish runners which take root and send up erect leaves and flowers on separate stalks. The leaves have numerous, sharply toothed segments, often as many as twenty or more on one leaf rib. The underside is silky with long silvery white hairs. The enlarged underside of the leaflet shows detail. Silverweed grows on wet, sandy or rocky shores.

ROUGH AVENS

Geum virginianum

Rose Family

Bennet and Herb-Bennet are other names given to this flower. It grows in low grounds, rocky banks, and at borders of dry woods. Rough Avens is a stout, branching plant two and a half feet or less in height. The stout stems and leaf stalks have bristly hairs on them. The lower and basal leaves are divided into blunt, shallowly-toothed segments. There may be from three to seven leaflets, but the terminal leaflet is larger than the side ones. Stem leaves rapidly reduce in size as they reach the summit of the plant. The five creamy-white or greenish-yellow *petals are smaller than the green sepals.* The sepals turn backwards as the flower matures. The dry, spherical, hairy fruit is equipped with hooks.

YELLOW AVENS

Geum aleppicum

Rose Family

This is a hairy geum with stem
leaves divided into wedge-shaped
leaflets and basal leaves with five to
nine leaflets. It grows in low
grounds, thickets, or moist meadows
to a height of from two to five feet.
The flowers have five broad, golden
yellow petals each of which is nearly
one-half of an inch long. Numerous
stamens and pistils in the center later
enlarge and form a round, bur-like
head. The leaves are variable. The
terminal leaflet of the basal leaves is
usually much larger than the side
ones. Small leaflets may be
interspersed with the larger ones.

YELLOW MOUNTAIN AVENS

Geum peckii

Rose Family

This geum is a small plant of
higher elevations. It grows in damp
rocky or peaty places, in gravel, or on
cliffs. It grows to be from six inches
to two feet in height. The leaves
have a round, sharp-toothed segment
at the end with one or more smaller
leaf segments on the sides. The basal
leaves are tufted and are on long
stalks. The flowers have five
spreading, yellow petals which are
longer than the sepals. The flowers are
about one inch broad and from one to
six flowers are at the top of the plant.

179

TALL HAIRY AGRIMONY
Agrimonia gryposepala
Rose Family

Tall Hairy Agrimony is a tall plant which is usually three or four feet tall, but sometimes reaches a height of six feet. It grows in rich woods, especially in rather open places. The stem and veins on the lower surface of the leaves are hairy, and there are broad, coarsely-toothed appendages of stipules on each side of the leaf stem where it is attached to the main stem. The large, bright-green leaves are divided into from five to nine leaflets with the end one being much larger than the side leaflets. The leaflets are thin, elliptical, and have toothed margins. Usually there are three pairs of tiny leaflets interposed with the larger ones. Small yellow flowers are in a long, narrow spike at the top of the stems. Each one is about one-fourth inch across and has five spreading petals. There are hooked bristles on the cup-shaped end of the flower stalks. These later form a bur which sticks to clothing when brushed.

AGRIMONY
Agrimonia striata
Rose Family

Agrimony is similar to Tall Hairy Agrimony, but is a taller, stiffer, and more robust plant with brownish, spreading hairs. It grows to a height of six feet at the borders of woods, in thickets, and along woodland paths. The stem that bears the flowers is densely hairy, but has no glands. Numerous leaves are divided into from seven to nine dull green leaflets with long-pointed tips. These leaflets are smooth on the top, covered with soft hairs on the bottom, and have toothed margins. Pairs of tiny leaflets are interposed with the larger ones. The tiny yellow flowers are crowded on a spike, and each one has five petals with a red circle of dots in the center. There are purplish bristles at the base of each flower. Note the cup-shaped bur with hooked bristles which forms on both of the Agrimony plants.

WILD SENSITIVE PLANT
Cassia nictitans
Pea Family

Wild Sensitive Plant is very similar to the Sensitive Pea but is smaller. It grows in dry sandy soil to a height of from six to twelve inches. There are from ten to twenty paired leaflets along a central rib. They are very sensitive, and the two sides will fold together if touched. From one to three small yellow inconspicuous flowers are borne on short pedicels (flower stems) at the leaf axils. The petals are only about one-fourth of an inch long and there are *only five stamens* instead of ten.

PARTRIDGE PEA or SENSITIVE PEA

Cassia fasciculata

Pea Family

This plant — also called Golden Cassia or Prairie Senna — is a slightly hairy, erect plant with from ten to fifteen pairs of tiny leaflets on each compound leaf. These are sensitive to the touch and will close together if disturbed. Large yellow flowers are on slender pedicles (flower stems). Each has five spreading petals with a purplish spot at the base. In the center there are ten long, drooping anthers. Four of them are yellow and six of them are purple. The plant grows in sandy soil and is from one to two feet in height. The seed pod is from one and a half to two and a half inches long. It may or may not be hairy.

WILD INDIGO

Baptisia tinctoria

Pea Family

Indigo is a smooth plant with numerous leaves in sets of three leaflets. They are gray-green in color and are often attached right on the main stem. The stem and leaves often have a bluish bloom on them. The leaves turn black when dried. The numerous pea-like, yellow flowers are in loose flower clusters at the ends of the branches.

182

RATTLEBOX

Crotalaria sagittalis

Pea Family

Rattlebox is an erect or leaning annual with many branches. It grows in dry sandy soil and rarely gets taller than one foot. The stems and the edges of the leaves are covered with soft hairs. The simple leaves — usually pointed at the tip and rounded at the base — are nearly stalkless, and grow alternately along the stems.

From two to four pea-like yellow flowers are at the tips of the branches. They are scarcely one-half inch long. The two lipped corolla about equals the calyx in length. The inflated oblong pod is about an inch long, and is nearly black at maturity. When completely ripe, the shiny seed inside will rattle when the pod shakes. Other names for the plant are Rattle-box, Loco-weed, and Wild Pea.

KIDNEY VETCH
LADY'S FINGERS

Anthyllis vulneraria

Pea Family

Kidney Vetch has tufted, downy stems which are from eight to fifteen inches tall. It may be found growing in fields and wastelands. The leaves are divided into from five to thirteen paired segments. The basal leaves often have fewer segments, and may even be reduced to a single enlarged leaflet at the end of the leaf stalk. The pea-like flowers are usually yellowish, but may vary from red to yellow, and are arranged in long-stalked clusters surrounded by conspicuous bracts. The five-toothed calyx is very hairy, much inflated, but narrowed at the mouth.

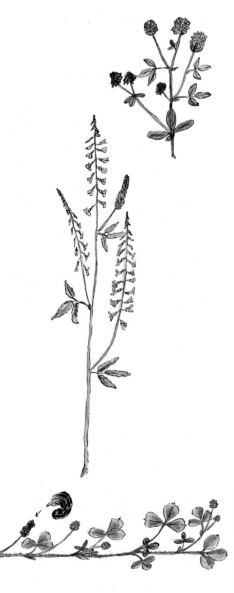

YELLOW HOP CLOVER

Trifolium agrarium

Pea Family

Hop Clover grows erect and up to eighteen inches tall in waste places and along roadsides. The small leaflets are in sets of three and have very short leaf stalks or are attached directly to the stem itself. The yellow flowers are arranged in a cylinder-shaped cluster at the end of the stem. As the flowers fade, the individual flowers turn brown and fold downward. This brown head looks similar to that of dried hops — hence the name of Hop Clover.

YELLOW SWEET-CLOVER

Meliotus officinalis

Pea Family

This tall bushy sweet-clover found along roadsides and in waste places grows to a height of from two to five feet. The leaves are divided into sets of three leaflets. The bright yellow flowers are arranged in numerous spike-like racemes which grow from leaf axils. This sweet-clover gives off an odor of new-mown hay.

BLACK MEDIC

Medicago lupulina

Pea Family

This common weed has downy stems which rest on the ground. It grows in waste lands, on lawns, and along roadsides. The leaves have three leaflets that are either blunt or have a tiny spine at the tip. The yellow flowers are in almost round flower heads, but are quickly replaced by clusters of twisted black seed pods.

BIRD'S FOOT TREFOIL

Lotus corniculatus

Pea Family

This perennial grows from a long root and may be found growing in waste places, along roadsides, and in fields. It is a short plant which varies in height to from three inches to two feet — though is commonly less than a foot. The stems are often in a reclining position. The leaves are divided into three leaflets at the tip with two smaller stipules at the base of the leaf stem; causing some authors to call it a five-part leaf. The pea-like bright yellow flowers have a tubular throat with a rounded standard at the top of the flower. The calyx lobes are equal and pointed and are nearly as long as the throat of the flower. From three to ten flowers are clustered at the tip of the plant. The slender pod suggests a bird's foot.

GOAT'S RUE

Tephrosia virginiana

Pea Family

This is a hairy plant with large two-colored, sweet pea-like flowers. The standard is yellow and the wings are pink. The leaves are divided into many pairs of leaflets with a single leaflet at the end. There are from nine to fifteen leaflets on each stem. Goat's Rue grows in sandy woods to a height of from one to two feet.

MILK VETCH

Astragalus canadensis
Pea Family

Milk Vetch is a coarse plant — one of a large and confusing genus. There are many species in our area and more out west. To identify which milk vetch you have found, it would be necessary to count leaf segments, observe the fruit, and consult more technical manuals. The Milk Vetch illustrated will serve as a "sample" flower. The leaves are divided into from seven to fifteen pairs of elliptical leaflets with one leaflet at the tip. The slender pea-like flowers are creamy white or pale yellow, about one-half inch long, and are arranged in clusters up to six inches long. The fruit is a pod from two-fifths to four-fifths of an inch long and about one-fifth of an inch thick. Milk Vetch grows along shores, in rich thickets, or open woodlands to a height of from one to five feet.

YELLOW FLAX

Linum virginianum
Flax Family

Yellow or Wild Flax grows in open woodlands, thickets, or clearings to a height of one and a half to three feet or more. It has fibrous, thread-like stems which may be reclining instead of standing upright. The thin leaves are long and pointed and the lower ones are opposite on the stem. Each small yellow flower has five yellow petals which last less than a day. The sepals remain to cup the fruit as it matures.

CREEPING WOOD-SORREL

Oxalis corniculata

Wood-sorrel Family

This oxalis is very similar to the Upright Yellow Wood-sorrel but it has creeping stems. It is more hairy, and the hairs are not pressed close to the stem as they are on the plant below.

UPRIGHT YELLOW WOOD-SORREL

Oxalis stricta

Wood-sorrel Family

This wood-sorrel varies greatly and is difficult to classify. It is an upright flower of fields, woods, and roadsides which is from three to fifteen inches tall. The stems have hairs pressed close to the stem. There are usually more than five and not more than ten bright yellow flowers in each cluster. Each flower is about one-half inch broad and has five petals.

The thin leaves are a yellow-green and are almost transparent. They have a pleasant sour taste and can be used in salads. Each leaf is divided into three heart-shaped leaflets. At night these three leaflets hang down in a closed position from the central mid-point. One way to identify this wood-sorrel from other wood-sorrels is to note the sharp angle formed by the straight, erect seed pods.

PALE TOUCH-ME-NOT
or JEWELWEED
Impatiens pallida
Touch-me-not Family

This touch-me-not is usually taller
and stouter than Spotted Touch-me-not
on page 156. It grows in wet shady
places in woods and along streams to a
height of from three to six feet. It has
yellow flowers with a shorter spur and
the stems are watery when bruised.
The flowers are from one to one and a
half inches long and hang in
horizontal position in loose clusters
from axils of leaves. The calyx and
corolla are the same color and are
difficult to distinguish from each other.
There are six irregular pieces — the
largest one extends backward from the
face of the flower and forms a deep sac
which ends in a little hooked spur.

PRICKLY MALLOW
Sida spinosa
Mallow Family

Prickly Sida, False Mallow, and
Indian Mallow are other names given
to this plant which grows in fields and
waste places. The plant has a slender,
erect, branching stem which is covered
with soft hairs and grows to a height
of from one to three feet. The small
leaves have a rounded base, pointed
tip, toothed margins, and are on leaf
stalks. There is a curved spine at the
base of leaf stem. The yellow flowers
are on short stalks arising from the
axils of the leaves. Each flower is from
one-fourth to one-half inch wide and
has five spreading, odd-shaped petals
and a calyx with five triangular,
pointed teeth.

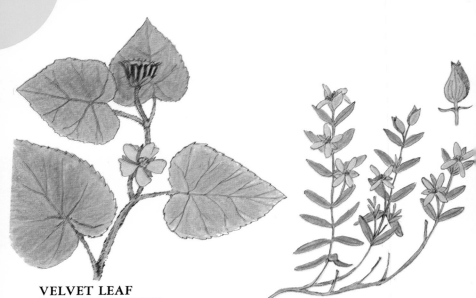

VELVET LEAF
INDIAN MALLOW
Abutilon theophrasti
Mallow Family

Velvet Leaf is a stout, branching annual which is covered with velvety hairs. It grows to a height of from two to six feet in rich soil of once-cultivated fields or vacant lots. Once this plant has become established, it continues to come up year after year even though conditions may not be adequate to produce mature seeds.

The leaves are heartshaped, have long stems, and the margins are toothed. Margins of lower leaves may not be toothed. Solitary, broad yellow flowers up to one inch across grow on flower stalks from the axils of the leaves. The fruit has a beautiful, perfectly symmetrical design on the top which gives the plant the names of Butter Print or Pie Marker. The sturdy stem has very tough fibers which cause some to call this plant Indian Hemp.

ST.-ANDREW'S CROSS
Ascyrum hypericoides
St. John's-wort Family

St.-Andrew's Cross is a low, rather shrubby plant with flattened stems and smooth, pale-green leaves. It grows in dry sandy or rocky soil to a height of from five to ten inches. The opposite leaves are linear to oblong, narrowed at the base and broader at the rounded tips. This plant is easily identified by its light yellow flowers with four narrow petals which form a cross. Each flower is about an inch or less across. The petals about equal the two outer pair of sepals. The inner pair of sepals is very small, or may be entirely lacking. The outer pair is large and surrounds the pod which forms after the petals fall. The flowers are solitary — either in the axils of the leaves or at the summit of the stem.

189

COMMON ST. JOHN'S-WORT

Hypericum perforatum

St. John's-wort Family

This plant grows along trails, roads, and in fields or open woods to a height of from two to three feet. The leaves are very numerous and are arranged in pairs — with smaller leafy branches often growing out of the leaf axils. The leaves have blunt tips and have translucent dots scattered on them. The bright yellow flowers are arranged in a rather tight terminal cluster. Each star-shaped flower is about one inch across and has five spreading petals with black dots at their margins.

PALE ST. JOHN'S-WORT

Hypericum ellipticum

St. John's-wort Family

This St. John's-wort is a frail plant which grows in low grounds, swamps, and along streams to a height of from eight to twenty inches. The simple, usually-unbranching stems rise from a creeping base. The thin, oval leaves are in pairs and are set close to the stem. They are blunt on the tip. The flowers are borne above the foliage in a branching cluster, but the *central flower of each cluster opens first.*

190

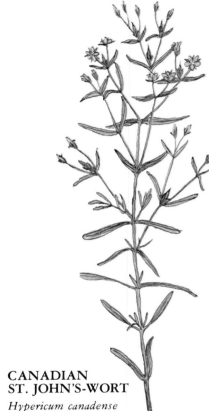

NORTHERN ST. JOHN'S-WORT

Hypericum boreale

St. John's-wort Family

This St. John's-wort has reclining stems with tips that curve upward. It grows in damp peat, sand, or shallow water to a height of from one to eighteen inches. The thin leaves are elliptic with rounded tips and no leaf stalks. There are three (sometimes five) nerves and the base of the leaf may slightly clasp the stem. Leaves on the lower stem are smaller than those higher up on the stem. Most leaves are in pairs, but there may be a whorl of leaves right below the branching flower cluster at the top of the plant.

CANADIAN ST. JOHN'S-WORT

Hypericum canadense

St. John's-wort Family

This St. John's-wort grows in moist, sandy soil to a height of from six to twenty inches. The slender, wiry stems are freely branching. The light, dull-green *leaves are very narrow* and generally have *three main veins*. Tiny, deep golden-yellow flowers are less than one-fourth inch broad, and they wither early in the day. The bud-like conical seed pods which follow the flowers are ruddy-red and are longer than the five-lobed green calyx which incloses it. The *pod is very pointed.*

191

ORANGE GRASS
PINEWEED
FALSE ST. JOHN'S-WORT

Hypericum gentianoides

St. John's-wort Family

This low, bushy plant has wiry, thread-like branches. It grows in sandy or sunbaked soil along roadsides to a height of from four to twenty inches. The minute leaves are awl-shaped and opposite each other at regular intervals along the stem.

The small yellow flowers are less than one-fourth inch broad. They are scattered among the erect branches, and open in the sunlight. There are three styles and five or ten stamens. After flowers fade, a three-part cone-shaped capsule forms. It is about one-fourth inch long, is red or purple, and has a sharp point.

LARGER CANADIAN
ST. JOHN'S-WORT

Hypericum majus

St. John's-wort Family

This St. John's-wort is very similar to the one at the left, but is stouter. It grows in wet or dry open soil to a height of from one to three feet. The paired leaves have *five or seven main* veins and are rounded — somewhat clasping — at the base. The conical seed capsule which follows the flowers is blunter than on the one at the left.

FROSTWEED

Helianthemum canadense

Rockrose Family

Frostweed usually has only one main stem with a flower at the top, but soon smaller, side branches will grow taller than the flower. It is a foot or more tall and has narrow pointed alternate leaves. The stem and leaves are hairy. The yellow flower has five large, overlapping petals and many stamens. It is about one inch across. Later in the season, clusters of flowers without petals appear on branches, are fertilized, but do not open. As fall approaches, the bark on the stem may split and release tiny strings of ice crystals, hence the name of Frostweed.

WOOLLY HUDSONIA
or FALSE HEATHER

Hudsonia tomentosa

Rockrose Family

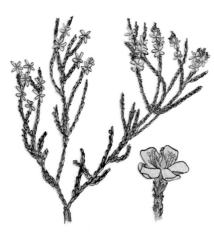

Hudsonia is a low, bushy, matted plant which is somewhat woody. It is a pale-colored plant with grayish-white hairs. It grows in sandy pine barrens or sandy shores, and is often found along the coast where little else will flourish — hence the name of Poverty Grass which it is called by some. The leaves are small and almost scale-like. They are pressed closely to the stem and overlap one another. There are numerous bright, yellow flowers on very short stalks or attached directly to the stem. The flowers are crowded along upper part of the branches. Each flower is about one-fourth of an inch across, has five oblong petals, numerous stamens in the center, and lasts only for one day.

flower is about one-fourth of an inch across, has five oblong petals, numerous stamens in the center, and lasts only for one day.

PRICKLY PEAR or DEVIL'S TONGUE
Opuntia humifusa
Cactus Family

Prickly Pear is also called Indian Fig. It grows in dry sand or rocks and forms carpets a yard and more across. Most plants will be in a prostrate position and spread by means of branching, fibrous roots. Prickly Pear is a succulent, eastern cactus with jointed, branching stems with long, reddish-brown bristles. From one to four spines are usually together, and they may be white or reddish at the base. The flower is yellow but sometimes has a red, star-shaped center. There are from eight to twelve petals. The fleshy fruit is club-shaped, not spiny, and is edible.

SEEDBOX or RATTLEBOX
Ludwigia alternifolia
Evening Primrose Family

Seedbox grows in swamps and wet places to a height of from two to three and a half feet. It is a smooth herb with many branches. It looks similar to a small evening primrose, but the four sepals which are as long as the four petals, do not bend backwards as they do on the primrose. The leaves are alternate, have toothless margins, and taper at both ends. Small, yellow flowers about a half inch broad are on short stalks in the leaf axils. The fruit is somewhat cube-shaped with wings at the margins. Seeds inside eventually come loose and rattle when the plant is shaken.

194

EVENING PRIMROSE
Oenothera biennis
Evening Primrose Family

Evening Primrose grows in fields, waste places, and along roadsides to a height of from one to five feet. The flowers have four broad yellow petals and a cross-shaped stigma in the center. The individual flowers are nearly two inches broad but usually close when exposed to bright sunlight. The flowers last only over night and new buds open in the morning. The long sepals are turned backwards towards the stem. The narrow, hairy leaves are alternate on the hairy stem. The stem is green, but turns reddish as the flower matures.

NORTHERN EVENING PRIMROSE
Oenothera parviflora
Evening Primrose Family

This primrose grows on sandy shores and in dry clearings to a height of from two to three feet. It usually does not branch. The simple stem has rather fleshy leaves, and red hairs which are broader at the base. The yellow flowers are from one to two inches broad and are in axils of upper leaves. The bracts on the back of the lower flowers are often larger than the flowers themselves.

SUNDROPS

Oenothera perennis

Evening Primrose Family

Sundrops are day-blooming plants with flowers similar to those on Evening Primrose only smaller. The erect or spreading stems are one or two feet tall with long, light green leaves which have untoothed margins. The hairy stem is reddish at leaf axils and a cluster of drooping buds at the top. The flower stalk straightens as buds open. There are two small sepals — joined at the tip — which fold backward as the flower blooms and look like a single heart-shaped sepal.

HOARY PUCCOON

Lithospermum canescens

Forget-Me-Not Family

Hoary Puccoon is found in open woods in dry sandy soil. It is from six to twenty inches tall and has curled-over clusters of yellow or orange funnel-shaped flowers. Each one is about one-half of an inch long. The leaves are very slender and are alternate on the stem. The stem and leaves are covered with stiff hairs.

HAIRY PUCCOON

Lithospermum croceum

Forget-Me-Not Family

This plant is larger and stouter than the one above, but is very similar. The flowers are larger and the corolla-tube is bearded at the base.

196

YELLOW PIMPERNEL

Taenidia integerrima

Parsley Family

Yellow Pimpernel grows in dry
woods, rocky hillsides and thickets to
a height of from one to three feet. It
can be distinguished from other
parsnips by the leaves. Each one is
divided into three or five parts and
each part is divided again into
smaller *untoothed leaflets*. The
slender, smooth stem may have a
whitish powder on it.

MEADOW PARSNIP

Thaspium trifoliatum

Parsley Family

Meadow Parsnip is a sparingly
branched plant of dry woods, thickets,
or banks. The toothed, stem-leaves are
divided into three leaflets and the top
ones are attached directly to the main
stem. The broad basal leaves are either
heart-shaped or round. This species can
be easily distinguished by the mature
fruit. There is both a purple-flowered
and a yellow-flowered variety of this
plant.

WILD PARSNIP
Pastinaca sativa
Parsley Family

Wild Parsnip has long been cultivated for its edible, long, fleshy roots. It is now a wide-spread and conspicuous weed growing along highways, in fields, and in vacant lots. It is an immense plant, sometimes reaching a height of five feet with lower leaves up to one and a half feet long.

It has a tough, prominently-ribbed stem which is almost impossible to break. The leaves are a dull deep green and are on long stalks. They are divided into coarsely and irregularly-toothed segments. The dull yellow flowers are in small clusters on slender stems. Many of these small clusters form a broad, flat-topped cluster.

PINESAP
Monotropa hypopithys
Wintergreen Family

This flower is described on page 344 in the brown section.

198

marshes, swampy spots or moist thickets and is from eight to twenty inches tall. The leaves, which are opposite each other on the stem, are long and pointed and are sometimes dotted with black. Often, little branches with more leaves will grow from the axils of the leaves after the flowers have begun to fade.

The flowers are about one-third of an inch wide and are arranged in a tall slender raceme at the end of the stem. Each flower has five yellow petals which have a ring of red or purple dots at the base of each petal. The pistil is easily seen protruding from the center of the ring of yellow petals.

(A) FRINGED LOOSESTRIFE

Lysimachia ciliata

Primrose Family

This plant grows in swamps, wet thickets, and on stream banks in full sun. It is often branched at the top, and reaches a height of from one to four feet. The yellow flowers have five fringed or toothed petals, and frequently face downward. The paired leaves have hairs on their leaf stems.

(B) SWAMP CANDLES or YELLOW LOOSESTRIFE

Lysimachia terrestris

Primrose Family

Swamp Candles is also known as Bulb-bearing Loosestrife. It grows in

(C) WHORLED LOOSESTRIFE

Lysimachia quadrifolia

Primrose Family

This loosestrife has star-like yellow flowers which are similar to the other two, but both the leaves and the flowers are arranged in whorls of four at regular intervals on the stem. Whorled Loosestrife grows in woods and thickets to a height of from one to three feet, but it usually is about eighteen inches tall.

TUFTED LOOSESTRIFE
Lysimachia thrysiflora
Primrose Family

This plant grows in cold swamps, springy marshes or bogs and is usually about a foot or more tall. Part of it may be in the water, however. The smooth stem is usually not branching and has paired leaves which are narrowed at both ends. The lower stem leaves are usually reduced to scales, for this part of the stem may be under water at times. The leaves are usually a paler color on the under side. From the lower or middle leaf axils, round clusters of flowers will grow on stalks. The corolla is deeply divided into five (rarely seven) long yellow petals with black dots on them.

MONEYWORT
Lysimachia nummularia
Primrose Family

Moneywort grows in moist ground of shores, damp roadsides, and especially near old dwellings. It is a beautiful, trailing plant from six to twenty-four inches long. The small, shiny, dark green leaves are in pairs and so are the golden yellow flowers. Each flower has five petals which may be spotted with black. This plant creeps along the wet ground rather than climb upward. It is easy to transplant to a wild flower garden and is lovely in a hanging planter.

200

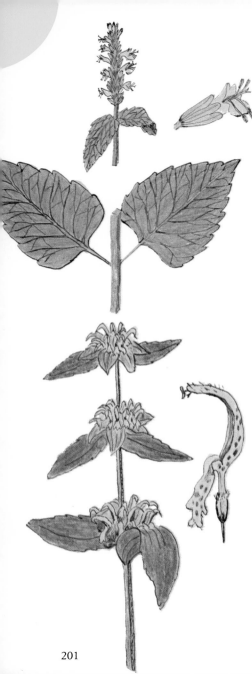

YELLOW GIANT HYSSOP

Agastache nepetoides

Mint Family

Yellow Giant Hyssop is a tall, erect perennial herb with stout, square stems. The stem is from two to five feet tall and is usually branching above the middle. This hyssop grows in rich thickets and borders of woods. The thin leaves are broad at the base, and pointed at the tips. The margins are toothed.

The greenish-yellow flowers are arranged in terminal clusters. There are numerous bracts beneath each row of flowers. Each flower is about one-third inch long — not much longer than the tubular, five-toothed calyx of sepals. The flower is two-lipped with a nearly-erect upper lip and a lower lip which is divided into three parts. Four stamens protrude from the throat of the flower — two of these curve upward and the other two curve downward.

HORSEMINT or DOTTED MONARDA

Monarda punctata

Mint Family

Horsemint grows in dry fields or sandy soils to a height of from one to three feet. It is a densely hairy plant with narrow, pointed leaves which narrow at the base to form stalks. The flowers are in terminal clusters and in clusters at axils of the leaves. The yellowish corolla is about an inch long and is spotted with purple. The high, arching upper lip is hairy and about the same length as the wide-jawed lower, lobed lip. There are showy, recurved bracts under each flower head. These showy bracts may be white or lilac.

RICHWEED
HORSE-BALM
STONEROOT

Collinsonia canadensis

Mint Family

Richweed grows in rich, wet woods to a height of from two to five feet. It is a coarse, bushy plant with a stout stem. The leaves and flowers have a pleasant lemony odor. The oil responsible for this odor has been used medicinally and the leaves have been brewed for tea. The name Stoneroot was given because its "root" — really a rhizome — was used medicinally in treating the affliction known as stone. The large, thick leaves have toothed margins and a pointed tip. The yellow flowers are in a loose, branching cluster at the top of the stems. The two-lipped corolla is pale yellow and is about one-half of an inch long. The delicately fringed lower lip is larger than the hooded upper one. The flower has two long divergent stamens and a prominent forked pistil.

CLAMMY GROUND CHERRY

Physalis heterophylla

Nightshade Family

Clammy Ground Cherry grows in dry woods in rich soil where the surface has been disturbed — like in clearings made for power lines. The plant is from one to three feet tall. The stems have sticky hairs on them. The plant grows from a slender, creeping rootstock. It is erect at first, but later in the season it is reclining as it spreads. The leaves are rounded or heart-shaped at the base with few teeth at the margins. The bell-shaped flower is yellowish with a brownish or purplish center. The face of the flower is somewhat five-lobed and each lobe may have a point in the center. The calyx lobes are triangular and will later enclose the edible, yellow berry. The fruit of this plant is very similar to the Husk Tomato which is grown in gardens.

BLACK HEN BANE or HOG'S BEAN

Hyoscyamus niger

Potato Family

Hen Bane grows in waste places and along roadsides to a height of from one to three feet or more. It is a clammy, ill-smelling, narcotic herb with a hairy stem and slimy, alternate, lobed or deeply-cut leaves. The Latin name indicates that it is poisonous to swine — and likewise to humans. The margins of the leaves and the mid rib are hairy. Upper leaves may clasp the stem. The dull-yellow or greenish-white flowers have a network of purple veins and are arranged in a one-sided, leafy spike. Each flower has a funnel-shaped corolla with five spreading lobes. The hairy, barrel-shaped calyx holding the flower has five points and later encloses the seed pod.

COMMON MULLEIN

Verbascum thapsus

Figwort Family

This gray-green woolly plant grows in waste places, fields, and along roadsides to a height of from two to six feet. It has a stout erect stem and large, thick, felt-like leaves that grow right into the stem. The saucer-shaped flowers are in a thick, club-like raceme. They have five yellow petals and are covered on the backside with whitish hairs.

CANKER-ROOT

Kickxia elatine

Figwort Family

Sharp-pointed Toadflax is another name given to this plant which grows in waste places, roadsides, and on sandy shores. It is a hairy, low, vine-like plant from six inches to two feet long which is usually lying on the ground. The upper leaves are on short petioles (leaf stems) and are triangular in shape with basal lobes spreading outward. The lower leaves are oval, quite veiny, and are in pairs. The solitary flowers are on thread-like stalks which are usually longer than the leaves. The pale yellow flower is very irregular and has a violet upper lip and a slender yellow spur.

204

BUTTER-AND-EGGS

Linaria vulgaris

Figwort Family

This member of the Figwort family is also known as Toadflax in some areas of New England. It is found growing along roads, in dry fields, waste places, and gravel pits. Its height varies from one to three feet depending upon the type of soil. The leaves are very numerous and are placed alternately around the stem. The snap-dragon-like flowers are of two shades of yellow and grow in long spikes at the end of the flower stalk. The corolla is pale yellow with an orange-yellow inflated center. The top and bottom petals are closed into a throat and there is a long narrow spur hanging down from the back of each flower.

MUSKFLOWER or MUSKPLANT

Mimulus moschatus

Figwort Family

Muskflower grows in wet places by streams, springs or ditches. It is a viny-type plant which is from six to twelve inches long. The hairy, musk-scented plant has creeping stems, paired leaves, and yellow flowers. The leaves are pointed at the tip, rounded at the base and have toothed margins. They may be one or two inches in length. The flowers have a funnel-shaped corolla about an inch long. On some plants, the flowers are striped with red or purple on the inside of the throat and on the outside of the tube. The calyx is hairy and has pointed teeth. Each flower is on a slender, hairy, flower stalk which is shorter than the leaves.

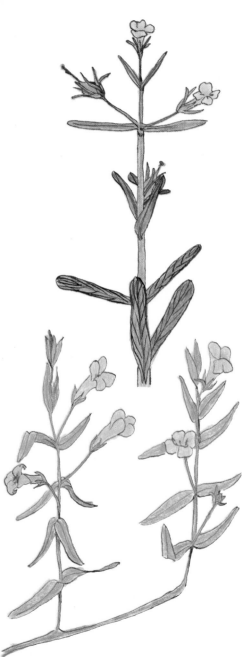

HEDGE-HYSSOP

Gratiola neglecta

Figwort Family

Hedge-Hyssop is more abundant than Golden Pert, but because of its small size and the places it grows, it is often overlooked. It is rarely up to a foot tall and grows in wet, muddy places. This low annual has a soft, loosely-branching stem and paired leaves. On some plants the leaves have slightly-toothed margins, but on other plants the margins are plain. The leaves have no petiole (leaf stem) but taper toward the base with the broadest part of the leaf being at the tip. The flowers are on stalks up to one inch long. The corolla is less than a half inch long. It has creamy-white or yellowish lobes and a honey-colored tube. The inside of the throat is bearded.

GOLDEN PERT or GOLDEN HEDGE HYSSOP

Gratiola aurea

Figwort Family

Golden Pert is a low plant found in ditches, swamps, and along shores of ponds and lakes in wet mud. It is usually less than a foot tall, but varies in height from three to fifteen inches. The leaves are in pairs and are about an inch long. They have three main nerves, untoothed margins, and a broad or clasping base. They do not have petioles (leaf stalks). The shiny, yellow flowers are borne singly on stalks arising at the leaf axils. The corolla is two-lipped but appears to be four-lobed. Actually, the upper lip is notched and the lower lip has three lobes. The flowers are about one-half inch long.

206

FALSE FOXGLOVE
Gerardia flava
Figwort Family

There are several false foxgloves in our area which vary only slightly in leaf structure and the amount of hairy covering or lack of it. The one given here will serve as a "sample flower" and those who wish more information may consult technical books for further identification.

False Foxgloves are large, erect, branching plants which may be from three to six feet in height. Most of them grow in dry woods — especially oak woods. The leaves are simple, but are deeply cut on some plants. Basal leaves may have side lobes. The large pale yellow flowers are very beautiful. They are funnel-shaped and are about one and a half to two inches long. The flower is slightly irregular and has five spreading lobes. The outside of the flower is smooth, but the inside of the throat is usually hairy. There are two pairs of stamens. The fruit is an oblong, smooth, pointed capsule.

NORTHERN or LANCE-LEAVED PAINTED-CUP
Castilleja septentrionalis
Figwort Family

Northern Painted-Cup is a paler species than Painted-Cup on page 148. It is a variable plant which is usually slender and non-branching. The oblong bracts at the top of the plant are really more showy than the flowers. They are somewhat fan-shaped and sometimes are shallowly three-lobed. These bracts are usually greenish-white, but may be yellowish or tinged with bronze or purple. The narrow light green leaves

are usually not lobed, and they taper at both ends. There are from three to five nerves on the leaves. The yellowish flowers are nearly hidden within the cluster of showy bracts (floral leaves) at the summit of the plant. The hooded upper lip is from two to four times as long as the lower lip, but the flower is about the same length as the bract. Flowers on some plants may be paler yellow, a yellow green, or greenish-white tinged with dull magenta. Northern Painted-Cup grows in damp, rocky soil or on bleak and rocky summits of mountains. It grows to a height of from six to twenty inches.

COW-WHEAT

Melampyrum lineare

Figwort Family

There are several cow-wheats in our area, but this narrow-leaved cow-wheat is a typical one. Some grow in dry woods and thickets, at the edges of fields, but this one is usually found in woods, bogs, or in peaty soils or by rocky barrens or ledges. The slender stem is widely branching with opposite, narrow, wide-spreading leaves. Lower leaves are simple or slightly toothed at base. Upper leaves may have several bristle-pointed teeth at the base. The irregular, tube-shaped corolla has an enlarged, rounded upper lip over a spreading lower lip with three teeth. There are four stamens in two pairs of unequal length. The calyx is four-toothed with the two upper teeth being longer.

YELLOW RATTLE
Rhinanthus crista-galli
Figwort Family

Yellow Rattle grows in old fields, waste places, and thickets to a height of from eight to twenty-four inches. It may have either a simple or a branching stem. The stem is four-sided and only two of the sides have hair on them. The flower has two lips. The upper lip is rounded and has teeth on the underside. The lower lip is divided into three lobes. The flower is mostly yellow, but sometimes the teeth of the upper lip are a darker color and sometimes there are dark spots on the lower lip. The flower is in a sac-like calyx which becomes more inflated as seeds form inside. The seeds will rattle when the plant is moved — hence the name of Yellow Rattle. The leaves are in pairs along the stem and have toothed edges.

SWAMP LOUSEWORT or SWAMP BETONY
Pedicularis lanceolata
Figwort Family

This betony grows in rich, limy meadows, shores, or in swampy areas to a height of twelve to thirty-four inches. It is also called Light Naples and Wood Betony, but Wood Betony really is Pedicularis canadensis which blooms in the spring and grows in woods and thickets. This plant has a smooth upright stem with opposite — or nearly so — deep-green leaves which are so finely cut they resemble those on a fern. The flowers are yellow and are in a thick, crowded, leafy spike at the tip of the stem. The upper lip is a pale, dull-yellow and is incurved with a beak at the tip. The lower lip is more erect and nearly closes the throat of the flower. The upper lip is *not toothed* as it is on Wood Betony which blooms in the spring. The calyx is two-lobed and toothed, and it embraces the flower.

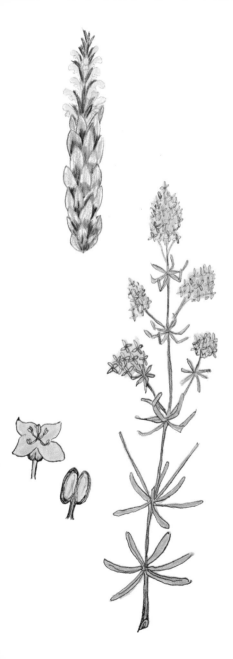

SQUAW-ROOT

Conopholis americana

Broomrape Family

This plant has tan colored tightly-fitting scales which are so stiff the plant resembles a pinecone. The plant is from three to eight inches tall and grows in rich woods in groups at the base of trees — especially oak trees. The plant lacks green leaves so is unable to make its own food. It is a parasite and lives off the food of other plants. There are many uneven pale yellow flowers which are about one-half of an inch long. The top part of the flower forms a hood over the stamens and three lobed lower petals. The irregular flowers protrude from between the stiff scales at the top of the plant.

YELLOW BEDSTRAW

Galium verum

Madder Family

Early Christians claimed that this was what filled the manger at Bethlehem — hence the name of Our Lady's Bedstraw. It has stiff, smooth, erect stems and leaves in whorls of six or eight. It is a slender plant with a smooth, squarish stem which may be somewhat woody at the base. It grows in dry waste places and borders of fields to a height of from eight to thirty inches.

The tiny yellow flowers are in small terminal clusters or on stalks arising from axils of the leaves. Each flower has four pointed lobes. The fruit is smooth, and the plant will turn black as it dries.

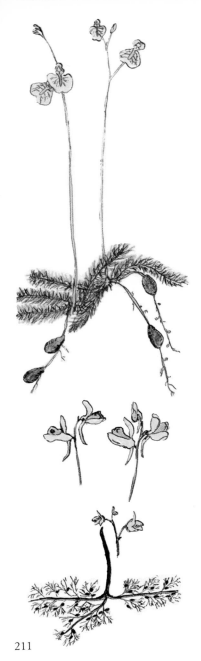

FLAT-LEAVED BLADDERWORT

Utricularia intermedia

Bladderwort Family

The bladderwort is rooted in shallow water of slow-moving streams, ponds or bogs. The stems are aquatic and horizontally submerged branches go out from the base of the flower stalk. The leaves are densely arranged alternately along separate leafstalks. There are no bladders among the leaf segments, but other rootlike leaves bear several large bladders. The naked flower-bearing scape is about eight inches high and bears from one to four yellow flowers that look similar to a snapdragon. The upper lip is triangular and about one-third of an inch broad. The bottom lip is a little larger and the spur is clearly visible.

HORNED BLADDERWORT

Utricularia cornuta

Bladderwort Family

This bladderwort has only a few small inconspicuous grass-like leaves which are embedded in the mud of bogs or sandy shores. The flower scape is brown and is from two to thirteen inches tall. There are from one to five bright yellow, fragrant flowers with a long spur hanging down. The lower lip of the flower is nearly two-thirds of an inch long and has a hood-like top part over it.

COMMON OR GREATER BLADDERWORT

Utricularia vulgaris

Bladderwort Family

This bladderwort has a spur which is shorter than the lower lip and filament-like leaves that float horizontally below the surface of the water. Unlike the Flat-Leaved Bladderwort, this plant has the small black bladders scattered throughout the leaf segments. They are not on separate leaf stalks. The flowers are yellow and small and are at the top of the bare flower scape.

NORTHERN BUSH-HONEYSUCKLE

Diervilla lonicera

Honeysuckle Family

Diervilla lonicera is from one to four feet tall and grows in dry or rocky soil in woods openings or at the edges of fields. This is the only honeysuckle with *toothed leaves*. The leafblades are oblong and pointed at the tip and are opposite each other on the stem. The trumpet-shaped flowers are pale yellow and grow in sets of twos or threes from the leaf axils and at the tips of the stems. The stamens protrude noticeably, and the petals fold way back.

GUMWEED or GUMPLANT

Grindelia squarrosa

Composite Family

Curlycup Gumweed is a variable plant which grows in dry soil. It varies in height from six inches to three feet. The stout stem branches at the top and the foliage is very sticky. The leaves are long and narrow, alternate on the stem, and are clasping at the base. They are usually toothed at the margins and are dotted with glands. The flowers are in rather large disks surrounded by yellow petal-like ray flowers up to one inch long.

Supporting these flower heads are conspicuous, gummy bracts with recurved spreading green tips.

212

CURVED-LEAVED GOLDEN ASTER
SICKLE-LEAVED GOLDEN ASTER

Chrysopsis falcata

Composite Family

This Golden Aster is a low coastal plant which often forms large, spreading mats on the sand of coastal plains. A distinguishing characteristic is the stiff, curved or sickle-shaped leaves. These are gray-green in color, and are crowded closely together along the stem. The stems are covered with a white wool and are from four to fifteen inches tall. The yellow flower heads resemble other types of asters, but the rays are a rich golden yellow. Each head is about an inch broad.

BROAD-LEAVED GOLDENROD

Solidago flexicaulis

Composite Family

This goldenrod is also called Zig-Zag Goldenrod because of the shape of the smooth stem. It grows in rich woods and thickets to a height of from one to three feet. The thin, very broad leaves have a long, pointed tip and narrow at the base into leaf stems. The leaf margins have sharp teeth, and the underside of the leaf may be slightly hairy. The heads of yellow flowers are in a short terminal cluster and in smaller clusters in the axils of upper leaves. The flower heads have only three or four yellow rays.

DOWNY GOLDENROD
Solidago puberula
Composite Family

This goldenrod grows in dry or sandy soil to a height of eighteen inches to three feet. It is a rather slender plant which is rarely branching. The slender stem is sometimes purplish, and a hand lens will reveal spreading hairs on the stem and the leaves. Basal leaves are sharply toothed and narrow at the base into leaf stalks. The upper stem leaves are narrow and pointed, and may or may not have toothed margins. The uppermost leaves are very slender and do not have stalks. Numerous yellow flower heads are arranged in a long, narrow cluster at the top of the plant. Each flower head is about one-fourth of an inch high with from nine to sixteen bright-yellow rays. The thin bracts under the flower heads have sharp points.

WREATH or BLUE-STEMMED GOLDENROD
Solidago caesia
Composite Family

This goldenrod grows in rich or dry woods and thickets to a height of from one to three feet. It is a smooth, slender goldenrod with a bluish or purplish stem which is covered with a whitish powder. The long, pointed leaves have sharply-toothed margins, but no leaf stem. The small flower heads are yellow and are in well-spaced, small clusters at axils of the upper leaves and in a terminal cluster at the top of the plant. There are only from three to five rays on each flower head.

SEASIDE GOLDENROD
Solidago sempervirens
Composite Family

This smooth, stout goldenrod grows in salt marshes, on sea beaches, along tidal rivers, and in sandy soil near the coast. The very leafy stem is rarely branching, but it may be in a leaning position. The plant varies greatly in height from two to six feet, depending upon soil conditions. The yellow-green leaves are smooth and slender. They are thick and rather fleshy and have toothless margins. The lower leaves are usually blunt at the tip and may be as long as twelve inches on a large plant. The lower leaves narrow at the base into a long leaf stem, but the narrow, pointed upper leaves have no leaf stalk. The heads of flowers are about one-fourth of an inch high and are arranged in a long, leafy, rather one-sided plume at the top of the plant. Each small head has from eight to ten showy yellow rays, and the bracts underneath are long and pointed.

CANADA or ROCK GOLDENROD

Solidago canadensis

Composite Family

This goldenrod grows on hillsides and thickets or along banks of streams to a height of from one to five feet. There are usually several plants together, because they spread by underground roots or runners. The stem is smooth at the base, but may be downy at the top. There are many leaves on the stem — sometimes with smaller leaves growing from axils of the larger leaves. The thin, pointed leaves have toothed margins, three nerves, and usually do not have leaf stems. The yellow flower heads are very small and are arranged *on one side* of spreading branches which form a large, loose cluster at the top of the plant. There are usually less than ten yellow rays, and the green bracts at the base are long, thin, and pointed. (See insert)

LANCE-LEAVED GOLDENROD

Solidago graminifolia

Composite Family

This goldenrod grows in damp to dryish shores and thickets to a height of from ten to forty-five inches. The stem usually is not hairy, and it does not begin branching until middle or upper part of the stem. The leaves are long, slender, and pointed. Sometimes smaller leafy stems will appear in axils of the larger leaves.

The yellow flowers grow in flat-topped clusters of about twelve to forty-five heads of flowers, and there are several variations of this plant.

216

LOW CUDWEED
Gnaphalium uliginosum
Composite Family

Cudweed is an insignificant low annual with a widely-branching, white, woolly stem. It grows in damp places or low ground and is usually less than a foot tall. The numerous leaves are linear and are sharply pointed on some plants and spoon-shaped on others. They often extend above the flower heads. Leaves are silver-grey in color. The tiny tubular flowers are arranged in heads in terminal clusters. The cluster is enclosed in wool. There are brownish scales at the base of the cluster.

ELECAMPANE or HORSEHEAL
Inula helenium
Composite Family

Horseheal is a large, woolly herb with a stout, thick root. It grows along roadsides and in fields to a height of from two to six feet. The woolly stems are stout and are usually not branching. The root is valued as a horse medicine. Hippocrates wrote that it was a stimulant to the human stomach and brain. The rough-hairy leaves are alternate on the stem, and are densely woolly on the under side. Lower leaves are on long petioles, but upper leaves have no stalk, and may clasp the stem. Yellow flower heads are large and showy with very thin yellow rays and a brown disk center. One flower head may be from two to four inches broad.

217

CUP PLANT or INDIAN CUP

Silphium perfoliatum

Composite Family

Cup Plant is a coarse tall plant with a stout, square stem which grows along river banks, or in rich woods and thickets to a height of from four to eight feet. The triangular-shaped leaves are in pairs and are joined at their bases, surrounding the stem and forming a leafy cup. The edges of the leaves may have a few, very coarse teeth. The large yellow flower-heads are two or three inches across. The central disk is made up of tubular flowers and around it is a fringe of long, narrow, yellow ray flowers . . . . the typical flower of members of the composite family.

OX-EYE or FALSE SUNFLOWER

Heliopsis helianthoides

Composite Family

Ox-eye grows in open woods and dry banks along streams to a height of from two to five feet. It is a robust plant with thin, opposite, oval-pointed leaves and terminal flower heads on long stalks. The leaves are thin and have evenly-toothed margins. They may be three to six inches long. Each flower head is supported by a flattened cluster of bracts. Each head has from ten to twenty yellow ray flowers and a rounded, yellow disk in the center.

218

BLACK-EYED SUSAN
Rudbeckia serotina
Composite Family

This well-known flower is also
called Nigger Heads and Yellow Daisy.
Some older books give the Latin name
as Rudbeckia hirta, but they are very
similar. It has rough, hairy stems and
leaves and grows to heights up to
three feet. The stem leaves are long
and narrow, but basal leaves are
broadly oval and are twice as long as
they are wide. A few showy flower
heads about two or three inches broad
are at the tips of the stout, terminal
flower stalk. There are spreading green
bracts below the flower head. Each
flower head has from ten to twenty ray
flowers which are notched at the tip.

GOLDEN GLOW or
CONEFLOWER
Rudbeckia laciniata
Composite Family

This tall coneflower grows in moist,
rich low ground in thickets which
border swamps or streams. It varies in
height from three to ten feet; is robust
and branching; and is not hairy. The
nearly-smooth, deep-green lower leaves
are divided into from three to seven
lobed segments and are on leafstalks.
The middle leaves are irregularly three
to five parted, and the uppermost
leaves are small and elliptical. The
golden yellow flowers have a greenish-
yellow, conical center with showy-
yellow, drooping rays. As the flower
matures, the center becomes more
conical and turns brownish. The flower
is large — the entire head may be
three or four inches broad.

219

WOODLAND or ROUGH SUNFLOWER

Helianthus divaricatus

Composite Family

This sunflower grows in dry openings, thin woods and thickets in dry shady places to a height of two to six and a half feet. It has an erect, smooth stem which may be simple or branching at the summit. Rough, opposite leaves are thick and are hairy on the under side. They have a broad, rounded base and taper to a pointed tip. Each has three main nerves and may have a short petiole or none at all. The flower heads are about two inches across and have from eight to fifteen yellow rays surrounding the yellow disk center.

THIN-LEAVED SUNFLOWER or TEN-PETALED SUNFLOWER

Helianthus decapetalus

Composite Family

This wild sunflower grows in moist woods and along streams to a height of from one to five feet. It is a tall, erect plant with many branches and large heads with yellow rays and brown or purplish disks in the center. Though called Ten-petaled Sunflower, it may actually have from eight to fifteen light-yellow rays. The thin leaves have pointed tips and toothed margins. The lower leaves are all opposite with slender leaf stalks, but the upper leaves are usually alternate and may be attached directly to the main stem.

220

JERUSALEM ARTICHOKE

Helianthus tuberosus

Composite Family

Jerusalem Artichoke is a large sunflower-like plant with broad, thick, rough leaves on branching, rough, hairy stems. It grows from thick, heavy tubers. These are similar to potatoes; and may be eaten in the autumn when they are ripe. Indians are said to have cultivated this plant and thus spread its range. It grows in rich or damp thickets and fields to a height of from six to ten feet. The lower leaves are oval-pointed and are usually opposite, but upper leaves may be alternate or in whorls of three. Each leaf is three-nerved and is up to eight inches long.

Flowers are in numerous heads with from twelve to twenty bright yellow ray flowers and a brownish center. The heads may be from two to three and a half inches across.

GIANT SUNFLOWER

Helianthus giganteus

Composite Family

This sunflower grows in swamps and wet fields to a height of from three to twelve feet. It is a very tall plant with a rough-hairy, dull-red or purplish stem with alternately-attached leaves. The lance-shaped leaves are very rough on the top, vary from two to six inches in length, but are seldom over an inch wide. The leaves are usually stalkless. The flower heads have greenish-yellow disks and from ten to twenty yellow ray flowers. They may be nearly three inches across.

GARDEN COREOPSIS

Coreopsis tinctoria

Composite Family

This annual has many branches and
showy flowers with yellow rays with
red-brown color at the base of each. It
is mostly escaped from cultivation in
the east, but is native further west. It
grows in low grounds to a height of
from one to four feet. The opposite
leaves are divided along a central rib
into narrow segments which are
sometimes divided again. The
numerous flower heads are in flat
clusters at the top of the plant. Each
flower head is on a slender stalk.

Coreopsis palmata is called STIFF
COREOPSIS. It is a more rigid plant
which grows in open woods and on
limy bluffs. The rigid leaves are
divided into three, stiff, narrow lobes
like crow's feet and are not as finely
disected as those on C. tinctoria. There
is no brown at the base of the petals.

Coreopsis auriculata can be
distinguished by its stalked leaves
which are mostly on the lower third of
the plant. The lower leaves are *not cut,*
but are ovate or roundish. They may
have two small lobes at their base.
This Coreopsis grows in rich limy
hardwoods and openings.

222

NODDING BUR MARIGOLD
or STICKTIGHT

Bidens cernua

Composite Family

Nodding Bur Marigold grows in swamps and around springs. It is usually about three feet tall, but varies in height from four inches to six feet. The opposite leaves are directly attached to the stem and are usually somewhat united around it. The long, narrow leaves are seldom more than an inch wide, and they have sparsely-toothed margins. Numerous flower heads — up to one inch broad — have from six to ten yellow rays around the yellow-brown disk centers, but sometimes these rays are missing. The fruits have four barbed awns instead of two as on Beggar-ticks. The tiny flower grows between these awns. (See insert) The heads are usually facing sideways rather than upwards.

BEGGAR-TICKS
BUR MARIGOLD
STICK-TIGHT

Bidens frondosa

Composite Family

Beggar-Ticks grows in moist soil to a height of from two to three feet. The stem is usually tinged with magenta or purple — especially at the leaf axils. The thin yellow-green leaves are divided into from three to five pointed segments with slender petioles (leaf stalks) and toothed margins. There are usually no ray flowers on the flower heads, but the yellow disk flowers are surrounded by from four to eight slender green bracts. The tiny little yellow flower is between the barbed awns.

TICKSEED-SUNFLOWER

Bidens aristosa

Composite Family

There are several Tickseed-Sunflowers in our area but all are similar to the one drawn. The leaves are divided into from three to five toothed segments. The showy yellow flowers have petal-like rays and the seeds are "achenes" with two barbed awns at the tips. Tickseed-Sunflowers vary in height from one to four feet and grow in wet places. The species differ only by technical characteristics, and the novice will have to refer to more technical manuals to determine which one he has found.

WATER MARIGOLD

Megalondonta beckii

Composite Family

Water Marigold is an aquatic plant with finely dissected submerged leaves and a few pairs of simple leaves above the water. The submerged leaves are opposite, but are finely dissected and give the appearance of being in a whorl. There is usually only one showy yellow flower head at the top of the plant. This head has from six to ten yellow ray flowers and is usually about an inch or so broad. The flower may not open fully (see insert). The dry seed usually has four rigid spreading awns which are downwardly barbed at the point. Occasionally the seeds may have from three to six such awns. Water Marigold grows in ponds and slow-moving streams. Most of the plant is under the water. It grows from two to eight feet long, depending upon how deep the water is.

224

YELLOW SNEEZEWEED or SWAMP SUNFLOWER

Helenium autumnale

Composite Family

This sneezeweed grows in thickets, swamps, wet meadows, and especially along rivers to a height of from two to five feet. It is a sturdy, branching plant with an angled stem, which — from a distance — looks like a Black-eyed Susan with *turned-back* yellow rays. The alternate leaves have pointed tips and toothed margins. The flower head has a globular green-yellow, button-like center with yellow rays with three teeth at the tip. Each head is one or two inches broad, and there are from ten to twenty drooping yellow ray flowers.

SNEEZEWEED

Helenium flexuosum

Composite Family

Sneezeweed looks like Black-Eyed Susan from a distance. It grows in clumps in rich thickets, meadows or roadsides to a height of from one to three feet. The stem is branching and has alternate leaves with wings on each side of the midrib.

What appear to be simple flowers, are really flower heads with brown disk flowers in the center and yellow ray flowers on the outside. Each ray has from three to five teeth on the tip. These rays point backwards from the brown button-like center.

PINEAPPLE WEED

Matricaria matricarioides

Composite Family

This branching, leafy plant grows in farm yards, along roadsides, and in waste places to a height of from six to eighteen inches. The leaves are a deep yellow-green and are deeply cut and re-cut. When the plant is bruised, it emits an odor similar to a pineapple.

The yellow-green flowers are in conical or pointed heads with green bracts surrounding the base of the head. There are not any rays as there are on most other members of this family.

TANSY

Tanacetum vulgare

Composite Family

Tansy grows along roadsides and in over-grown fields near old farms or dwellings. It is a tall, strong-scented plant which grows to a height of from two to four or more feet. It has long been used for medicine and is now used for tansy wine or tansy tea. Tansies were cakes made of eggs and tansy leaves to be eaten during Lent by people in some Catholic churches. The deep green fern-like leaves are divided into long, slender, toothed lobes. The yellow or orange-yellow flower heads are composed of tiny flowers which are all tubular. The button-like disks *have no rays* and are arranged in a flat-topped cluster at the top of the plant.

DUSTY MILLER
Artemisia stelleriana
Composite Family

Dusty Miller has showy, silver-gray foliage and is often used as a border in home gardens. The leaves are deeply cut and are covered with a white wool. It has escaped cultivation and is now found growing "wild" where it forms handsome rosettes or large mats on dunes and along sea beaches. The greenish yellow flowers are on a spike above the showy foliage and bloom in August. The flower heads are in an upright — not a nodding or drooping — position. The plant varies in height up to two and a half feet.

ARNICA
Arnica mollis
Composite Family

Arnica is a more westerly or northerly plant usually, but there are two types found in our area. The arnica shown is a tufted plant which grows to a height of from two inches to two feet. It grows on ledges, along mountain streams, and in wet rocks or cliffs at higher elevations. It may be found on gravelly shores of alpine lakes or ponds. Each hairy stem has from three to five pairs of leaves with a pointed tip and toothed margins. The lower stem leaves may have only short stalks (petioles), but the basal leaves are on long petioles. Showy yellow flower heads are at the tips of the stems. The yellow rays are one-half inch long or longer. Each ray is really a complete pistillate (female) flower. There are three teeth at the tip of each petal-like ray.

COMMON GROUNDSEL
Senecio vulgaris
Composite Family

This branching, leafy "weed" grows from six inches to two feet in height and has soft thick leaves which are coarsely toothed. It is similar to the ragworts below, but the flower does not have the showy, flat, yellow rays of the ragwort. The stem and leaves are smooth. The outer bracts under the yellow flower head are tipped with black.

TANSY RAGWORT, STINKING WILLIE or STAGGERWORT
Senecio jacobaea
Composite Family

Tansy Ragwort grows in fields and pastures or along roadsides to a height of from two to nearly four feet. It is a coarse, somewhat woolly biennial with a tough, erect stem and finely-cut leaves. It is a pasture weed which appears to be avoided by grazing animals. The alternate, deeply-cut leaves are similar to the leaves of Tansy (see page 226). The lower leaves have leaf stems, but upper leaves are smaller and are attached directly to the stem. At the top of the plant is a showy, flat-topped cluster of yellow flowers. The heads have both disk and ray flowers — about twelve or fifteen ray flowers on each head.

228

ROBBIN'S RAGWORT
Senecio robbinsii
Composite Family

This ragwort resembles the one
below, but the blades of the basal
leaves are different. The blade is either
a long oval or a long arrowhead shape
with a pointed tip. Some of the larger
leaves have a few ragged lobes on each
side of the midrib. The flowers are
very similar, but are paler in color.

GOLDEN RAGWORT
Senecio aureus
Composite Family

This ragwort is from one to three
feet in height and grows mostly in wet
places. The daisy-like flower heads are
about three-fourths of an inch across
and have from eight to twelve yellow
ray flowers on each head. The narrow
stem leaves are deeply cut but the
basal leaves are either heart-shaped or
egg-shaped with toothed edges. The
broad basal leaves have long leaf stalks
and are sometimes reddish on the
underside. The entire plant is smooth
when it is mature — but is apt to be
somewhat hairy during early growth.

YELLOW THISTLE
Cirsium horridulum
Composite Family

This woolly yellow thistle is native
to our area and grows to a height of
from one to four feet. It grows in open
places, especially in salt marshes and
on sandy coastal shores. The leaves are
very deeply cut and have extremely
sharp bristles. The flower is usually
yellow and is surrounded by a circle of
prickly leaf-like bracts. These bracts
are soft tipped.

NIPPLEWORT, SUCCORY or DOCK-CRESS

Lapsana communis

Composite Family

Nipplewort grows along roadsides and in waste places to a height of from one to nearly four feet. It is a stiff, erect, leathery plant which branches at the top. The top of the plant is usually smooth, but the lower part may be hairy. There is no basal rosette of leaves, but the lower stem leaves are thin and have toothed margins and petioles. They may be from two to four inches long and there are usually from two to six small lobes on the side of the petiole. The upper leaves are long and narrow, are smaller in size, and have no petiole. The small yellow flower heads have from eight to twelve ray flowers in each one. The tip of each ray is toothed or jagged.

LAMB SUCCORY

Arnoseris minima

Composite Family

This member of the composite family is easily identified by the swollen stem below the yellow flower heads. The flowers have very short, flat rays and the leaves are very coarsely toothed. It grows to a height of from six to fourteen inches along roads or in sandy waste places.

230

CAROLINA DWARF DANDELION

Krigia virginica

Composite Family

This is a small, slender dandelion with a single yellow blossom which looks like a hawkweed flower. The head is much smaller — about one-half inch broad — and there are no reflexed outer bracts at the bottom of the head. Instead of the bracts, there are scales and bristles. The leaves in the whorl at the base are usually not all alike. The early spring leaves are often entire and not toothed, while those that develop later do have the dandelion-like toothed leaves. Sometimes the plant becomes branched later in the season.

COMMON DANDELION

Taraxucum officinale

Composite Family

The dandelion is probably the best-known of all wildflowers. Though it is considered to be a pest by most people who have lawns, the leaves may be cooked as greens, the blossom is delicious when dipped in batter and fried, medicine is made from its roots, and wine is made from its flowers. The narrow green leaves with jagged edges are attached to the root. Buds form in the center and then rise on milky, hollow stems and open to form a shiny golden head. There are reflexed outer bracts at the base of the flower head. The flower head is actually made up of many perfect flowers. When these yellow heads dry up, a white puffball forms.

RED-SEEDED DANDELION
Taraxacum erythrospermum
Composite Family

This dandelion differs in several ways from the common Dandelion. It has smaller heads, red seeds, leaves that are narrower and more deeply cut, and the green bracts at the base of the flower head are pointed out instead of being curved backwards. This Dandelion grows in dry fields and is from two to eight inches tall.

FALL DANDELION or HAWKBIT
Leontodon autumnalis
Composite Family

Fall Dandelion grows in fields and along roadsides to a height of from seven inches to two feet. It is a small dandelion with a tall forking or branching flowerstalk. There are tiny bracts or scales about one half inch apart along the upper stalk. The stem is very wiry and is not hollow as the stem is on the common dandelion. The basal leaves are dull green and smooth. They are narrow and have blunt lobes on the sides. The light, golden-yellow flower head stands erect and is about an inch broad. Usually there are two or three heads on the same flower stalk, but occasionally there is only one. The yellow rays appear to be cut off sharply at the tips.

CAT'S-EAR

Hypochoeris radicata

Composite Family

Cat's-Ear has yellow dandelion-like heads about an inch wide. It grows in grassy areas, is from eight to sixteen inches tall, and has scale-like bracts on the stem. The bracts under the flower head are of different lengths and overlap each other. There is a circle of jagged and hairy leaves at the base.

YELLOW GOAT'S BEARD

Tragopogon pratensis

Composite Family

Goat's Beard grows in fields, waste places, and along roads to a height of eight inches to three feet. It has narrow grass-like leaves which clasp the smooth stem. Below the pale yellow flower heads are long, pointed bracts. These lengthen and turn backwards as the round seed head forms.

TWO-FLOWERED CYNTHIA or VIRGINIA GOAT'S BEARD

Krigia biflora

Composite Family

This goat's beard grows in moist woods, fields, and along roadsides to a height of from eight to thirty-two inches. Usually only two yellow-orange flower heads will be on a plant, one on each part of the forked stem. The basal leaves have long petioles and may be either smooth, jagged, toothed, or lobed like those of a dandelion. There is usually only one upper leaf which embraces the smooth flower stalk. Circling the yellow flower head are from nine to eighteen upright green, pointed bracts. As the flower ages, these bracts turn backward.

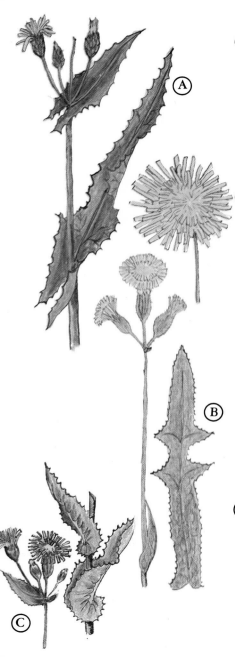

(A) COMMON SOW-THISTLE

Sonchus oleraceus

Composite Family

This troublesome weed has *smooth bracts* and flower stalks, and the base of the leaves have *pointed lobes* which clasp the stem. It grows in waste places, fields, and along roads to a height of from one to eight feet.

(B) FIELD SOW-THISTLE

Sonchus arvensis

Composite Family

This sow-thistle is similar to Common Sow-thistle but blooms later and has a different type of leaf. It grows in fields, along roadsides, on gravelly shores, and in waste places to a height of from one and a half to four feet. It creeps and spreads by means of underground rootstalks. The stems have many prickly-edged leaves which clasp the stem with their heart-shaped bases. The yellow blossoms look much like those of a dandelion, but are not as full and rounded. To distinguish it from Common Sow-thistle, look for *glandular hairs on the green bracts* under the flower head and on the flower stalks.

(C) SPINY-LEAVED SOW-THISTLE

Sonchus asper

Composite Family

This sow-thistle is similar to the other two, but has *rounded "ears" or lobes at the base of the leaf* which surrounds the stem. The margins of the leaves on this plant are very spiny.

234

WILD LETTUCE
Lactuca canadensis
Composite Family

Wild Lettuce grows in thickets, along roadsides, and in woodland clearings to a height of from three to eight feet. It is a tall, smooth, extremely variable plant which may have a whitish powder on it. There is usually a basal rosette of leaves, but other leaves vary in size and shape. Lower ones are deeply lobed while upper ones may not be lobed at all. Leaves on large plants may be ten or more inches long. Many insignificant, yellow flower heads are in long, branching clusters at the top of the plant. Each head is about one-fourth of an inch across, and is similar to a dandelion blossom. The yellow flower heads sometimes turn purplish with age.

HAWK'S-BEARD or SMOOTH HAWKSBEARD
Crepis capillaris
Composite Family

Hawksbeard is a branching, dandelion-like plant which grows in fields, waste places and poorly-kept lawns. It is usually less than a foot tall. At the base of the plant is a circle of shiny dandelion-like leaves which are deeply toothed or cut and are narrowed at the base. The upper stem leaves are narrow, deeply-cut, and clasp the stem with arrow-like lobes. Numerous flower heads are on slender flower stalks at the top of the plant. The stem is simple at the base, but it is very branching at the top of the plant.

235

KING DEVIL

Hieracium pratense

Composite Family

This plant is similar to a Devil's Paintbrush only it is yellow. King Devil is from one to three feet tall and grows in fields and along roadsides. The stems and bracts under the flower heads are covered with black, bristly hairs. The stem sometimes has a few tiny reduced leaves, but usually it is leafless. The narrow basal leaves are from two to ten inches long and taper as they reach the stem. The leaves are hairy on both sides. There are numerous yellow flower heads at the top of the stem.

RATTLESNAKE WEED

Hieracium venosum

Composite Family

This plant is similar to hawkweeds but may be easily identified by the reddish or purple veining on the green leaves. The elliptical basal leaves have long hairs and the underside is often purplish or reddish. The smooth stem (or stems) is from one to two and one-half feet tall and is usually branching at the top. There are numerous yellow flowering heads at the top — sometimes as many as forty flowers on a large plant. The green bracts holding the heads are not hairy. It grows in open woods and clearings.

PANICLED HAWKWEED
Hieracium paniculatum
Composite Family

This hawkweed grows in dry open woods to a height of from one to three and a half feet. It has a slender, leafy lower stem, but there are no leaves after the stem starts to branch. The plant is usually smooth, but may be hairy at the base. The leaves are thin and have slightly-toothed margins. The leaves may be on petioles (leaf stalks). A dozen or so small yellow flower heads about a half inch broad are on slender stalks that *branch horizontally* from the main stem.

ROUGH HAWKWEED
Hieracium scabrum
Composite Family

This hawkweed grows in dry soil of open woods, clearings, and pastures to a height of from one to three feet. It is a coarse, sturdy plant which is thickly covered with glandular hairs. The red-tinged stem is stout and leafy up to where the flowers begin. There is *no basal tuft* of leaves at flowering time. The hairy, oblong, leaves are from two to four inches long and are blunt at the tip. They get smaller as they ascend the stem. The leaf margins may be sparingly toothed on some plants. Flowers are in numerous small, yellow flower heads about one-half inch broad. Each flower head is on a densely-hairy reddish flower stalk.

LARGE-LEAVED PONDWEED

Potamogeton amplifolius

Pondweed Family

Pondweeds are mostly submerged plants, sometimes with some floating leaves. There are about thirty-five species in our area, all of which are highly variable in appearance making them difficult for amateurs to identify — other than to recognize them as "one of the many pondweeds." Exact identification requires the ripe fruits. The pondweed shown here is the largest and coarsest of the pondweeds and has two kinds of leaves. The submerged leaves are long and are usually folded lengthwise with wavy edges and are curved into a position like a sickle. They have a definite midrib and stipules the color of wax paper. The upper leaves are on long stalks; are oval in shape, and may be floating on the water. As in the case of most pondweeds, the inconspicuous flowers are in long, club-shaped spikes which are raised to the surface of the water where floating pollen grains can fertilize them. There are no true petals or sepals but there are four stamens and four green outgrowths which look like petals. The flowers are in a whorl around the spike.

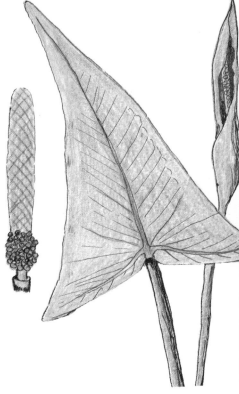

SPIKE GRASS or
SEASIDE ARROW-GRASS

Triglochin maritima

Arrow-Grass Family

Spike Grass is a narrow-leaved plant
with round, hollow, slender leaves
which are sheathed at the base with a
whitish sheath. It usually grows in salt
marshes, but may be found in fresh
marshes or along the shore. It varies
in height to from six inches to two
feet. The small, whitish flowers have
six concave, petal-like parts and are in
long clusters at the top of a jointless
stalk. This spike-like cluster may be up
to twelve inches long on larger plants.
The fruit is oval with six recurving
tips (or rarely only three) and splits
open when ripe.

GREEN ARROW-ARUM

Peltandra virginica

Arum Family

This wild flower is a member of the
Arum family, as is the Skunk Cabbage,
the Wild Calla, and the Jack-in-the-
Pulpit. This is a fairly large family of
plants, many of which grow around
the water. All of them have small
flowers crowded around the bottom of
the spadix and usually covered or
protected by a spathe. The Green
Arrow-Arum is a large flower which
often grows right in the water of lakes
and streams. The plant is often one

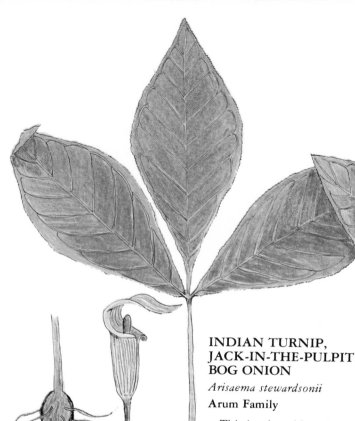

INDIAN TURNIP,
JACK-IN-THE-PULPIT,
BOG ONION

Arisaema stewardsonii

Arum Family

This is a later-blooming species of Jack-in-the-Pulpit which is sometimes found growing in wet woods and swampy thickets until early August. It grows to a height of from one to two and a half feet tall. Mature plants have two leaves, each of which is divided into three shiny, pointed leaflets. Young plants may only have one three-part leaf. The flowers are minute, in a ring around the base of the spadix (Jack) inside of the spathe (the pulpit). The spathe is green and is strongly ribbed with white ribs. The arching hood is pointed and is usually green and white striped, though occasionally there may be purple on it.

and one-half feet high. The green pointed spathe grows about five inches long. If this spathe is pulled apart, the long green spadix with tiny flowers clustered at the bottom may be seen. The leaves are shaped like an Indian Arrowhead — hence the name. These leaves sometimes grow to be twenty inches long. The berries, which develop at the base of the spadix, are green.

FALSE HELLEBORE or INDIAN POKE

Veratrum viride

Lily Family

This stout plant is from two to six feet tall and can be found growing in low wet land or swamps. It has a single stem with broad, clasping leaves which are heavily ribbed in a length-wise direction. Leaves are alternate on the stem. The yellow-green flowers have six petals and are star-shaped. They are arranged in a large, much-branched panicle at the summit of the stem. Each flower is about two-thirds of an inch broad. All parts of this plant are highly poisonous.

BUNCHFLOWER

Melanthium hybridum

Lily Family

Bunchflower is restricted to upland regions and is not common. It is found in southern New England in open woods and on slopes. It varies in height from two to five feet. It has a tall, slender, leafy stem which grows from a thick rootstalk. The Latin name comes from the mixture of flowers on the same plant; some are staminate (male), some are pistillate (female) and some are perfect and contain both male and female parts. The leaves are linear to oval-pointed, and are not folded or ribbed. The lower leaves clasp the stem, but the upper leaves are much smaller and do not clasp. The "bunch" of flowers at the top of the plant may be a foot or more in length. There are three sepals and three petals which look very much alike. They are greenish to cream colored, but turn darker as they age. Each petal-like part has a narrow stalk-like base and wavy edges. A hand lens will reveal the two dark glands at the base of each petal. A stamen is attached to the base of the claw on each petal.

TWISTED STALK

Streptopus amplexifolius

Lily Family

White Mandarin and Liverberry are two other common names given to this plant. It grows in cold, moist woods and thickets to a height of from one to three feet. A distinctive characteristic to look for when trying to distinguish this Twisted Stalk from other Twisted Stalks, is the sharp kink in the tiny flower stalks. White Mandarin has a zig-zag stem with alternate, oval, pointed leaves which embrace the stem. A single bell-shaped flower (rarely two) hangs on a kinked stalk below each leaf. The flowers are generally greenish-white and the petals and sepals are about one-half inch long. The insides of the petals are often spotted with purple. The tips of the petals turn backwards at the tip. The fruit is a bright, fleshy, inedible berry.

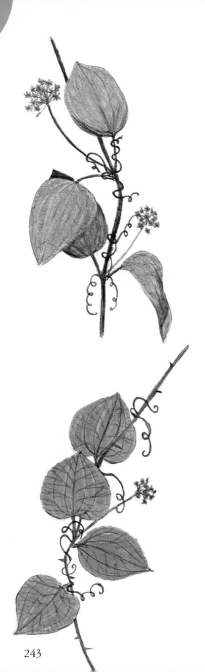

CARRION-FLOWER

Smilax herbacea

Lily Family

Carrion-flower is a freely branched shrub which climbs by tendrils. It grows in moist soil of open woods, roadsides, and thickets and is often as long as six feet. The leaves are rounded or heart-shaped at the base but are pointed at the tip. They are very broad and have nerves which run lengthwise and also veins which are not running lengthwise. The leaves are pale green and have a gray-green waxy substance which may be rubbed off. The small yellow-green flowers have six petals and are arranged in umbels which arise from the axils of the leaves. The flowers emit an odor of carrion (rotting flesh). The male (staminate) flowers are on one plant and the female (pistilate) flowers are on another.

GREENBRIER

Smilax rotundifolia

Lily Family

This high-climbing shrub grows in open woods, thickets, and along roadsides. It has a green, four-angled stem which is scattered with stout thorns. The vine is often evergreen and climbs by means of tendrils. The leathery leaves are a shiny green color and are broadly triangular or heart-shaped.

They have lengthwise nerves plus net-like veins. The part of the stem which bears the flower cluster arises from the axil of the leaves. The staminate flowers and the pistilate flowers are on separate plants. The berries are blue-black.

WILD YAM

Dioscorea villosa

Yam Family

Wild Yam is the only member of
this more southern family which is
native to New England. It is a large
vine — often ten feet or more in
length — which twines over shrubs in
moist thickets or ditches. It has a
smooth stem and heart-shaped leaves
which have prominent veins and ribs.
Most of the leaves are alternate, but
the lower leaves may be arranged in
whorls of three. The delicate yellow-
green flowers are only from one-eighth
to one-fourth of an inch broad. Male
and female flowers are in separate
clusters on the vine.

LONG-BRACTED ORCHIS or FROG ORCHIS

Habenaria viridis

Orchid Family

The distinctive characteristic of this
orchid is the long green bract under
each blossom. The lower bracts may be
up to three times as long as the flower
itself. Frog Orchis grows in woods and
thickets and rich meadows and shores
to a height of from six to twenty-four
inches. The slender stem is very leafy
with blunt lower leaves and pointed
upper leaves. The green flowers may
be tinged with bronze on some plants.
Each flower has a forked lip and a
short rounded spur.

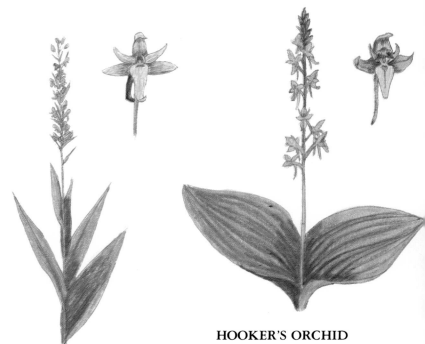

HOOKER'S ORCHID

Habenaria hookeri

Orchid Family

Hooker's Orchid grows in woods to a height of from eight to sixteen inches. It has two large, roundish leaves which are up to six inches long and five inches wide. The orchid-like flowers are yellowish-green and have a long tapering spur at the base. The spur may be nearly an inch long. The sepals and lip are about one-half inch long, but the side petals are much shorter. Flowers are arranged in a slender raceme at the top of the stem. There are no bracts on the stem and the flowers are not on separate pedicels (stems), but attached directly to the main stem.

NORTHERN GREEN ORCHIS

Habenaria hyperborea

Orchid Family

This tall, leafy orchis grows in bogs, woods, and thickets to a height of from eight to forty inches. The flowers are green or yellowish-green and are in a compact spike-like raceme with small leaf-like bracts intermingled with the flowers. The three sepals at the back of the flower are larger than the two side petals. The side petals are long and narrow and are directed forward. The lower petal forms a lip. There is a spur about the same length as the lip which curves inward towards the stem.

ROUND-LEAVED ORCHIS

Habenaria orbiculata

Orchid Family

This orchid grows in the woods —
often in deep pine woods — to a
height of from one to two feet. It has
two large, round, flat leaves at the base
of the flower stalk. These leaves are
usually spreading flat on the ground
and are silvery on the bottom side and
green on the top. The flowers are in a
loose cluster at the top of the stem.
Each greenish-white flower has a long
tapering lip which is *not fringed* and is
usually shorter than the spur. The
slender spur may be an inch and a half
long on larger plants.

RAGGED ORCHIS or GREEN FRINGED ORCHIS

Habenaria lacera

Orchid Family

Ragged Orchis grows in old fields,
clearings, dry or wet meadows, and wet
woods to a height of from eight to
thirty-two inches. The lower leaves are
alternate and are oblong with pointed
tips. The upper leaves are reduced to
pointed bracts. The flowers are in a
loosely-flowered spike at the tip of the
stem. They are fragrant and are
yellowish-green or white shaded to
yellowish. The lower lip is cut nearly
to its base into three clawed, spreading
divisions. Each division is deeply
fringed.

GREEN ADDER'S MOUTH

Malaxis unifolia

Orchid Family

This orchid grows in dry or moist woods, borders of swamps or bogs, or on gravelly slopes. It varies in height from four to twelve inches. The stem is simple and bears a single, pointed, dark-green leaf about mid way which clasps the stem. The flowers are in a dense cluster at the top of the stem. The lower sepals are spreading, but the upper one is long and erect. The two side petals are thread-like and are sometimes drooping. The lower lip is broad and is three-toothed at the tip. The lip is above when the flower opens, but as the flower stalk twists and grows, the upper petal is then brought into a lower position.

STINGING NETTLE

Urtica dioica

Nettle Family

This is a branching weed which should not be touched because it is covered with coarse, stinging hairs. It grows in waste ground where the soil is light or loosely packed. It has a hollow, four-angled stem which is from two to four feet. The stem is fibrous but gives off a watery juice if it is broken. The opposite leaves have long stalks and are coarsely toothed. The tiny greenish flowers have four petal-like parts. They are in branching clusters which originate in the leaf axils. The staminate (male) and the pistillate (female) flowers are often on separate plants.

WOOD NETTLE
Laportea canadensis
Nettle Family

Wood Nettle grows in rich woods and along banks of streams to a height of from one and a half to four feet. It is a perennial herb with large, toothed leaves which are strongly veined. The thin, hairy leaves have a slender-pointed tip and toothed margins. There are stinging hairs on the stems and on the leaf stalks. The large, loose flower clusters of tiny flowers are often longer than the stalks of the leaves. The lower flowers in the cluster are staminate (male) and the upper ones are pistillate (female). The staminate flower has five sepals and stamens, while the pistillate one has only four sepals with the inner two being much larger.

RICHWEED, CLEARWEED, or COOLWEED
Pilea pumila
Nettle Family

Richweed grows in swampy, shady places — often on or near old logs — to a height of from six inches to two feet. It is a rather weak plant which wilts quickly when it is picked. The branched stems are smooth and succulent and look clear and almost transparent. The lustrous leaves have pointed tips, toothed margins, *three main veins,* and long, slender stalks. The tiny, greenish flowers are in four diverging clusters at the axils of the leaves. These clusters are usually curved or drooping and are usually *shorter than the leaf stalks.*

248

FALSE NETTLE, BOG HEMP
Boehmeria cylindrica
Nettle Family

False Nettle is a smooth (or sometimes hairy) plant with a simple stem and pointed leaves. It is similar to Nettle on page 247, but it has *no stinging hairs*. False Nettle may be found growing in shady places where the soil is moist. It grows to a height of from sixteen to forty inches.

The thin, oval leaves taper to a point and have toothed margins. They are chiefly opposite each other on the stem, are on a long stalk, and have three main nerves.

Tiny flowers are densely clustered into long spikes at the axils of the leaves. Male and female parts are in different flowers on separate plants, or may be in separate clusters on the same plant. The long green flower clusters frequently bear smaller leaves at their tips.

SOUR or CURLED DOCK
Rumex crispus
Buckwheat Family

There are several docks in our area. The one shown is a stout erect plant that grows along roads and in wastelands to a height of from one to four feet. It has many stems which are tough and fibrous and have a corky center. The leaves have a prominent midrib on the under side and the margins are very wavy. The large pea-green flower cluster at the ends of the branches is made up of many smaller branching clusters. There are small leaves intermingled with the winged flowers. There is a brown fringe around the stem at the axils of the leaves.

SHEEP SORREL or RED SORREL

Rumex acetosella

Buckwheat Family

Sheep Sorrel grows in acid soil in wastelands, roadsides, and unkept lawns, to a height of from four to twelve inches. The stem is erect and may be either simple or branched. The leaves are variable, but are usually arrowhead-shaped with three lobes. They have a very acid or sour taste. The flower heads are very minute and are in small clusters separated by empty spaces on the stem. The flowers are green, but often turn reddish-brown as they mature. Male flowers are yellow. Sometimes the spike-like flower cluster is half as tall as the entire plant.

GARDEN SORREL or GREEN SORREL

Rumex acetosa

Buckwheat Family

This sorrel is larger than Sheep Sorrel and the upper leaves clasp the stem. The lower lobes of the leaf point backwards. The flower spikes are larger and more compact. This sorrel grows in fields and along roads to a height from six to twenty-four inches.

250

KNOTWEED

Polygonum prolificum

Buckwheat Family

There are many different species of knotweeds, but all are tiny-leaved plants with insignificant flowers tucked in the leaf axils. The minute flowers are either single, in pairs, or in sets of three. The variety shown is a coastal variety. The leaves get very veiny when dry, and the flowers can scarcely be seen.

WATER PEPPER, COMMON SMARTWEED

Polygonum hydropiper

Buckwheat Family

Water Pepper is a common branching annual which has reddish stems and is intensely peppery to the taste. It grows in damp soil and along shores to a height of one or two feet.

The narrow lance-shaped leaves have wavy margins and prominent veins. The leaf stalk is fringed with tiny bristles where it is attached to the main stem. The flowers are in slim, greenish, nodding or arching clusters at tips of the branch or arising from axils of the leaves. The calyx is green or red-tipped and is covered with dark spots. There are no true petals.

MILD WATER PEPPER

Polygonum   hydropiperoides (not shown)

Buckwheat Family

Mild Water Pepper is very similar to the above, but the nodding clusters of flowers are more pinkish and the leaves do not bite the tongue if chewed. The calyx is rose or purplish, and it *is not dotted.*

FRINGED BLACK BINDWEED

Polygonum cilinode
Buckwheat Family

This bindweed grows in rocky places, dry thickets, or in borders of woods and is a twining, reclining, or high climbing vine which may be as long as ten feet. The Latin name *cilinode* is the clue to the distinctive characteristic. It means "with ciliate or hairy nodes," and indeed, this plant has a ring of bristles or a fringe at the base of the stipules at each leaf axil. The broad leaves have a heart-shaped base and a pointed tip. Some lower leaves may have lobes that point away from the mid-rib. The leaves are on long stalks, and there are soft hairs on the underside. The flowers are in long clusters on stalks arising at the leaf axils. There are no true petals, but the calyx has petal-like parts which are white or may be pink tinged.

CLIMBING FALSE BUCK-WHEAT

Polygonum scundens
Buckwheat Family

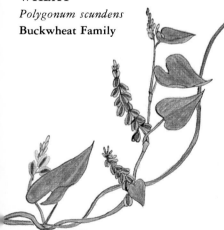

Climbing False Buckwheat grows in moist thickets and along country lanes. It is a twining and climbing vine which may be from eight to twelve feet long. It has a smooth, reddish stem which climbs over bushes and has become a troublesome weed in vegetable gardens. The clusters of winged fruit are actually more showy than the clusters of insignificant, greenish or pinkish flowers. There are no true petals, but the calyx has five petal-like parts with colored margins and conspicuous flaps on the keels on the back. A green, winged, three-angled seed pod follows the flower. The leaves are heart or arrow-head shaped, and are alternate on the stem.

LAMB'S QUARTERS
Chenopodium album
Goosefoot Family

Lamb's Quarters — also called Pigweed — is a branching weed with stout red-streaked stems. It grows in fields, gardens, and in wastelands to a height of from one to three feet. The upper stem leaves are thin, long, slender, but untoothed. The basal leaves are large, diamond-shaped, coarsely toothed, and mealy-white on the underside. The small greenish flowers are in dense clusters on separate stems which grow from axils of leaves.

STRAWBERRY BLITE
Chenopodium capitatum
Goosefoot Family

This erect plant is from six to twenty-four inches tall and is branched from the base. It grows in woodland clearings, along roads, and in wastelands. It is often found in great quantity after a fire. The basal leaves have long leaf stems (petioles) which are often longer than the blade itself, but the upper stem leaves have very short petioles. The leaves are triangular in general outline, but have irregular teeth. The flowers are in tight, round clusters at the top of the stem and in axils of upper leaves. When in the seed stage, the fruit looks like a bright, red berry.

ORACHE
Atriplex patula
Goosefoot Family

There are several species of orache in our area. Most are weedy plants

which grow to a height of up to forty inches. The plant is mealy and is often reddish. The leaves have petioles and are either opposite or alternate on the stem. The flowers are in the upper nodes on nearly leafless spikes. Both staminate and pistillate flowers are intermingled. Orache grows in alkaline soil and waste lands. Young, tender leaves of orache are very good when cooked as greens in the spring.

SLENDER GLASSWORT

Salicornia europaea

Goosefoot Family

This glasswort is the most common species found in salt marshes or in salty, inland soil. It may be either erect or sprawling and is a slender plant. The joints are longer than they are wide. The flowers are in groups of three in the joints, but the central flower is broader than the two side ones. See page 102 in the pink section.

PIGWEED, RED ROOT, or GREEN AMARANTH

Amaranthus retroflexus

Amaranth Family

This rough, yellow-green or gray-green plant is a common weed in cultivated fields, waste soils, and roadsides. The oval-pointed leaves are rough, have untoothed margins and are on long stalks. Tiny purplish or greenish flowers are hidden among bristle-like bracts in long spike-like clusters. These clusters are in the axils of the leaves and at the top of the plant. The tops of the spikes are rounded. The plant varies greatly in height, but is usually one or two feet tall.

254

SILVERLING or SILVER WHITLOW-WORT

Paronychia argyrocoma

Pink Family

Silverling grows on or near acid rocks, mostly at higher elevations. It is a freely-branching herb which forms broad tufts from three to eight inches tall. The erect stems are covered with silvery hairs which are pressed closely to the stem. The paired, flat, linear leaves have one nerve and are silky. There are two silvery-white appendages at each side of the base of the leaf. Tiny flowers are hidden behind conspicuous, large, silvery bracts. The petals are merely teeth between the five hairy sepals. There are five stamens — one in the middle of each sepal. Each green sepal has an erect bristle at the tip.

DITCH or VIRGINIA STONE-CROP

Penthorum sedoides

Saxifrage Family

Ditch Stonecrop grows in ditches, wet places, and on river banks to a height of from eight inches to two feet. It is a curious wildflower with an erect stem which is sometimes reclining at the base. The light-green, alternate leaves are pointed at both ends and have finely-toothed margins. They have short leaf stalks or none at all. The small yellow-green flowers are in two or three slender, bending clusters. Each flower is one-fifth of an inch broad. It has a five-part calyx, but usually there are no petals. If present, the petals are small and linear. Five pistils are joined together at the base and the fruit is a distinctive five-lobed capsule with five spreading tips or horns.

NAKED MITREWORT or BISHOP'S CAP

Mitella nuda

Saxifrage Family

Bishop's Cap grows in cool woods and mossy bogs and is seldom taller than seven or eight inches. It is a dainty plant with a nearly-leafless, hairy stem. The basal leaves are somewhat round in general outline, but have large-toothed margins. The flowers are insignificant until viewed with a hand lense. (See the enlargement) The greenish-white or greenish-yellow flowers are perfectly lovely. They are symmetrically perfect. There are ten yellow stamens surrounding the pistil, and five fragile thread-like fringes which are really the petals of the flower.

256

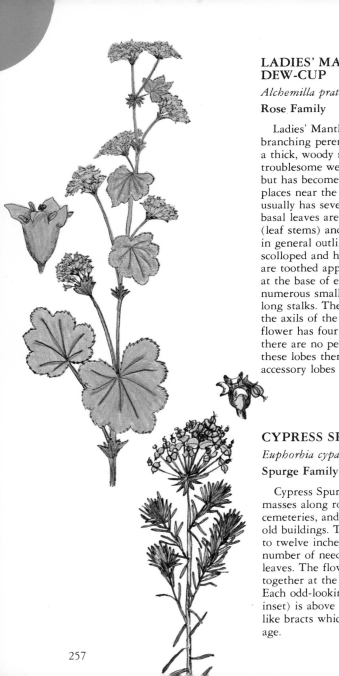

LADIES' MANTLE, DEW-CUP

Alchemilla pratensis

Rose Family

Ladies' Mantle is an erect and branching perennial which grows from a thick, woody root. It is sometimes a troublesome weed. It is from Europe, but has become naturalized in grassy places near the coast. Each plant usually has several hairy stems. The basal leaves are on slender petioles (leaf stems) and are somewhat round in general outline. The margins are scolloped and have small teeth. There are toothed appendages called stipules at the base of each petiole. There are numerous small flowers in clusters on long stalks. These stalks originate in the axils of the leaves. Each small flower has four lobes in the calyx, but there are no petals. Between each of these lobes there may be smaller accessory lobes or bractlets.

CYPRESS SPURGE

Euphorbia cyparissias

Spurge Family

Cypress Spurge grows in dense masses along roads, in fields, and cemeteries, and around foundations of old buildings. The stems are from six to twelve inches tall and have a great number of needle-like, pale-green leaves. The flowers are clustered together at the summit of each plant. Each odd-looking flower cluster (see inset) is above a pair of yellow petal-like bracts which may turn red with age.

257

LEAFY SPURGE

Euphorbia esula

Spurge Family

Leafy Spurge resembles Cyprus Spurge but is taller and less leafy. The narrow leaves are broader than those of the Cypress Spurge, and there are not as many leaves on the stem. There are numerous smaller alternating bracts *below the top* flower umbel, whereas the flowers of the Cypress Spurge are all at the top. Though the illustration does not indicate, the Leafy Spurge is much larger than the Cypress Spurge.

THREE-SEEDED MERCURY COPPERLEAF MERCURY-WEED

Acalypha virginica

Spurge Family

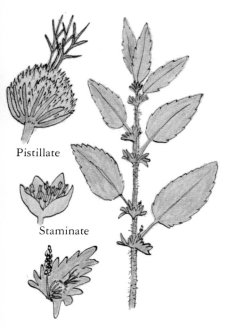

Pistillate

Staminate

This is a rather delicate plant with an erect stem and branches which are densely covered with short uncurved hairs. It grows in dry soils of woods and thickets to a height of from six inches to two feet. The plant is usually green, but may be purple-tinged. The long, pointed leaves are thin, have toothed margins, and are on leaf stems which are one-third to one-half the length of the leaf blade itself.

Small yellowish-green staminate (male) flowers and pistillate (female) flowers are on separate spikes. The staminate flowers are tiny and are in an upright spike with only a few (sometimes only one) female flower at the base. Both spikes are within the same fringed leaf-like bract which is at the leaf axils.

258

POISON IVY, POISON OAK

Rhus radicans

Cashew Family

Poison Ivy is a well-known plant with as many as thirty common names. It is very widespread and grows at edges of woods and in openings or dry thickets. It is an upright or trailing shrub which climbs by means of clinging rootlets which attach themselves to trees, stone walls and rocks. It is a dreaded shrub which causes an itching and weeping rash to some who touch it. It is especially poisonous if touched during the night or in early summer when the sun is not shining upon it.

The leaves are divided into three, somewhat four-sided, pointed leaflets, the end leaflet usually being longer stalked than the other two. The underside of the leaf can be either smooth, or covered with soft hairs.

The flowers have five greenish or yellowish-white petals. Flowers are in loose clusters at axils of leaves. Later in the season there will be a cluster of whitish, berry-like fruits with a hard or stony center.

WOODBINE or VIRGINIA CREEPER

Parthenocissus quinquefolia

Vine Family

This plant is also called False Grape and American Ivy. It is a beautiful climbing or trailing vine which grows in woods and thickets, often on rocky banks. It climbs by means of tendrils and aerial rootlets. The long-stalked leaves are divided into five leaflets with pointed tips and coarsely-toothed margins. The upper surface is dull or dark green, but the underside is pale. Usually the leaves are not hairy. The flowers are very tiny, but there may be from twenty-five to two hundred of the inconspicuous flowers in a spreading, flat-topped cluster. Each small flower has five thick, concave petals which are yellow-green or whitish-green in color. The leaves have conspicuous veins, and both the leaf stalk and the stalk holding the flower cluster are deep red. The leaves turn a brilliant deep red in autumn and the berries turn blue in October.

CLIMBING BITTERSWEET

Celastrus scandens

Staff Tree Family

Other names for this plant are Waxwork, Shrubby Bittersweet, and Staff-Tree. It is a twining, woody vine which ascends nearby trees or poles to a height of twenty-five feet or more. If there are no trees near-by, it will trail along the ground until it finds some support. It grows in rich soil, especially along streams, old stone walls, or roadsides. It is more commonly found at higher elevations.

The light-green, egg-shaped leaves are smooth on both sides. They are pointed at the tip, but are rounded at the base. They grow alternately along the stem, but may be in ranks because of the way the stem twists. Tiny greenish-white flowers are in loose terminal clusters. The petals are finely toothed along the margins. Five stamens are inserted on the margin of the cup-shaped disk at the base of the calyx. The capsule is yellow or orange, but as it dries, it splits and turns backward to expose the showy red seed covering inside. These showy clusters are prized by those who make dried-flower arrangements in the fall.

MANY-FRUITED LUDWIGIA

Ludwigia polycarpa

Evening Primrose Family

This erect plant grows in swamps and along shores of ponds to a height of from one to three feet. The leaves are very narrow, are pointed at both ends, and are alternate on the stem. Insignificant greenish flowers grow in the leaf axils. Four greenish petals are minute. The capsule is top-shaped and is somewhat four-sided, and has linear or awl-shaped leaflets at its base.

WATER PURSLANE

Ludwigia palustris

Evening Primrose Family

This common aquatic species may be found growing in shallow water in swamps and ditches. It is a creeping or floating plant with reddish stems and paired, glossy, red-veined leaves. It is less than a foot long. Tiny inconspicuous four-parted flowers are tucked in the leaf axils. They usually have no petals, but if the plant is found growing on land, then the flowers may have four rudimentary petals. Each flower has four stamens. The fruit has four long, green bands on it.

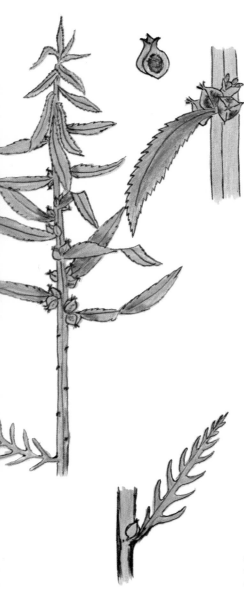

MERMAID WEED
Proserpinaca palustris
Water Milfoil Family

Mermaid Weed is a very leafy aquatic plant with creeping stems at the base and upright square stems at the tips. Leaves are alternate and small flowers are attached directly to the main stem at leaf axils. Flowers may be solitary, or in groups of from two to five. There is one leaf beneath each flower cluster. The stem leaves only have toothed margins, but submerged leaves have deeply cut margins and a sharp, black, rigid spine in their axils.

There are no petals on the flowers, but each flower does contain both male and female parts. The tube of the calyx is attached to a three-sided ovary as shown in enlargement. After flowering, the ovary develops into a three-winged, three-sided nut-like fruit.

Mermaid Weed grows in shallow water in wet swamps or along shores to a height of from eight to twenty inches.

CUT-LEAVED MERMAID WEED
Proserpinaca pectinata
Water Milfoil Family

Cut-Leaved Mermaid Weed is very similar in habitat and growth, but is smaller. The stem leaves as well as the submerged ones are deeply cut. This is the distinctive characteristic used in identification.

262

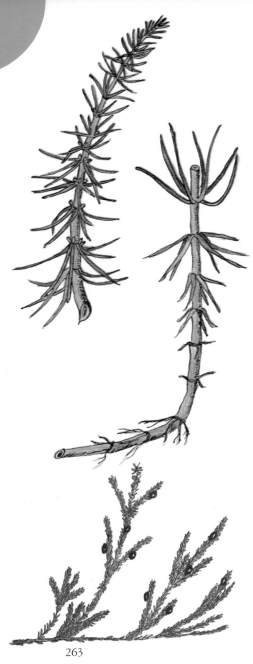

MARE'S TAIL or BOTTLEBRUSH

Hippuris vulgaris

Water Milfoil Family

Mare's Tail is also called Joint-Weed. It grows in shallow pools, in swamps and bogs, or in margins of lakes and streams in cool regions of New England. It varies in height from eight to twenty inches. It is a lax, fleshy plant without much rigidity. The erect stems rise from creeping, underground or underwater stems. The leaves are long and slender and are arranged in whorls of from six to twelve at each joint on the stem. The submerged leaves are longer and thinner than the leaves above the water line. The leaves usually reduce in size at the very base of the stem. Minute flowers are in the middle and upper axils. The calyx is barrel-shaped and there are no petals. The flower is usually perfect, but sometimes will only have the female parts. The fleshy fruit is small, one-celled, and has one hard, stony seed inside.

There are only two species in our area. *Hippuris tetraphylla* is similar, but smaller. There are only from four to six slender leaves in each whorl on this plant.

CROWBERRY

Empetrum nigrum

Heath Family

This much-branching, woody-stemmed plant forms a thick spreading mat over rocks and bare ground. It is an arctic plant which grows at higher elevations and along ocean cliffs and banks to a height of less than six inches. Numerous needle-like leaves

263

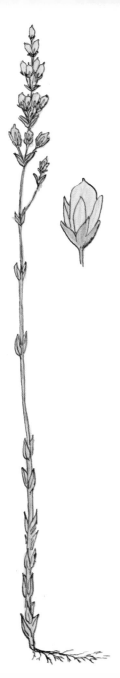

are crowded on the stems. The leaves are less than one-fourth inch long. The minute flowers have three sepals and three petals. They are pink only near the base and are predominantly creamy-green. They are tucked in the axils of the tiny leaves. The fruit is black and berry-like and ripens in July. The berry is edible, but it is rather dry and tasteless.

YELLOW BARTONIA or SCREW-STEM

Bartonia virginica

Gentian Family

Screw-stem is a rather stiff, wiry, yellowish-green plant which is usually not branching, though some plants may have a few erect branches at the summit. The stem sometimes twists and bends. This plant grows in moist acid soil or in soil that was wet earlier in the spring but has since dried. It reaches a height of from four to eighteen inches.

Opposite scale-like leaves are on the stem. These pairs are close together at the base of the plant, but are farther apart near the top. The funnel-shaped corolla has four greenish-white petals inside of the yellow-green calyx. Each flower is less than one-fourth inch long.

GREEN MILKWEED

Asclepias viridiflora or *Acerates viridiflora*

Milkweed Family

This milkweed is a hairy plant which may be upright or reclining. It grows in dry rocky or sandy soil in openings. It is usually from one to three feet tall. The thick, oval, pointed leaves are slightly rough. They may be alternate or opposite on the stem, but most of them are usually opposite. Green flowers are arranged in several densely-flowered umbels in the axils of the leaves. The slender fruit is called a follicle and is long and pointed.

FIGWORT

Scrophularia marilandica

Figwort Family

This figwort grows in thin woods and thickets to a height of from three to seven feet. It is a smooth perennial with a slender, four-sided stem with grooves, and curious, sac-shaped flowers. The slender-stemmed leaves have a rounded base and toothed margins which taper to a point. The small flowers are clustered on long, nearly-leafless branches. The two-lipped corolla is green on the outside and shiny, brownish-magenta on the inside. There are four normal stamens inside and one deep purple one that is sterile. See page 345 in the brown section for another Figwort.

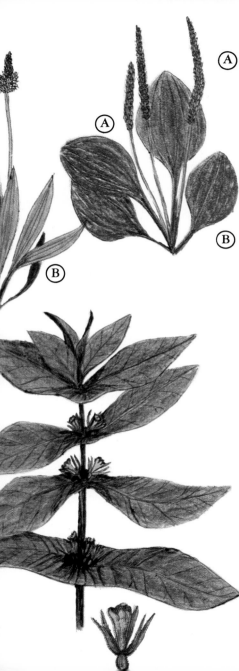

(A) COMMON PLANTAIN

Plantago major

Plantain Family

Common Plantain grows in dooryards, lawns, and waste places to a height of from six to eighteen inches. It has thick, broad, dull-green leaves at the base of the plant. The tough leaf stalks are grooved and are often longer than the leaf blade. Tiny flowers are in long, tight-clustered flower spikes.

(B) ENGLISH PLANTAIN

Plantago lanceolata

Plantain Family

English Plantain grows in dooryards, along roadsides, and in wastelands to a height of from nine to twenty-four inches. It has slender three-ribbed leaves, and a grooved stalk with a short, dense spike of flowers at the tip.

FEVERWORT

Triosteum perfoliatum

Honeysuckle Family

Other common names are Wild Coffee, Horse-Gentian, and Tinker's-Weed. The plant grows in rocky, open woods and clearings to a height of from two to four feet. The paired leaves join together around the stem which is downy with gland-tipped hairs. The flowers are set in the axils of the leaf on an egg-shaped ovary. The petals are greenish, dull yellow, or dull purple, and make a funnel-shaped hairy flower with five erect lobes surrounded by five, long, hairy sepals. The fruit is a red-orange, hairy, berry-like cluster with three nutlets.

266

BUR or STAR CUCUMBER

Sicyos angulatus

Gourd Family

Bur Cucumber grows in damp soil
along hedges, streams or in low thickets.
It is an annual vine which trails or climbs
by branching tendrils to a length of
fifteen to twenty-five feet. The angled
stem has clammy hairs on it. The thin,
broad leaves are rough on both surfaces.
They have a heart-shaped base and five,
sharply-pointed lobes. The small,
greenish flowers have five petals and
five sepals. The male flowers are in loose,
elongated clusters on long stalks. They
have a five-toothed, cup-shaped calyx
tube and a five-part corolla. The female
flowers are in tight heads on shorter
stalks. After pollination, the female
flowers develop into an oval, prickly fruit
with one seed inside. The cluster of these
prickly seeds looks somewhat like a bur.

BURWEED MARSH ELDER

Iva xanthifolia

Composite Family

High Water Shrub and Marsh Elder are two other names given to this shrubby, branching plant. It is tall and hairy, and grows to a height of from three to six feet in moist or rich soil. The thick, rough leaves are opposite, have long stalks, and toothed margins. Each leaf has three main nerves. Small insignificant flowers are in crowded, branching clusters. Each flower is greenish-white and is in a nodding position. The male and female parts are in separate flowers, but are combined in the same cluster. The corollas of the flowers are very small, or are totally lacking.

COMMON RAGWEED

Ambrosia artemisiifolia

Composite Family

This plant is also called Hogweed, Roman Wormwood and Bitter-weed. It is a varible plant which has become a despised weed because it causes some to suffer with hay fever. Ragweed grows in dry soil, in cultivated fields, or unkept lawns and gardens to a height of from one to six feet depending upon richness of the soil. The plant may be either simple or branched and may be either smooth or hairy. The leaves are very thin and are divided into many deeply-cut leaf segments which are arranged on each side of a common rib. Leaves are both alternate and opposite on the stem. The upper surface of the leaf is usually smooth. The inconspicuous green flowers have no petals. Flowers are in numerous elongated clusters at the ends of the branches.

268

SEA BURDOCK or BEACH CLOTBUR

Xanthium echinatum

Composite Family

Sea Burdock grows on beaches, in hollows in dunes, or at the borders of salt marshes near the coast. It is a coarse, rough annual with a purple-mottled stem from six to twenty-four inches tall. The alternate leaves are broad, tough, and coarse. They may be slightly lobed or unlobed with a wavy margin which may or may not have teeth. The greenish heads of inconspicuous flowers are either pistillate (female) or staminate (male). The staminate flowers are in heads at the ends of the branches. The pistillate flowers are in the axils of the upper leaves. Staminate flowers have tubular corollas, but the pistillate ones have no corolla at all. The olive-shaped, drab green or pale brown burs have prickles which are hooked at the tips. They are densely hairy with reddish hairs. These burs are clustered in axils of the upper leaves where the pistillate flowers were.

SPINY CLOTBUR or SPINY BURWEED

Xanthium spinosum

Composite Family

This plant is similar to the above, but the shiny leaves are tapered at both ends and are dark on top and downy white on the underside. The leaves are conspicuously veined with white, and there is a *three-pronged yellow or orange spine* on each leaf axil. The flowers and burs which form later are similar to those on the above plant.

MUGWORT, MOTHERWORT WORMWOOD

Artemisia vulgaris

Composite Family

Mugwort is a branching, smooth-stemmed, erect plant which has become established as a weed in waste places, thickets, and along stream-banks, roads, and railroad tracks. It is from one to three and a half feet tall. The stem may be greenish or purplish. The leaves are dark green and smooth on the top, but white-woolly on the underside. Each leaf is deeply cut into linear lobes with deeply cut or toothed margins. The lower leaves have stalks (petioles) and have from four to eight small lateral leaf segments at the base. The upper leaves are linear with no cuts and no petioles. The inconspicuous greenish flowers are in numerous heads in compound spikes at the top of the plant.

ROMAN WORMWOOD

Artemisia pontica

Composite Family

A similar plant (not shown) is a slightly woody, rather shrubby plant with gray hairy stems and numerous grayish leaves crowded on the stem. The leaves are divided into narrow lobes which are then divided into toothed segments. The leaves are gray and hairy on the underside. The plant rarely flowers, but when it does, the heads are hemispherical rather than in spikes as in the plant above. These heads nod at the end of the pedicels (flower stems).

ASIATIC DAY-FLOWER

Commelina communis

Spiderwort Family

Asiatic Day-flower is a reclining plant with erect tips. The stem creeps along the ground and roots at points where the leaves are attached. It often is found growing in colonies because broken stems will take root and make new plants. The dark-green, fleshy leaves are contracted at the base to form sheaths around the main stem. The irregular flowers are one-half inch wide. They are in clusters within a folded bract at the top of the erect stem. This folded or hooded spathe incloses the flowers. The two side petals are deep or violet blue and have claws. The front petal is white and much smaller. Three unequal stamens are bent inward. There are three other smaller, sterile stamens. The flower lasts only one day before it fades.

SPIDERWORT

Tradescantia virginiana

Spiderwort Family

This wild flower may grow to be three feet tall and grows in shady areas of cool, rich, moist woods or along the edges of swamps and lakes. At the end of the flowerstalk, there is a large cluster of oval greenish buds which open one or two at a time. As one flower fades, other buds will open. The flowers are usually blue, but may be violet, rose, and rarely white. Each flower has three large petals and six showy yellow stamens which protrude from the center. The flower itself is between one and two inches wide. The leaves are long and pointed. They are shiny green in color and grow to be a foot or more in length.

271

PICKEREL WEED

Pontederia cordata

Pickerelweed Family

Pickerel Weed is an aquatic herb
which is frequently found growing
along borders of ponds, streams, and
shallow lakes. The roots are embedded
in the mud beneath the water and the
thick flower stems may emerge up to a
foot and a half above the surface of the
water. The leaves are arrowhead-
shaped and are deeply veined. They
may be from two to ten inches long
and from one to six inches wide. They
are thick, glossy, and dark green. The
numerous flowers are violet-blue and
are arranged in a dense spike. Each
tubular flower is about one half inch
long. It is curved and has two lips. The
upper lip has three lobes — the
middle lobe is largest — and the lower
lip has three linear, spreading lobes.
There are two yellow spots at the base
of the upper lobe in the throat of the
flower.

MUD PLANTAIN

Heteranthera reniformis

Pickerelweed Family

Mud Plantain grows in ponds or wet
mud and is usually creeping in mud or
floating on shallow water. It has wide,
dark-green floating leaves and
five-petaled white or pale blue
flowers. The kidney-shaped leaves are
on long leaf stalks. There may be three
to ten flowers in the cluster, but
usually there are only a few. There are
three unequal stamens in the throat of
the flower.

BLUE-EYED GRASS

Sisyrinchium angustifolium

Iris Family

There are several blue-eyed grasses in our area, but all are similar to the one shown. This one grows in moist meadows and along shores and is from four to thirteen inches tall — usually less than a foot. The flat stems are twisted and the blue-green leaves are very narrow like grass. The leaves on this blue-grass are usually shorter than the flower stalks. The blue or purple flowers are on long stalks at the top of the plant. Each has six petals with a bristle or point at the tip. The center of the flower is beautifully marked with a six-pointed white star outlined in golden yellow. Three united stamens are in the center of the eye.

WILD LUPINE

Lupinus perennis

Pea Family

This plant grows straight upwards in dry or moist sandy soil in open areas and along roadsides. It is often as tall as two feet. The leaves are arranged in groups of from seven to ten segments which extend outwards from a central point. The numerous blue flowers are arranged in racemes at the top of the plant. The flowers are pea-like with the bottom lip about twice as long as the top one.

MONKSHOOD or WOLFBANE

Aconitum uncinatum

Buttercup Family

Monkshood is a tall plant with deeply-cut leaves and showy, blue irregular-shaped flowers. It is an escape which now has become naturalized in low woods and on damp slopes in New England. I saw it growing in eastern Maine along the coast near Lubec. The plant may be from two to four feet tall. The firm, thick leaves are usually broader than they are long and have long stalks. The blue flowers are in loose, branching clusters at the top of the plant. One of the larger sepals forms an erect, hooded, conic structure which looks like a helmet. The tip of the "helmet" is slightly beaked. There are from two to five petals, some of which are concealed within the hood. There are numerous stamens inside.

ALFALFA

Medicago sativa

Pea Family

This plant is low and is often found lying on the ground. It is as long as one and one-half feet and grows in fields and along roadsides. It is often grown as a forage crop for cattle. The leaves are clover-like and in groups of three. The tube-shaped flowers are from one-fourth to one-half inch long and vary from blue to violet. Each flower is on its own tiny stem called a pedicel, but gathered together into a cluster. One distinguishing feature is the seed pod which twists or coils into a spiral. It has from one to three complete turns and is covered with fine hair. See page 299 in lavender section for more information.

274

FLAX
Linum usitatissimum
Flax Family

This delicate slender plant grows in fields and waste places to a height of from nine to thirty inches. The alternate leaves are very narrow and pointed, and have three veins which go lengthwise on the leaf. The flowers have five sepals, five petals, and five stamens. The petals may be blue, white, or yellow, but are most commonly pale blue with a yellow center.

LAPLAND RHODODENDRON
Rhododendron lapponicum
Heath Family

This is a dwarf rhododendron which grows in higher elevations of New England and New York. It is a freely branching shrub, not much taller than a foot. The leaves are less than an inch long. The leaves are oval, leathery, evergreen, and are scaly on the underside. The bright purple flowers are in small clusters at the ends of the branches — usually only two or three in a cluster. Each flower is less than three-fourths of an inch broad. The pistils and stamens are very noticeable.

FRINGED GENTIAN
Gentiana crinita
Gentain Family

Fringed Gentain is one of our most beautiful, late-blooming flowers. It is an annual whose seeds are easily blown or washed away so that it may be in one field one year, but not there the next season. It is becoming extremely rare and *should not be picked*. It grows in low wet meadows, damp thickets, or along brooks and blooms from late August through to November. It may be from four to forty inches tall, but its common height is about a foot.

The narrow stem leaves are opposite

and lance-shaped, but lower leaves may be somewhat broader. Large bright-blue flowers are in an upright position on long stalks at the tips of the stems. The funnel-shaped corolla is about two inches long, and is at first closed and twisted. Later, it may open to show four beautiful, fringed lobes. The four teeth of the calyx are unequal — two narrow teeth and two very wide ones.

CLOSED GENTIAN or BOTTLE GENTIAN

Gentiana andrewsii

Gentian Family

Bottle Gentian is a smooth upright plant with many stems tufted at the base of the plant. This gentian grows in moist, shady places in meadows. It is usually ten or twelve inches tall, but may grow to be two feet tall. Pairs of narrow, pointed leaves are on the stem, but there is a whorl of from four to six leaves directly under the flower cluster. Showy deep-blue flowers are clustered at the tip of the stem, or may sometimes be in axils of leaves. The oblong corolla remains closed at the mouth. Gentians are becoming scarce in our area and should not be picked.

NARROW-LEAVED GENTIAN

Gentiana linearis

Gentian Family

Narrow-leaved Gentian is similar to Bottle Gentian. The very slender leaves have smooth margins, three nerves, and are pointed at both ends. The porcelain-blue to blue-violet flowers are erect and are opened a bit at the tip to show the rounded flower lobes. This gentian grows in wet meadows, wet woods, or bogs and is from six to twenty-four inches tall.

276

MARSH FELWORT

Lomatogonium rotatum

Gentian Family

IVY-LEAVED MORNING-GLORY

Ipomoea hederacea

Morning-Glory Family

JACOB'S LADDER

Polemonium vanbruntiae

Phlox Family

Felwort grows in wet places near the sea — often growing right in with beach grasses. It may be from six to fifteen inches tall, but is usually less than a foot in height. This small plant may be simple or branching. It has opposite, fleshy leaves. The lower leaves are spatulate shaped, but the upper stem leaves are long and narrow. The flowers are on long stalks which arise from leaf axils. The corolla may be porcelain blue or white and is about an inch across. The pistil in the center is distinguished by the fact that it has no style. The calyx has four or five very narrow, unequal parts.

This morning-glory is a hairy, trailing vine with three-lobed leaves which resemble leaves on English Ivy. It grows in fields and along roadsides and has established itself as a weed in cultivated land. The flowers are on long peduncles (flower stalk) and are funnel-shaped with a somewhat five-sided face. They are usually light blue when they first open, but the face of the flower becomes redder as it ages. The tube usually remains white. The calyx has five hairy sepals which abruptly taper to a long, slender tip.

Jacob's Ladder is found in wooded swamps, bogs, and along streams. The stout erect stem is hairy and from one to three feet tall. The loose clusters of blue-violet bells are at the ends of the branches. The five white-tipped stamens protrude noticeably from the center of the blossom. Each flower has five rounded blue lobes and a white center with wine-colored veins in it. The leaves are subdivided into untoothed leaflets. There are from four to nine pairs of sharply pointed leaflets and an odd leaflet at the tip of the leaf stalk.

COMFREY

Symphytum officinale

Borage Family

See page 142 in pink section for details.

SMALL BUGLOSS

Lycopsis arvense

Borage Family

Small Bugloss grows in fields and along sandy or dry roadsides or near unkept dwellings to a height of from one to two feet. It is a rough-bristly plant with a branching stem and lance-shaped, hairy leaves. The light, blue-violet flowers are crowded into long, leafy clusters. The corolla is funnel-shaped with a curved tube and the calyx is nearly as long as the blue corolla.

VIPER'S BUGLOSS or BLUE-WEED

Echium vulgare

Borage Family

Viper's Bugloss is a rough bristly weed which is erect and branching. It grows to a height of up to two feet in places where soil is poor and little else will grow. It sometimes takes over areas like old roadsides, old parking lots or old railroad beds.

The long pointed leaves are alternate along the hairy round stem. Leaves are very close to the stem at the top of the plant, but larger leaves at the bottom of the plant narrow into long petioles (stalks) and have smaller leaves growing in their axils. There are red spots on the upper stem from which white hairs grow. The showy flowers

are bright blue and are arranged along one side of a curled flower branch. The pink buds open one at a time — starting from the bottom of the cluster. As seeds form and new flowers open, the curled branch straightens and lengthens. The trumpet-shaped flowers have five unequal spreading lobes. One pink pistil and five long red stamens protrude from the center of the throat of the flower.

SEASIDE BLUEBELLS or MERTENSIA

Mertensia maritima

Borage Family

Sea Lungwort, Oysterleaf, Oyster Plant and Sea Mertensia are other names given to this plant. It is a relative of Garden Bluebells, but instead of standing erect, it lies on the ground and often forms thick mats. The spoon-shaped leaves are thick, fleshy, and are bluish-grey in color. They have a waxy covering on their upper surface. The leaves are said to have a taste similar to the taste of oysters. The buds and flowers are pink at first, but turn blue as they age. Flowers open a few at a time, so there is usually a mixture of pink and blue flowers on the plant. They are somewhat bell-shaped and about one-third of an inch long. The nutlets which form afterwards are smooth and shiny. This plant grows on sandy or rocky beaches along the coast, and blends right in with the rocks. The spreading stems may be as long as forty inches.

279

TRUE FORGET-ME-NOT
Myosotis scorpioides
Borage Family

This small plant has delicate flowers with five sky-blue petals and a yellow eye. The flower is less than one-third of an inch across. The stem forks at the top and has two coiled clusters of buds. As the buds open, the cluster uncoils. The hairy, blunt leaves are attached directly to the hairy stem on alternate sides. Forget-Me-Not grows along brooks and in cool wet places to a height of from six to twenty-four inches, but usually less than a foot.

SMALLER FORGET-ME-NOT

(Not shown) is similar but has smaller flowers less than one-fifth inch broad.

STICKSEED

Lappula echinata
Borage Family

Beggar's Lice, Bardanette and Burseed are other names given to this plant. It grows along roadsides and in waste places to a height of one or two feet. It is an erect, rough, hairy or grayish annual with spreading, long, coiled clusters of minute flowers. Light, gray-green hairy, linear leaves are scattered along the slender branches. Basal leaves are widest at the tip. The blue corolla is funnel-shaped with a short tube and five pointed lobes. The flowers are in long, leafy clusters which uncurl as the flowers bloom. The nutlets which form after the flowers fade have a double row of prickles at the margin and a prickly base.

280

FALSE PENNYROYAL

Isanthus brachiatus

Mint Family

This low, slender, branching annual herb grows in dry or limy soil to a height of from six to twenty inches. There are clammy hairs on the plant. The oblong leaves are pointed at the tip and at the base and only have a very short petiole. The margins are usually toothless, but may have a few teeth. Each leaf has three conspicuous ribs. The blue, funnel-shaped corolla has five nearly-equal, spreading lobes. The flower is just a bit longer than the cup-shaped calyx. The pistil is much longer than the stamens and protrudes from the throat of the flower; thus the plant must be cross fertilized by bees.

BLUE CURLS or
BASTARD PENNYROYAL

Trichostema dichotomum

Mint Family

Blue Curls is a stiff, branching plant which is covered with minute hairs and is easily recognized by its four, very long, downward-curving blue or violet stamens. This plant grows in dry, open soil to a height of from six inches to two feet. The oval paired leaves are narrowed at the base into short leaf stems. The margins are untoothed. Upper stem leaves get gradually smaller, and larger leaves may have pairs of smaller leaves growing in their axils. From one to three flowers are grouped together at the tips of short branches which rise from axils of the leaves. The corolla is usually blue or violet, but may be pink or even creamy-white. The calyx has five unequal lobes. The three upper sepals are long and the two lower ones are very short; but, after the fruit is set, the stalk twists so that the short lower sepals are on the top.

BUGLE or BUGLEWEED

Ajuga reptans

Mint Family

Bugle has creeping, leafy stolens which have broad leaves with wavy margins. An erect flower stem grows to a height of twelve or fifteen inches and bears a spike of flowers at the tip. Bugle grows in fields, wastelands, or sometimes along roadsides. The lower leaves are tufted at the base of the upright flower stem. These are rounded at the tip and taper at the base to a long-margined petiole (leaf stem). The stem leaves are much smaller and have little or no petiole.

The irregular blue-purple flowers have two lips. The upper lip is short and the lower lip has three spreading lobes. The middle lobe is larger and is usually cut in the middle. The calyx is barrel-shaped and has five lobes. The flowers are in clusters in the axils of upper leaves and in terminal spikes.

HOODED SKULLCAP

Scutellaria churchilliana

Mint Family

This skullcap grows on sandy or gravelly shores, and has an upright stem which forks or branches at the summit. The angles of the stem are hairy. The thin leaves are rounded at the base, pointed at the tip, coarsely toothed at the margins, and hairy at the nerves on the underside of the leaf. The flowers are in long, leafy clusters on stalks which arise from the axils of the upper leaves. A solitary flower is in the axil of each leaf, but the leaves are paired, so the flowers are in pairs. The two-lipped corolla is blue-violet.

282

MARSH SKULLCAP

Scutellaria epilobiifolia

Mint Family

This species grows in swampy thickets, at shores, or in wet meadows to a height of from one to three feet. It has single pale-violet or blue flowers which grow in the leaf axils. The leaves are very short-stalked or even stalkless — attached directly to the main stem and are slightly toothed.

MAD-DOG SKULLCAP

Scutellaria lateriflora

Mint Family

This skullcap is very similar to the other skullcaps already shown in full, so only a close-up of the flowers is shown. It grows in rich thickets, meadows, and in wet woods to a height of one or two feet. It has a smooth, square stem which is upright, branched, and may be twisted. Mad-Dog Skullcap is easily distinguished from the other skullcaps because the *flowers are in one-sided spikes.* Flowers may be in pairs at each node. The little two-lipped flowers are about one-fourth of an inch long and are in cup-shaped, hairy, toothed calyxes. Four stamens are located under the arched, upper lip. After the flowers pass, odd little hood-like calyxes containing four white seeds hang from the delicate stem. Though it is a mint, it is not aromatic.

DOWNY WOOD MINT

Blephilia ciliata

Mint Family

This mint grows in moist and dry woods to a height of from one to three feet. The leaves are almost stalkless and have white down on the bottom. The flowers are pale blue with purple spots. They are in whorls in a cylindrical head, but are separated by a row of fringed, dark-colored bracts. The two-lipped flower has an untoothed, hood-like upper lip and a three-lobed bottom lip.

283

BLUE GIANT HYSSOP
Agastache foeniculum
Mint Family

This plant has erect, branching stems up to forty inches tall. It grows in dry upland woods. Blue tubular flowers are in spikes at the top of the stem and at the ends of the branches. They also appear as little pin-cushion-like clusters in axils of upper leaves. The tiny flower has two pairs of protruding stamens. Two stamens point upwards and two stamens point downwards. The pistil extends straight outward. (See enlargement). The leaves are toothed and pointed at the tip, but are very broad or rounded at the base. The leaves emit an odor of anise and are woolly white on the underside.

AMERICAN PENNYROYAL
Hedeoma pulegioides
Mint Family

Other names for this plant are Pudding Grass and Mock Pennyroyal. It grows in dry fields and open woods to a height of a foot or more. It is an erect, branching, aromatic plant with a square stem and opposite leaves. The leaves are usually more than an inch long. They are often purplish on the underside and are covered with silky hairs. Several flowers are clustered together in whorls in the axils of upper leaves. Each flower is two-lipped with an erect, notched upper lip and a spreading three-part lower lip. The lower lip is usually marked with deep purple markings. The hairy calyx has three short teeth on the top and two long curved teeth underneath. There are only two fertile stamens. This plant has the taste and odor of true pennyroyal.

284

APPLE-OF-PERU

Nicandra physalodes

Nightshade Family

Apple-of-Peru grows in old fields or
waste places near old dwellings to a
height of from two to five feet. It is a
coarse annual with thin leaves and
solitary bluish flowers on flower stalks
at the top of the plant, or from axils
of leaves. The margins of the leaves
are deeply lobed and lower leaves
narrow at the base to form leaf stalks.
The bell-shaped flowers are an inch or
more long, and the face is somewhat
five-lobed. There are five stamens. The
five parted calyx incloses the nearly-
dry berry which forms after the flower
fades. These berries, especially the
seeds, are poisonous. Some say they
can be used as a fly-poison.

BLUE TOAD FLAX

Linaria canadensis

Figwort Family

This erect plant is from four to
thirty inches tall and grows in dry
sandy soil. The shiny leaves are very
narrow and are scattered along the
stem. The small bluish flowers are
tubular and arranged in long racemes.
The entire flower is about one-third
inch long and has a slender spur at the
base. The lips are much longer than
the tube and the bottom lip has two
short white ridges on it. Around the
base of the plant is a circle of runners
with tiny leaves.

NORTHERN SPEEDWELL

Veronica alpina

Figwort Family

This northern plant extends southward into northern New England, but is confined to certain mountains. It has a hairy, erect stem which stands up to a foot tall. The leaves are oval or rounded, in pairs, and sometimes have short stalks. The margins may be toothed or untoothed. The corolla is dark blue and the flowers are in short clusters at the top of the plant. The flowers are typical veronica flowers (See enlargement p. 287 Veronica americana), but are much darker blue or lavender in color. Look for this in wet moss and cold ravines at high altitudes.

MARSH SPEEDWELL

Veronica scutellata

Figwort Family

This speedwell grows in wet places, shores, and in swamps to a height of six to twenty inches tall. It is a weak, usually hairless perennial with slender, creeping stems. The paired leaves are long and narrow, are stalkless, and the margins may be toothed or toothless. The base of the leaves may slightly clasp the stem. The flowers are in several long clusters *on zig-zag stems.* The corolla is similar to the other veronicas, but it is lilac or lavender-blue, and the bottom lobe is much narrower than the other three. The capsule is flat and is much broader than it is tall.

286

AMERICAN BROOKLIME

Veronica americana

Figwort Family

American Brooklime grows in
shallow water near springs, in swamps,
or on banks of streams to a height of
from six to fifteen inches. It is a
smooth, fleshy or succulent perennial
with a creeping or reclining base. The
hollow, smooth stem sometimes creeps
along the ground and finally becomes
erect and branching. The light green
leaves are narrow and pointed with
short, flat stalks and slightly-toothed
margins. The frail flowers on slender
stalks are in long, loose clusters with
from four to thirty flowers in each
cluster. The four petals are blue-violet
to lilac and usually have a white or
lighter-colored center. The lower,
middle lobe is narrower than the other
three. There are two spreading
stamens which (on this veronica) may
be light purple.

BIRD'S-EYE SPEEDWELL

Veronica persica

Figwort Family

This veronica is a lower, more
spreading plant which grows on lawns,
along roadsides, and in waste places.
The oval to roundish leaves are more
coarsely-toothed at the margins. The
bright blue corolla has a paler lower
lip and a paler or yellow center. The
petals are usually striped with darker
blue lines. The flower is about one-half
inch broad.

VENUS' LOOKING-GLASS
Specularia perfoliata
Bluebell Family

This erect plant has simple stems from six to thirty inches in height. The leaves are numerous and clasp the stem. The egg-shaped leaves are hairy and are toothed at the edges. The flowers are violet-blue with five spreading lobes. They are from one-half to three-fourths inch broad and are not bell-shaped like the harebell. Each blue flower is tucked individually inside of the cup-like leaf; but occasionally two or three flowers are together. Look for Venus' Looking-Glass in open woods, old fields, and along roadsides.

CREEPING or EUROPEAN BELLFLOWER
Campanula rapunculoides
Bluebell Family

Bellflower is an erect, stout-stemmed plant which spreads by means of slender rootstalks. It grows in wastegrounds, thickets, fields, and along paths or lanes to a height of from one to three feet. The leaves have pointed tips and toothed margins. Upper leaves have very short stalks (petioles) or none at all. The lower leaves are heart-shaped at the base and have petioles. Larger leaves may be as long as six inches on larger plants. The flowers hang downward along the tip of the stem — forming a long, loose, one-sided cluster. The lovely bell-shaped flowers are a deep blue (sometimes purplish) and may be one to one and a half inches long. Each is deeply cut into five pointed lobes which spread outward.

288

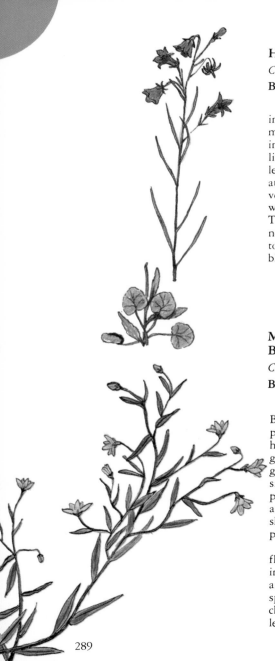

HAREBELL
Campanula rotundifolia
Bluebell Family

This plant is from six to eighteen inches high and grows in dry meadows, on cliffs, on beaches, and in grassy places. It has wiry hair-like stems and long linear stem leaves. Sometimes the stem is hairy at the base. The basal leaves are very small and round, and often wither away before flowering time. There are from one to several nodding bell-shaped flowers at the top. They vary in color from violet blue, to blue, to white.

MARSH BELLFLOWER
BEDSTRAW BELLFLOWER
Campanula aparinoides
Bluebell Family

This flower — also called Marsh Bluebells — is a slender, branching plant with weak stems. The stems have short rasping bristles on them. It grows in grassy swamps, wet grassy ground, and swales to a height of from six to twenty-four inches. The long pointed leaves are rough at the mid rib and on the margins. The leaves have shallow-toothed margins and no petioles (leaf stalks).

The single white or very pale blue flowers are scarcely one-third of an inch broad. They are bell-shaped but are deeply cut into five, pointed, spreading lobes. The flowers are chiefly at the tips of the spreading, leafy branches.

MARSH BLUEBELLS

Campanula uliginosa
Bluebell Family

Marsh Bluebells (not shown) is similar to Marsh Bellflower, but the stems are stiffer and less spreading, and the bell-shaped flowers are bluer. The leaves are very thin and barely — if at all — toothed at the margins. It grows in swales and wet thickets.

(See p. 289)

SHEEP'S BIT

Jasione montana
Bluebell Family

Sheep's Bit grows in fields and roadsides to a height of from six to twenty inches. It is a small, leafy herb with several stems rising from a single root. Tiny flowers are clustered in roundish, terminal heads on a long peduncle (flower stalk). Beneath each head is a circle of many bracts. The plant as a whole may be erect or reclining or leaning. The alternate leaves are very narrow and hairy. The tiny blue flowers which make up the flower head are rather tubular with five narrow lobes. The anthers are united at their bases to form a ring around the style of the pistil. The calyx has five pointed lobes.

GREAT LOBELIA or
BLUE CARDINAL FLOWER

Lobelia siphilitica

Bluebell Family

This is the largest blue lobelia and may be found growing in swamps or in moist places in low, rich woods. It is usually from one to three feet tall. The leafy, slightly-hairy stem is stout and usually does not branch. The light green leaves are long and pointed at both ends. The margins may be untoothed or irregularly toothed. The blue-violet flowers are nearly an inch long. Each flower is two-lipped with a deeply-cut, erect upper lip and a spreading, lobed lower lip which is striped with white. The calyx is covered with stiff hairs.

BROOK or
KALM'S LOBELIA

Lobelia kalmii

Bluebell Family

This lobelia grows in wet meadows, bogs, shores, on wet banks or wet ledges to a height of from four to sixteen inches. It is smaller than some other lobelias and has a slender, branching stem with narrow, blunt-tipped leaves. The upper leaves are linear and may have some teeth on the margins. Basal leaves are wider and hairy and are on longer petioles (leaf stems). The light blue flowers are two lipped and have a conspicuous white center. They are loosely scattered along the upper part of the stem. The fruit capsule is *not inflated,* but is top-shaped or globular.

WATER LOBELIA
WATER GLADIOLE

Lobelia dortmanna

Bluebell Family

Water Lobelia is an aquatic
perennial with numerous white fibrous
roots and a slender, erect stem. It
grows in borders of warm ponds, often
growing in sandy soil right in the
shallow water. It is usually less than a
foot tall, but may reach a height of two
feet.

The leaves are linear and fleshy and
are tufted at the base of the hollow
stem. This tuft of leaves is usually
submerged in water. The pale blue,
two-lipped flowers are in a loose
elongated cluster towards the summit
of the stem. They are about a third of
an inch long, and the lower lip has
three spreading lobes.

CHICORY

Cichorium intybus

Composite Family

Chicory grows in fields and along
roadsides to a height of four or five
feet. It has small, oblong-pointed
leaves with toothed margins. The
leaves have no leaf stalks, but are
attached directly to the rigid stem. The
basal leaves are similar to the leaves of
a dandelion. The blue flower-heads are
scattered along the stem and have very
little — if any — flower stalk. The
blue rays are square-tipped and
fringed. Sometimes the rays on the
flower head are pink or white, but
most often they are clear blue.

SLENDER BLUE FLAG

Iris prismatica

Iris Family

This iris grows in wet lands and marshes — especially near the coast — to a height of from one to three feet. A single flower stem rises from the tip of last year's runner and is usually surrounded at the base with remnants of last year's leaves. The new leaves on the stems are almost grass-like. The flower is pale bluish or blue violet. The three showy blades hanging downward — the sepals — are veined with deep purple and are yellow at the base. The three petals stand upright in the center.

HOOKER'S IRIS or BEACH-HEAD FLAG

Iris hookeri

Iris Family

This iris (not shown) grows in dense clumps on rocky slopes, ocean beaches and coastal banks in Eastern Maine. The leaves are about a half inch wide and up to sixteen inches tall. The flower is similar to the one above, but the purple sepals which hang downward are wide and have a white blotch at the base. The small petals are rolled into tubes above the sepals.

BLUE FLAG

Iris versicolor

Iris Family

Blue Flag is a showy plant which grows in marshes, stream borders, and other wet places. The stems are round, smooth, erect, and from two to three feet tall. The leaves are usually shorter than the flower and are at the base of the plant. The flowers are violet blue and have six clawed segments which are joined together at the center. The three outer parts are variegated with yellow and white and are beautifully veined with purple. They curve down and inwards. The inner three are smaller and curve upwards over the center of the plant.

293

LARGE PURPLE FRINGED ORCHIS

Habenaria psycodes var. grandiflora

Orchid Family

This orchid has many rose-purple or lavender to pink flowers in a cylindrical cluster at the top of the stalk. It has large lower leaves which are oval at the base and pointed at the tip, and upper leaves which are small and linear. The orchid grows in woods and meadows to a height of from one to five feet. The sepals are oval and the petals are spatulate shaped and are finely toothed. The lip is deeply three-parted and each lobe is fan-shaped, and so deeply toothed that it appears to be fringed. The lip is up to three-fourths of an inch long. There is a tubular, hollow spur which extends backwards or downwards from the base of the flower.

LARGE TWAYBLADE

Liparis lilifolia

Orchid Family

This orchid has two broad, elliptical basal leaves and many dull, mauve — almost brownish at times — flowers with very broad lips. The narrow lateral petals are greenish to pale purple and are usually rolled and twisted under the lip. The pale-purple lip is flat and broad. The sepals are greenish white. This orchid grows in rich, mossy woods or ravines to a height of from four to twelve inches.

294

SPOTTED CORALROOT

Corallorhiza maculata

Orchid Family

Spotted Coralroot is a rather inconspicuous orchid with no green foliage. It has a brown-purple or yellowish stem which may grow as tall as thirty inches. Several scales are pressed closely to the stem, and these are the only leaf-like parts. The plant does not make its own food. It grows in dry woods along with Indian Pipe and Pinesap, and is more commonly found in spruce woods or on wooded upland slopes. The slightly fragrant flowers are in a raceme of from a few to as many as thirty-five flowers. The sepals and lateral petals are crimson-purple. The white lower lip has two thin lobes, and is spotted with crimson or magenta near the base. Flowers on larger plants may be up to three-fourths of an inch long.

STRIPED CORALROOT

Corallorhiza striata

Orchid Family

Striped Coralroot is similar to the other two on this page. It grows in limy or rich woods to a height of twelve inches or more. The purplish flower stalk is stouter, and the flowers may be pinkish, purplish, yellowish, or whitish, but all are *striped with purple*. The sepals, side petals and lip are all about one-half inch long. The lower lip is elliptical and is *not lobed*.

SMALL CORALROOT or LATE CORALROOT

Corallorhiza odontorhiza

Orchid Family

Small Coralroot is similar to Spotted Coralroot above, but is only from six to fifteen inches tall. This coralroot is also a root parasite and has no leaves with chlorophyll to make its own food. The raceme of flowers is shorter — only from two to four inches long. There are from six to twenty flowers at the top of the slender purplish flower stem. The flowers are mainly purplish. The sepals and petals are marked with purple lines. The broad white lower lip is as long as the petals and may be notched at the outer tip. The lower lip is spotted with purple or magenta.

VIRGINIA SNAKEROOT
Aristolochia serpentaria
Birthwort Family

Virginia Snakeroot grow in woods to a height of from eight to twenty-four inches. An underground stem sends up stalks which bear large heart-shaped leaves and curious-looking flowers. The flowers are solitary on slender, scaly branches at the base of the leafy stem. The flowers may be either dull green or brownish purple, but are usually madder-purple. It has an enlarged base and flares out at the face to make an irregular three-lobed face. Inside of the throat are six stamens and a pistil. The face is smooth, but the s-shaped throat is hairy.

WATERSHIELD
Brasenia schreberi
Water-lily Family

The Watershield grows in ponds and in slow-moving streams. It has oval floating leaves which are from two to four inches long. The leaves are slimy-coated on the bottom and are attached to a long slimy submerged stem which is often as long as two yards. The plant has small dull purple flowers with either three or four petals and three sepals. Each flower has its own stout flower stalk which is attached to the main stalk.

296

SEA ROCKET

Cakile edentula

Mustard Family

Sea Rocket is a seaside mustard which is easily identified by its fleshy stems and distinctive pods. Sea Rocket is a much-branched plant with small leaves which are broadest near the tip. These leaves may be toothed or have wavy margins. The small four-petaled flowers are pale purple or may vary to white. The unusual pod is from one-half to three-fourths of an inch long. Each pod has two seeds in separate compartments. One seed faces up and the other seed faces down.

Sea Rocket is wide-spread and grows in a reclining position in spreading clumps in the sand along beaches or the sea coast. It is from six to twelve inches in height.

DAME'S ROCKET

Hesperis matronalis

Mustard Family

This plant is also known as Dame's Violet and Mother-of-the-Evening. It is a tall plant — sometimes three feet or more — which grows along roadsides and in open woods. The leaves are pointed, toothed, and attached to the stem with a short stalk (petiole). The beautiful, four-petaled blossoms are up to an inch across and vary from white through pink to purple. The flowers at the bottom open first, and as seed pods form, the top part of the stem lengthens so other buds may have room to open. The seed pods are very narrow and may be as long as five inches when they are mature.

PITCHER-PLANT

Sarracenia purpurea

Pitcher-Plant Family

Pitcher-Plant has hollow pitcher-like leaves which are from four to twelve inches long and are usually half filled with water. The leaves are heavily veined and the spreading rim of the leaf is lined with downward-pointing hairs. The leaves trap insects which enter and the plant then digests the soft parts of the insects. The insects also furnish food for larvae of flies which help to cross-polinate the flowers. The single rose-purple flower is about two inches broad and hangs down from the flower stalk which is from one to two feet high. There are five spreading greenish sepals and five purple petals which curve inward to inclose the flattened yellow center and the umbrella-like stigma. Pitcher-Plants grow in sphagnum bogs.

THREAD-LEAVED SUNDEW

Drosera filiformis

Sundew Family

See page 32 in the white section for description.

LIVE-FOREVER: GARDEN ORPINE or FROG'S BELLIES

Sedum purpureum

Orpine Family

This "wildflower" is generally an escape from gardens, but it has become established along roads, in fields, and on open banks. It grows in bunches and may be from ten to eighteen inches tall. It is a rather common, many-stemmed plant with a stout, light-green or brownish stem and very smooth fleshy leaves with rounded teeth at the margins. Children often rub them to separate the membranes and then inflate the leaves to form "purses" or "frog's bellies." The leaves are either alternate or in whorls of three and are usually covered with a whitish powder. Red-purple flowers are in thick flat clusters at the tops of the stems. Each small flower has five purple-red, wide-spreading petals and five shorter sepals.

PURPLE AVENS

Geum rivale
Rose Family

Purple Avens grows to be from one to three feet tall. It may be found growing in bogs, swamps, or wet meadows. The slender brown stem bears a loose, branching cluster of purple flowers — usually with three in each cluster. The flowers are somewhat cup-shaped, up to an inch broad, and hang in a downward position from the tip of the flower stalk. The larger leaves at the bottom of the plant have six main parts. The bottom four leaflets are in pairs, but the end leaflet is much larger and broader than the others. Four tiny leaflets are paired on the stem between the larger leaflets. Stem leaves have only three parts. The fruits have hooks on them.

ALFALFA or LUCERNE

Medicago sativa
Pea Family

This plant is a bushy perennial which grows to be a foot or two in height. The young shoots may be hairy, but mature plants are not. The three leaflets are toothed towards the blunt tips and are narrowed at the base. The end segment is usually stalked. Short clusters of lavender pea-like flowers are at the tips of long flower stalks (see p. 274).

NAKED-FLOWERED TICK-TREFOIL

Desmodium nudiflorum

Pea Family

This trefoil is similar to the one on p. 118, but a tall *leafless flower stem* rises from the root and holds a cluster of very small magenta-pink or lilac flowers. The leaves are divided into three leaflets but these leaves are *on separate stalks* and are not attached to the same stem which bears the flower cluster. The flowers are similar, but are smaller. The broad upper petals of the flower are notched at the apex, and are turned backwards. The narrow side ones are lilac and white. The pod is hairy, but has fewer jointed divisions, usually only three sections.

PANICLED TICK-TREFOIL

Desmodium paniculatum

Pea Family

Panicled Tick-Trefoil is similar to the above, but has *smooth stems.* The leaflets on the three-part leaves are narrow. Each leaf has a *long leaf stalk.* The purple flower is smaller — only about one-fourth inch long. The pods have from four to six joints and are somewhat angled below, but are *curved at the top.*

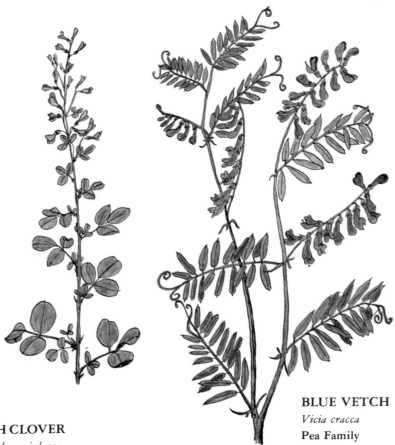

BLUE VETCH
Vicia cracca
Pea Family

BUSH CLOVER
Lespedeza violacea
Pea Family

Bush Clover grows in dry woods in clearings or openings to a height of from one to three feet. It is a tall upright plant with a branching stem which is sparsely hairy. The leaves are on long petioles (leaf stalks) and are divided into three small leaflets which are hairy on the underside. The small, pea-like flowers are clustered loosely together on slender stalks at the tips of the stems.

Blue Vetch grows in fields or meadows and along roadsides and has climbing or trailing stems which may be up to a yard long. The leaves are divided into many, small, paired leaflets. Tendrils are at the end of each leaf stalk. The blue to lavender tubular flowers are crowded together on flower stems which originate in the leaf axils. Each pea-like flower is slender and about one-half inch long.

301

HAIRY or WINTER VETCH
Vicia villosa
Pea Family

This vetch grows in fields and along roadsides where it has escaped from cultivation where it was grown for fodder. The entire plant is clothed in soft hairs. There are from six to ten pairs of leaflets on each divided leaf and each leaflet has a spine or point at the tip. On upper, not-fully-developed leaves, the leaflets may not be in pairs. The pea-like flowers are usually bicolored and may be either bluish with white or violet or lavender with white. The long narrow flower is longer than the ones on blue vetch — sometimes nearly an inch long. A distinctive characteristic is the way in which the flower is attached to the stem. Careful inspection shows that the flower is *attached under the bulge of the calyx,* not at the end. The calyx is pointed and hairy, with a bulge only on one side.

MARSH PEA or VETCHLING
Lathyrus palustris
Pea Family

This Marsh Pea can be distinguished from Beach Pea, on page 119 in pink section, by the wide, flat wing on each side of the stem. The bracts at leaf axils are not the large, arrowhead shape as on Beach Pea, but look like two triangles joined together on each side of the stem. Marsh Pea grows in meadows and marshes and along the shores.

302

GROUND NUT

Apios americana
Pea Family

Ground-nut is a large climbing or twining plant which sometimes completely covers near-by shrubs. The name refers to the underground stem (rhizome) which has thickened places to form a series of small tubers. These tubers are edible and indeed quite tasty when properly cooked. They were used for food by both the Pilgrims and the Indians in early times. The smooth leaves are divided into five or seven segments along a central rib, with one pointed segment at the tip. The irregular, purple-brown, fragrant flowers are about one half inch long. They are arranged in dense clusters at axils of leaves. The keel is sickle-shaped and coiled. The four upper teeth of the calyx are very short.

WILD BEAN

Phaseolus polystachios
Pea Family

Wild Bean grows in dry pine or oak woods or in sandy thickets. It is a twining or trailing vine which may be from five to twelve feet long. The leaves are divided into three roundish leaflets with pointed tips. Each set of three leaflets is on a long leaf stem, but each leaflet also has a short stalk of its own — the leaflet at the tip having a longer stalk than the two side ones. The small reddish-purple flowers are loosely arranged on a long, slender flower stalk. The cluster may be from four to eight inches long, but the flowers themselves are quite small — scarcely more than one third of an inch long. The two-lipped, pea-like flower is long, and the upper petals curve backward. The petals which form the keel are spirally coiled at the tips. The seed pods are a bit curved, and coil as they open.

WILD PEANUT
HOG PEANUT

Amphicarpa bracteata
Pea Family

Wild Peanut is a slender-stemmed
vine which climbs or twines over other
plants and shrubs. The twining stems
may be from one to eight feet long.
The stems have brownish hairs on
them. Wild Peanut grows along
shadowy lanes in damp woods or moist
thickets. The leaves are divided into
three pointed (somewhat four-sided)
leaflets. The flowers are in nodding
clusters and vary in color from pale
lilac, to purplish, to white. The plant
has two kinds of flowers. The upper
ones are perfect — that is — they
contain all of the parts. The lower
ones are rather unattractive, and
though they do not have petals, they
still contain the reproductive parts
which will yield ripe seeds. The seed
pod is about an inch long.

VIOLET WOOD-SORREL

Oxalis violacea
Wood-Sorrel Family

This fragile plant grows in open
woods and fields to a height of from
four to eight inches. The stems are
brownish and the leaves have three
inverted, heart-shaped leaflets which
often fold along the center crease. On
this species of oxalis, the center point
and the underside of the leaves are
reddish or purplish. There are several
flaring flowers on each stem. The five
petals are rose-purple to violet and the
"eye" is yellow-green with fine purple
veins. The seed pods split open with
force and scatter seeds in all directions.

SMALL-FLOWERED CRANESBILL

Geranium pusillum

Geranium Family

This cranesbill is a weak, much-branched plant which has become established as a weed in fields, wasteplaces, and along roadsides. It is usually from four inches to two feet in height, though it is often in a reclining position. The leaves are deeply cut into from four to nine lobes which are then lobed at the end. The leaves have long leaf stalks. The five slightly-notched petals are pale purple or bluish-lilac. There are *only five stamens* instead of ten as in other geraniums. Each flower is only about one-fourth inch broad. See pages 120-121 in the pink section for other geraniums.

CROSS-LEAVED MILKWORT

Polygala cruciata

Milkwort Family

This milkwort is also called Marsh Milkwort or Marsh Polygala. It grows in moist places at margins of marshes and bogs and in salt marshes along the coast. The square stem may be branched or simple and has linear leaves which are nearly all in whorls of four which form a cross. The greenish or purplish-pink flowers grow in short, thick spikes at the tips of the branches. The spike has green bracts in it which remain even after flower and seeds fall. The flower is very irregular and the sepals actually look like the petals. The large colored "wings" are somewhat heart-shaped and the tiny greenish flowers are in the center. (See insert) The whole plant is rarely taller than fifteen inches, and it is usually much shorter than that.

FIELD MILKWORT

Polygala sanguina

Milkwort Family

This flower may be either pink or purple. Look in the pink section on page 123 for details.

PURPLE TOUCH-ME-NOT

Impatiens glandulifera

Touch-me-not Family

Purple Touch-me-not is very similar to the yellow one on page 188. It is a tall, coarse plant which has escaped from cultivation. It grows at the edges of old lawns, fields, waste places, and in roadside thickets to a height of about six feet. The leaves are either opposite or in whorls. They are long and narrow, have a pointed tip, and sharply-toothed margins. Many flowers hang from a long flower stalk (peduncle). The purple-red sepals unite to form a spurred sac and the two purple petals protrude from it. The top petal folds back over the conical sac and the bottom petal — which looks like two petals — hangs downward.

WATER WILLOW
SWAMP LOOSESTRIFE

Decodon verticillatus

Loosestrife Family

Water Willow is not a willow, but is
does have willow-like leaves. It is a
showy shrub about three or four feet
tall which grows in swampy areas or
in shallow water at the edges of ponds
and streams. The arching stems may
be as long as eight feet, and sometimes
root at the tips and form new plants.
The leaves are paired, or may be in
circles of three or four. Each leaf has a
short stalk. The magenta flowers are
clustered in the axils of the upper
leaves. The base of the flower is bell-
shaped, but there are five spreading
petals at the "rim" of the cup. There
are ten magenta stamens. Five of them
are long and protrude far from the
center of the flower. The other five are
much shorter. Another name for this
flower is *Water Oleander*.

HYSSOP-LEAVED
LOOSESTRIFE

Lythrum hyssopifolia

Loosestrife Family

This loosestrife is smaller, from six
to twenty-four inches tall, and is
sometimes branched at the base. The
pale green stem leaves are narrow and
alternate. The flower is tiny, pale
purple and is trumpet-shaped. (See
enlarged flower). The six petals at the
top are shorter than the tubular throat.
At the base of the flower is a tiny leaf.
Flowers are usually solitary, but are
sometimes paired in the leaf axils.

WING-ANGLED LOOSESTRIFE

Lythrym alatum

Loosestrife Family

This is a close-up view of a loosestrife which grows in swamps, wet meadows, or ditches to a height of from one to four feet. It is a tall, branching plant with four-angled stem and lance-shaped paired leaves. The upper stem leaves are dark green and may be alternate instead of in pairs. Leaves are blunt at the base, but pointed at the tip. The purple or pink flowers have six spreading petals. There are two different kinds of flowers on the same plant. The drawing is an enlargement and the actual flowers are usually less than one-half inch broad.

PURPLE LOOSESTRIFE

Lythrum salicaria

Loosestrife Family

This tall beautiful weed grows in large colonies in swampy meadows, shores, marshes, and roadside ditches and makes a stunning display of lavender or magenta when all of the flower spires are in bloom. The stems are from two to five feet tall, are four-angled, and are very branching. The dark-green foliage is downy. Lower leaves are usually in pairs, but are sometimes whorled in threes or fours. The flowers are one-half to two-thirds of an inch long and are in a dense, terminal, spike-like cluster. This spike also contains numerous small leaves which look like bracts. The blossom may have either four or six petals and it has twice as many stamens as there are petals.

CLAMMY CUPHEA or BLUE WAXWEED

Cuphea petiolata

Loosestrife Family

Cuphea is from one to two feet tall
and grows in dry soil of open woods
and sandy fields. It has sticky, reddish
hairs and paired leaves on long leaf
stalks (petioles). The flowers are
magenta or red-purple and are
attached singly or in pairs in the axils
of the upper leaves. The flowers have
six uneven, clawed petals which
protrude from the hairy, ribbed calyx
which is about one-half of an inch
long. This hairy calyx has an odd sac-
like protuberance on the upper side so
that — at quick glance — one might
think the stem is attached to the side
of the flower instead of at the end.

SEA LAVENDER

Limonium nashii

Leadwort Family

Sea Lavender grows in salt marshes
or along ocean shores to a height of
from one to two feet. This plant has
leafless, branching flower sprays which
give a splash of lavender to the bleak,
rocky shores. The thick basal leaves are
broad at the tip and narrow to a long,
slender petiole (leaf stalk). Tiny five-
petaled lavender flowers are arranged
in a single line along one side of the
branch. Each flower is enveloped by
thin bracts, and five stamens are
attached to the base of the petals. The
spray of lavender flowers dries nicely
and will retain its color long into the
winter for winter bouquets.

CENTAURY or LESSER CENTAURY

Centaurium umbellatum

Centaury is a smooth, erect annual which came from Europe but is now naturalized in our area. It is a small delicate plant with several short branches. It grows in damp places in meadows and wastelands to a height of from six to twelve inches. Elliptical, light-green leaves are in pairs along the stem. Upper leaves may be more linear in shape. Small, tubular, rose-purple flowers are not more than one half inch broad and have five, spreading lobes. The tube of the corolla is long and slender. Flowers are arranged in branching clusters at the summit of the stem and branches.

STIFF GENTIAN

Gentiana quinquefolia

Gentian Family

Stiff Gentian is found in rich woods, wet gravelly banks, or damp fields in mountainous areas. It is a slender — usually branching — plant from one to two feet tall which blooms in late August to November. It also is called Agueweed and Gall-of-the-earth.

The middle and upper stem leaves are opposite. They are pointed at the tip, but partly clasp the stem by their rounded bases. From three to seven nerves are prominent on the underside of the leaf. The stem has four ridges. The upright flowers are smaller than those on Closed Gentian and are grouped together in tight clusters of five or more at the tops of the stem. The flowers are funnel-shaped and have four or five lobes with a bristle at the tip of each. The color of the flower varies from pale blue to lilac or pale purple to greenish-white.

310

PURPLE MILKWEED

Asclepias purpurascens

Milkweed Family

Purple Milkweed is very similar to the Common Milkweed on page 138, but the leaves are more pointed and the flowers are a deep magenta-red or purple in color. The stem is very leafy and is usually not branching. The oval leaves are on short stalks and have fine hairs on the underside. They have noticeable veins and taper to a point. This plant grows in dry fields and thickets to a height of from two to four feet. Several flower clusters are on each plant.

See the enlargement of the single flower and petal, which is the typical flower of all milkweeds. The reddish hoods are nearly as long as the anthers in the center. The enlarged petal shows the slender horn which is on the inside of the petals.

SPURRED GENTIAN

Halenia deflexa

Gentian Family

This gentian grows in moist woods and thickets to a height of from six to twenty inches. It is a leafy annual with a simple stem — rarely branched — with long spaces between the paired leaves. The basal leaves are wider at the tips and narrow into long slender petioles (leaf stems), but the stem leaves are oval-pointed and are attached directly to the main stem. They have either three or five distinct veins. The flowers are purplish or greenish white. Each has four erect lobes and four *spurs pointing downward.*

BLACK SWALLOW-WORT
Cynanchum nigrum
Milkweed Family

Black Swallow-wort is a smooth tropical vine. It has a twining stem which climbs to a height up to seven feet. The leaves are in pairs along the stem. They have untoothed margins, pointed tips, and are on petioles (leaf stalks.)

Small purplish-brown flowers are in short-stalked clusters arising from the axils of the leaves. The five-petalled corolla is star-shaped and spreading. The fruit is a slender, floss-filled pod similar to those of milkweeds.

COLLOMIA
Collomia linearis
Phlox Family

Collomia is a small erect plant with sticky hairs. It grows in dry, open places or gravelly shores to a height of from three to eighteen inches. The narrow leaves are alternate on the stem. The upper ones have no stalks, but the lower ones may have petioles (leaf stalks). The flowers resemble those of the phlox, but are much, much smaller. They are arranged in leafy clusters at the top of the stem. The corolla is funnelform with five lobes and a very slender tube. The color varies from lilac to white.

MOSS PHLOX or MOSS PINK
Phlox subulata
Phlox Family

This plant varies greatly in color from white to pink to blue-purple. See page 140 in the pink section for a description.

VIRGINIA WATERLEAF or JOHN'S CABBAGE

Hydrophyllum virginianum

Waterleaf Family

This hairy plant grows in rich woods and along streams to a height of from one to three feet. The flowers are white or pale violet and are in coiled clusters which unroll as they bloom. The stamens protrude far beyond the petals, giving a "fuzzy" appearance to the cluster. The barrel-shaped flower is made up of five petals which do not flare outward. The calyx is pointed and bristly. The flower clusters are on long stalks high above the leaves. The leaves, which often appear stained or water spotted, have from five to seven lobes with jagged teeth. The stem is reddish at the joints.

HOUND'S TONGUE

Cynoglossum officinale

Borage Family

This downy plant has a "mousy odor." It grows in fields, waste places, and along roadsides to a height of from two to three feet. The flowers have five petals and are dull reddish-purple and about one-third of an inch across. The hairy, four-part fruit has hooked bristles which cause it to stick to animals and clothing of people as they pass by. The lower leaves have stalks, but the upper ones are attached directly on the main stem.

BLUE VERVAIN or SIMPLER'S JOY

Verbena hastata

Vervain Family

Blue Vervain grows in swales, ditches, damp thickets and fields to a height of from three to seven feet. It is a common, erect plant with narrow, lance-shaped leaves. The hairy leaves have stalks and are toothed at the margins. The lower leaves may have

313

two lower lobes which point outward from the midrib. The flowers are in pencil-like spikes with many such spikes in a group at the top of the plant. Only one or two whorls of flowers open at a time, and as one whorl fades, a higher one opens. Though called Blue Vervain, the tubular *flowers are never blue,* but more violet or deep lavender. The tubular corolla has a five-cleft rim.

HOARY VERVAIN

Verbena stricta

Vervain Family

Hoary Vervain grows in fields, rocky open places, or along roadsides to a height of from one to four feet. The tall stem may be simple, but is usually branching. The leaves are thick, coarsely toothed, and have very short stalks (or none at all) where the base of the leaf is attached to the main stem. The stems and leaves are densely covered with fine white hairs. The flowers are arranged in long, thick, compact spikes, and only part of the spike is opened at one time. Each flower is funnel-shaped with either a straight or a curved tube. It has two lips with five lobes. The color is a pale purple or a rosy-pink. This is one way to tell it from Blue Vervain which is similar, but has deep blue flowers.

NARROW-LEAVED VERVAIN

Verbena simplex

Vervain Family

This smaller vervain is from four to twenty inches tall and is usually sparingly branched. It has slender spikes of lavender or light purple flowers. It is easily distinguished from other vervains by its long, lanceolate leaves which taper to a stalkless base.

314

PURPLE GIANT HYSSOP FIGWORT

Agastache scrophulariaefolia

Mint Family

Purple Giant Hyssop has a square stem. It grows in rich woods and thickets and along fences where it often reaches a height of six or seven feet. The leaves have a heart-shaped base, toothed margins, and a pointed tip. The leaf stems and lower surface of the leaves are hairy. At the tips of the stems are spikes of two-lipped purple flowers with numerous green bracts below them. The tubular flower is about one-half inch long and has a broad lower lip with a two-part upper lip cupped above it. Four stamens protrude from the throat.

GROUND IVY or GILL-OVER-THE-GROUND

Glechoma hederacea

Mint Family

Ground Ivy is a lovely little trailing mint that can be found growing in damp places, fields, and unmowed lawns around old buildings and trees or stumps. The trumpet-shaped blossoms are blue or light purple and are located in the axils of the leaves. The blossoms are about ½ inch long. The upper lip stands erect and is notched in the center. The lower lip has three spreading lobes which are spotted with dark purple. The leaves have a heart-shaped base, are deeply scalloped or toothed along the edges, and are arranged in pairs along the stem. Their surface is downy and the veins are very noticeable. The leaves vary in size, depending upon the richness of the soil and how early they appear. Those which appear later often have leaves which are more than an inch broad, while those blooming very early have tiny leaves.

315

SELF HEAL OR HEAL-ALL
Prunella vulgaris
Mint Family

   This is a common weed which is from four to twenty-four inches tall and grows in just about any type of soil. The hairy leaves are in pairs, but vary greatly in shape. Usually they are long with a blunt point at the tip. The tubular, two-lipped flowers are arranged in cylindrical spikes at the top of the plant. The flowers protrude from among many wide bracts. The color of the flowers varies from violet-blue to pink or even white and the color of the bracts varies from shades of brown to shades of red or green.

BLACK or FETID HOREHOUND
Ballota nigra
Mint Family

   Black Horehound is a green, erect, branching weed which grows in waste places to a height of from one to three feet. The weed is hairy and is often ill-scented. It was once prescribed for ulcers and as a treatment for the bite of a mad dog. The coarsely-toothed leaves are on stalks. The purplish flowers are clustered in axils of leaves. The flower has a hooded upper lip and a three-lobed lower lip. The upper lip is hairy. The funnel-shaped calyx (see enlargement) has five short teeth. The calyx is hairy at the base and at the edges of the teeth. The anthers protrude from the throat of the flower in pairs.

316

SPOTTED or VARIEGATED DEAD NETTLE

Lamium maculatum
Mint Family

HEDGE NETTLE or WOUNDWORT

Stachys palustris
Mint Family

This dead nettle grows along roadsides and in waste places to a height of from eight inches to nearly two feet. It is a slender hairy plant which rises from creeping stems. The erect flower stems are often forked or branching. The broad leaves are in pairs and have rounded teeth and long petioles. Usually there are long whitish blotches along the mid rib of the leaves. There are from six to fifteen rose-purple flowers in small clusters in leaf axils. Each flower is two lipped and has a short tube which is constricted near the base. The upper lip is strongly arched over the lower lip. The side lobes on the lower lip are very small.

This is not really a nettle. It is a downy plant with long hairs on the stem and calyx and it has a *rank smell*. It grows in ditches, wet ground, low meadows and along shores to a height of two or three feet. The paired leaves are rounded at the base, pointed at the tip, and toothed at the margins. They are covered with downy hair. Upper leaves have no leaf stem, but lower ones may be stalked. The magenta or rose-purple flowers are two-lipped and are mottled with dark and light tones of the same color. The tubular flower has a large hooded upper lip and a spreading, three-lobed lower lip. (See insert) The flowers are arranged in circles around the stem with from six to ten in each whorl. There are green bracts and a pair of leaves beneath each whorl and together they form a long, loose, leafy spike at the top of the plant. The hairy calyx may be maroon on some plants.

WILD BERGAMOT or HORSE-MINT

Monarda fistulosa

Mint Family

Wild Bergamot grows in dry woods and clearings or dry thickets to a height of from two to nearly four feet. It is very similar to Oswego Tea on page 146, but the flowers are pinkish to pale lilac. The square stems are usually branching, have opposite leaves, and flowers in compact heads at the tops of the stems. The leaves are rather gray-green in color, have petioles, pointed tips, toothed margins, and long hairs on the underside. The flowers vary in color, but are usually pinkish or yellowish-pink. The arching upper lip is hairy at the tip. The bracts below the flower cluster are lilac to white, not red as in Oswego Tea.

PURPLE BERGAMOT

Monarda media

Mint Family

This bergamot resembles Wild Bergamot but the bracts below the flower cluster are purplish and the flowers are a deeper reddish-purple. The foliage is a brighter green, and the plant may or may not be sparsely hairy.

BASIL

Satureja vulgaris

Mint Family

Basil has square, creeping stems from which hairy, flowering branches rise from one to two feet. The paired leaves are hairy and slightly toothed. The numerous, tubular, lipped flowers are pale purple or pink. They are in dense heads at the tips of the branches with a pair of leaves below each head. The cluster looks wooly for there are white hairs on the calyx and bracts.

318

HYSSOP
Hyssopus officinalis
Mint Family

Hyssop grows along roadsides and in dry soils of waste places to a height of from one to three feet. Usually there are several stems growing together from a woody base. The narrow, paired leaves are stalkless and are pointed at both the tip and the base. The pale purple or bluish flowers are in dense clusters in axils of upper leaves. Each one is a two-lipped funnel-shaped flower with an erect upper lip and a spreading three-cleft lower lip. Four stamens protrude from the throat of the flower. Two stamens are long and two are short.

WILD MARJORAM
Origanum vulgare
Mint Family

This plant grows along roadsides, in old fields and in thin woods to a height of from two to three feet. It is an upright, hairy, rather bushy plant with purplish-red flowers crowded into dense clusters. Red-purple bracts are clustered together with the flowers. The round to oval-pointed leaves have no petioles and untoothed margins. The two-lipped corolla is tubular with an erect, slightly-notched upper lip and a spreading, three-lobed lower lip. The lower pair of stamens project upward beyond the petals. Marjoram grows profusely on roadsides in Connecticut, and was used as a medicinal tea by colonists. It is not the plant used for the herbs called marjoram and oregano.

319

CREEPING THYME

Thymus serpyllum

Mint Family

Wild Thyme is not the thyme used as an herb in cooking. This species which is now found growing "wild" is really a garden escape. It is a creeping, much branching plant which may be from four to twelve inches long. The flowers are in short spikes at the tips of the erect branches. The flat leaves are strongly-veined, have untoothed margins and are on short leaf stems in pairs. The purple or white flowers are about one-fourth of an inch long. The upper lip is erect and rather flat — with a notch at the tip. The lower lip is spreading and has three lobes. There are four straight stamens protruding from the throat of the flower.

BUGLE WEED

Lycopus virginicus

Mint Family

Bugle Weed grows in rich moist soil to a height of from six inches to two feet. It is a mint-like weed with a minutely-downy stem and sharply-toothed leaves which may be tinged with purple. The stem is slender and four-sided. The leaves are in pairs and taper to a long stalk. The light-purple, tubular flowers are in whorls around the stem at the leaf axils.

CUT-LEAVED WATER HOARHOUND

Lycopus americanus

Mint Family

This plant is much like Bugle Weed above and grows in the same wet places. The stiff, erect stem may be branching or simple, and it is generally not hairy. The upper leaves are toothed, but the lower ones are deeply cut. The small, whitish, cup-shaped flowers are clustered together around the stem at leaf axils.

320

SPEARMINT
Mentha spicata
Mint Family

This mint has square erect stems up to twenty inches. The long, pointed, toothed leaves are attached directly on the main stem in pairs. The pale violet or pink flowers are in slender spikes at the ends of the stem and the upper branches. The long stamens protrude noticeably from the throat of the tiny, two-lipped flower. This plant grows in wet places and is widely cultivated for use as a flavoring.

PEPPERMINT
Mentha piperita
Mint Family

Peppermint grows in wet soil of shores, wet meadows and roadsides to a height up to three feet. It is a smooth, branching plant with purplish stems and fragrant leaves which *taste hot when chewed*. The paired lance-shaped leaves have a pointed tip, rounded base, and toothed margins. The whorls of flowers are in dense terminal clusters separated by short lengths of stem at regular intervals. The side spikes of flowers become longer than the middle spike as the plant matures.

CORN, FIELD,
or **WILD MINT**
Mentha arvensis
Mint Family

Wild Mint grows in dry waste places or along damp shores to a height of from six inches to two feet. The erect, square stem is branching, has hairs on the angles and a *strong mint odor*. The paired leaves have blunt-toothed margins, pointed tips and taper to a short petiole. Tiny white or pale lavender flowers are in whorls at the leaf axils.

ELSHOLTZIA
Elsholtzia ciliata
Mint Family

Elsholtzia is a smooth plant with a square stem, grows along roadsides and in old fields, and is one or two feet tall. The egg-shaped leaves have long leaf stalks and large-toothed margins. The pale purple flowers are in tight spikes in the axils of the leaves and at the tip of the stem. Each tiny flower is funnel-shaped, has four petals, and is slightly two-lipped. There are four stamens protruding from the throat. The hairy calyx has four equal teeth.

BEEF-STEAK PLANT or PERILLA
Perilla frutescens
Mint Family

This rank-smelling plant is found growing along roadsides, in wastelands and dry woodlands, and especially near old dwellings. After the petals have fallen, the dry sepals and leaves make a curious metallic sound when they are brushed against. The plant is erect and branching and may have a purple stem. The large, egg-shaped coarsely-toothed leaves are usually purplish on the under side and veins, have a bronze-green tone on the upper surface, and are on long stalks. The plant varies in height from one to three feet. The tiny flowers are dull white or purplish and are arranged in long, loose clusters at the tips of the branches. A small leaf-like bract is beneath each flower. The corolla has five nearly-equal lobes and is somewhat two-lipped. The outside of the upper lip is hairy, and there is a woolly ring inside of the throat.

HORSE-NETTLE
Solanum carolinense
Nightshade Family

Horse-Nettle is a large branching plant which grows in sandy soils, fields, and in waste places. It grows to a height of from one to four feet. The stems are erect and very spiny. The leaves are rough and have from two to five large teeth on each side. The central rib or vein of the leaf is also spiny. There are several flowers together in one cluster. Each flower has five pale violet or white petals which are curved backwards from the yellow-orange cluster of anthers in the center.

BITTERSWEET
Solanum dulcamara
Nightshade Family

Bittersweet — also called Purple Nightshade — is a weak climbing or reclining vine-like plant which grows in moist thickets throughout our area. The stem is often as long as six or eight feet. The flowers are similar to Horse-Nettle, but are smaller. The five swept-back violet petals surround the orange beak-like center. The top leaves are simple and pointed, but the larger lower leaves have two small lobes at the base. The fruit is a red, egg-shaped berry which is borne in drooping clusters.

KENILWORTH IVY

Cymbalaria muralis

Figwort Family

Kenilworth Ivy is an escape from cultivation and grows wild in wasteplaces and along roadsides. It grows readily in crevices of ledges or in rocky places. It is easy to transplant because it is so hardy. It is a small, low, trailing plant with tiny ivy-like leaves on long stalks. The margins of the leaves have roundish lobes, and the base of the leaf is indented. The delightful flowers look like velvet. They are on long stalks which rise from the axils of the leaves. The irregular corolla is violet with a yellow palate and a short spur at the back.

DWARF SNAPDRAGON

Chaenorrhinum minus

Figwort Family

Dwarf Snapdragon is a small, branching annual which has hairs and glands all over it. It grows along roads and railroad tracks or in waste places to a height of from two to sixteen inches. Most flowers of this genus are found in the Mediterranean area, but this one now grows wild in America.

The leaves are narrow, pointed and untoothed. The upper leaves are alternate and are narrower than the lower leaves which are usually opposite. Flowers are born singly on long stalks which rise from axils of the leaves. The corolla is lilac colored with a yellow center. It is about one-half inch long and has two lips. The upper lip is arched above the lower lip, and the throat is open. The spur at the back of the flower is much shorter than the body of the flower itself.

324

HAIRY BEARDTONGUE

Penstemon hirsutus

Figwort Family

There are over fifteen species of this plant in our area but all have one common characteristic — a tufted stamen which nearly fills the throat of the tubular flower. This species grows in rocky woods and dry fields to a height of from one to three feet. The stems stand erect — usually several coming from the same rootstalk. In most species, the tops of the leaves and the stem are hairy. The leaves are long, slender, pointed, and have toothed margins. The pale lavender petals are fused into a slender tube about an inch long. The inside of the tube is covered with pale hairs. The upper lip is two-lobed and erect, but the lower lip points straight out.

MONKEY FLOWER

Mimulus ringens

Figwort Family

Square-stemmed Monkey Flower grows in wet fields, swamps, along stream banks, and in low meadows to a height of from one to three feet. The upright stem has many branches and paired leaves with irregularly-toothed margins, and flaring lobes on each side. The two-lipped flowers are usually blue-violet, but may vary from white, to lavender, to light blue. The mouth is closed by a yellow palate which has two ridges. The upper lip arches over the spreading, lobed, lower lip. The pistil and the four stamens are white. The green calyx is sometimes marked with purple.

SEASIDE GERARDIA or SALT-MARSH GERARDIA

Gerardia maritima

Figwort Family

This gerardia grows in salt marshes along the coast. It is usually from four to sixteen inches in height. It is a green to purplish succulent plant which may be simple or branching. The stem is four-angled. The thick, linear leaves are fleshy and have blunt tips. The flowers are rose-purple and vary from one-half to three-fourths of an inch in length. There are from two to ten flowers in a raceme above the foliage. The flowers *are not downy.*

SMALL-FLOWERED GERARDIA

Gerardia paupercula

Figwort Family

This gerardia grows in damp open ground, along shores, and in bogs and is commonly less than two feet in height. The erect stems are four-angled and smooth. It may be branching towards the top of the plant. The dry-textured leaves are smooth, pointed, and almost threadlike they are so narrow. The flowers are funnel-shaped and are on very short flower stalks. The corolla is rose-purple to pink and is darker spotted in the throat with two yellow lines beneath. Soft hairs are in the throat of the flower.

326

EYEBRIGHT

Euphrasia canadensis

Figwort Family

Eyebright is a small plant less than ten inches tall which grows in fields and along paths or lanes. It is usually a simple, non-branching plant. The paired leaves have toothed edges and very short stalks. Small inconspicuous flowers grow in axils of the upper leaves. They are really lovely when viewed through a hand lens. The corolla is two-lipped. The upper lip is hooded over the broad, spreading three-lobed lower lip. The upper lip is violet tinged and the bottom lip is white with lavender or bluish markings. See page 77 in white section for another Eyebright.

BEECHDROPS or CANCER-ROOT

Epifagus virginiana

Broom-rape Family

Beechdrops is an inconspicuous, brownish, much-branched plant which is found on wooded slopes under beech trees upon whose roots it feeds. Scattered along the branches are small scale-like leaves, but there are no true green leaves. It may grow to be from six to eighteen inches tall, but most commonly it is about a foot tall. Small flowers grow in the axils of the bracts. The slim tubular flower is whitish with purple-brown stripes. Sterile upper flowers are two-lipped and have four teeth. The lower flowers do not open, but they are the ones which form the fruits.

PURPLE BLADDERWORT

Utricularia purpurea
Bladderwort Family

UPSIDEDOWN BLADDERWORT

Utricularia resupinata
Bladderwort Family

BUTTERWORT

Pinguicula vulgaris
Bladderwort Family

Purple Bladderwort grows in quiet ponds and muddy streams. It has small pea-like lavender or purple flowers on a leafless stalk. It grows to a height of from two to six inches.

The leaves are like tiny filaments and are usually submerged in mud or water. There are tiny bladders attached to the filaments. There are from one to four flowers on the plant. Each is two-lipped. The upper lip is flat or concave and the lower lip has three lobes and a yellow spot at its base.

This tiny plant forms mats with slender, horizontal creeping stems below the surface of the water. It has an upright flowering stem with one cup-like notched bract below each flower. This bladderwort grows in wet soil or in shallow water at margins of ponds and lakes. It is usually less than six inches tall.

The underground leaves are usually linear, but may be slightly forking. They have tiny traps or bladders on them. The threadlike flower stalk bears one single light purple flower at the top. The bottom lip is broad and round and larger than the top one. There is a cone-shaped spur and the flower appears to be resting upside-down on the summit of the flower stalk.

Butterwort is a small plant from two to six inches tall which grows on wet rocks and in wet meadows or bogs. It has a circle of yellowish-green leaves which are shaped like a football. The edges of the leaves usually roll inward. Small insects are often caught on the greasy surface of the curled leaves. The solitary flower at the top of the leafless stem is very similar to a violet. It has five purple petals and a spur. It is about one-half of an inch long.

328

WATER-WILLOW

Justicia americana

Acanthus Family

This plant grows in margins of rivers and lakes or on wet shores to a height of from one to three feet. It has slender willow-like leaves in pairs. The flowers are in small, long-stemmed clusters which rise from the axils of the leaves, and may be higher than the leaf tips. Each flower is bicolored — the notched upper lip arches over the lower, spreading, three-lobed lip. The lower middle lobe is fiddle-shaped at the base and its sides are reflexed. The upper lip is usually pale violet or reddish-purple, and the lower lobes are white with red-purple marks.

LONG-LEAVED HOUSTONIA

Houstonia longifolia

Madder Family

This houstonia is a small, low, tufted plant which grows in dry open or rocky places or in gravelly soil to a height of from five to ten inches. The basal leaves are blunt-tipped and have very short stalks. Stem leaves are opposite and are long with a pointed tip. Leaves have only one nerve and may be up to one inch long. The pale purple or pinkish flowers are in clusters of three or four. The trumpet-shaped corolla is about one fourth of an inch long with four pointed lobes. There are four stamens in the center. The green calyx also has four pointed lobes.

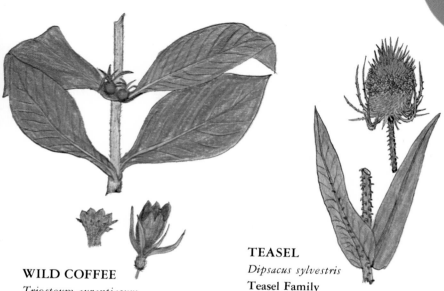

WILD COFFEE

Triosteum aurantiacum

Honeysuckle Family

This plant is also called Scarlet-Fruited Horse Gentian and Tinkerweed. It is very similar to Feverwort on page 266 but the flowers are reddish-purple and the paired *leaves are not joined around the stem*. This variable plant grows in woods and thickets to a height of from two to four feet. The hairs on the stem are glandular, and there is generally a ridge connecting the leaves across the stem. From one to three flowers are in the leaf axils. The lower surface of the leaves is densely hairy. The purple-red corolla (see insert) is tubular and distinctly two-lipped with five parts. It is wider at the tip. The inferior ovary is beneath the flower itself and the green sepals may be almost as long as the tubular flower. The fruit which forms after flowers fade is a bright orange red, and the sepals persist on top.

TEASEL

Dipsacus sylvestris

Teasel Family

Teasel is a tall, heavy-set, prickly-stemmed plant which grows in old fields and pastures or along roadsides to a height of from two to six feet. The upper leaves are paired and embrace the stem. They are often prickly along the margins. The lower leaves are oblong and may be a foot or more long on larger plants. The lilac-colored flowers are in a dense, terminal, spiny, cylindric head which is from two to four inches long. Spines packed between the tiny lavender flowers give the appearance of an egg-shaped pin cushion. The individual tubular flowers are less than one-half inch long and are four-cleft on the face. There is a cluster of long, narrow leaves at the base of the flower head, and each leaf curves gracefully upward. The ripened seed head is a bur-like body with barbed awns. It was supposedly used at one time for carding wool.

330

FIELD SCABIOUS
Knautia arvensis
Teasel Family

Field Scabious grows in cultivated fields, wasteplaces, and along roadsides to a height of from one to three feet. It is a hairy, simple or little-branched plant with lilac flowers in a terminal head. Pincushion is a very fitting name given to this plant in England. It is related to Teasel on page 330 but has hairs instead of prickles.

The hairy basal and lower leaves have petioles and may be deeply-lobed or not lobed at all. The margins may or may not have teeth. Upper stem leaves are usually deeply cut. There are noticeable hairs between the flowers in the pincushion-like flower head. The tiny flowers are lavender and have four lobes. The stamens protrude from the throat of the tubular flower. The outermost flowers on the head are longer and larger and almost look like rays.

INDIAN TOBACCO
Lobelia inflata
Bluebell Family

Indian Tobacco grows in dry open fields, along roadsides, or in open woods to the height of one or two feet. The stems are hairy and are usually branched. The plant is said to be poisonous if taken internally, but it has been used for medicine and Indians smoked its dried leaves. The leaves are alternate, oblong-pointed, and have slightly-toothed margins. The small blue or purple flowers grow in a long, loose, leafy cluster at the top of the plant. Each flower has an inflated base and is tucked into leaf axils. The lower lip of the flower is hairy at the base. The calyx forms an inflated seed pod with pointed tips.

NEW YORK IRONWEED
Veronia noveboracensis
Composite Family

Ironweed grows in moist, low fields and marshy places near the coast to a height up to six or seven feet. The stem is usually downy with numerous long, pointed leaves and a showy cluster of purplish flower heads at the top of the plant. It is a very difficult plant to photograph to get the true shade of purple. Most photos come out too pinkish. The long leaves are pointed at the tips and may have toothed or plain margins. There are from three to fifty tiny flowers in each thistle-like flower head. The flowers are all thread-like and there are no rays. The brownish-purple to greenish bracts form a cup-shaped base to each head. These bracts have long, slender bristle tips.

SCLEROLEPIS
Sclerolepis uniflora
Composite Family

This is a slender, creeping aquatic herb with whorls of linear leaves and a single terminal head made up of many small purplish flowers. It grows in shallow ponds and streams or in sandy or peaty swamps, and may be one or two feet long. The base may be in a reclining position, but the simple, unbranched tip is always upright. The firm leaves are linear, unstalked, and are arranged in whorls of four or six. Each leaf has only one nerve. The submerged leaves are merely thread-like. Each flower (see insert) is tubular and has five lobes at the top. The forked style protrudes from the throat of the flower.

SPOTTED JOE-PYE-WEED
or TRUMPET-WEED

Eupatorium maculatum

Composite Family

Joe-Pye-Weed is a stout, tall plant which grows to a height of from two to ten feet in damp thickets and meadows or along streams. The stem is deep purple or purple-spotted and is *not covered* with a whitish bloom as are other Eupatoriums. The leaves taper at both ends and have short stalks. They are rough and veiny and the teeth on the margins may be either sharp or blunt. The tubular purple-pink flowers have long protruding styles and are arranged in flat-topped clusters at the top of the plant. There are several other joe-pye-weeds which are quite similar.

NEW ENGLAND BLAZING STAR
or GAY FEATHER

Liatris borealis

Composite Family

This blazing star grows in open woods, clearings, or thickets to a height of from one to three feet. It has simple stems with alternate leaves and handsome rose-purple flower heads. The leaves are usually smooth, but may be sparsely hairy on the underside at the midrib. The flowers are in heads which have long stalks. From thirty-five to sixty tiny flowers are in each head. Under each head are overlapping, spreading bracts which have broadly rounding tips with a dark margin. There are other blazing stars, but this is the most common in our area, and the others are very similar to it.

CLIMBING HEMPWEED
Mikania scadens
Composite Family

Hempweed or Boneset grows in swampy thickets and along streams or in moist woods. It is one of the very few climbing vines of the composite family and may grow from five to fifteen feet in length. The triangular or heart-shaped leaves grow in pairs along the smooth, twining stem. Leaves may be from two to four inches long, and are on slender stalks nearly as long as the blade itself. The flowers are in clusters at ends of stalks which originate at leaf axils. Each cluster is made up of many small flower heads. Each head has four tubular pink or lilac flowers with four narrow bracts beneath.

HEART-LEAVED ASTER
BLUE WOOD ASTER
Aster cordifolius
Composite Family

Heart-leaved Aster is from one to five feet tall and grows in rich soil of open woods and clearings and is commonly found on slopes. It has a smooth stem with many branches. The rough leaves are broadly heart-shaped, deeply notched at the base, and have sharp-toothed margins. Leaves may be from two to six inches long and are on slender leaf stalks (petioles). The top surface of the leaves and the veins beneath are scattered with hairs. The small aster flower heads are only about five-eighths of an inch broad and are arranged in dense terminal clusters. There are from twelve to twenty pale blue-violet or bluish-white petal-like rays on each tiny flower head.

334

NEW ENGLAND ASTER

Aster novae-angliae

Composite Family

This handsome species of aster is often transplanted into cultivation. It grows in fields and thickets, along roadsides and shores, and in moist soil of low meadows to a height up to eight feet, but is more commonly four or five feet tall. This aster has stout hairy stems and sharp-pointed leaves. The stalks holding the flower heads have glands which may be easily seen through a hand lens. The leaves have untoothed margins and they clasp the stem at their heart-shaped base. The showy petal-like rays are usually bright purple, but there is a pink form. (See page 152.) The flower heads are in close, flat clusters at the tips of leafy branches. The bracts under the flower heads are recurving.

PURPLE-STEMMED ASTER

Aster puniceus

Composite Family

This aster is usually a sturdy plant with bristly, reddish or purplish stems and rough leaves that slightly clasp the stem at their base. It is a variable plant which may have either toothed or toothless leaves, and may sometimes have a smooth, green stem. It grows in swamps, wet thickets, or moist meadows to a height of from two to eight feet. It has a wide range and often crosses with other asters which makes identification very difficult. The petal-like rays are usually light violet or violet-blue, but may vary to pink and even white. The flower heads are an inch or more across, and have from twenty to forty rays which may be one-half inch long or longer.

335

SHOWY ASTER
LOW SHOWY ASTER

Aster spectabilis

Composite Family

Showy Aster is a short, hairy plant beset with glands. It grows in sandy soil of pine barrens near the coast, especially in southern New England. It varies in height from six to thirty inches, but is usually less than two feet tall. The long-stalked, lance-shaped basal leaves have toothless margins, but the stem leaves *have no stalks*. Stem leaves are rough, may have a few teeth, and are much smaller than the basal leaves. The flower heads have bright violet petal-like rays which may be an inch long. Each head will have from twenty to thirty rays and is well over an inch broad.

NEW YORK ASTER

Aster novi-belgii

Composite Family

This showy aster grows in swamps, moist places, and by salt marshes to a height of from one to three feet. It is a slender-stemmed aster which usually has many branches. A distinctive characteristic is the bracts under flower head with tips that spread or *curve downward*. The firm smooth leaves are slender and lance-shaped, have clasping bases, and margins with no teeth or only slightly toothed. The flowers are about three-fourths of an inch broad and each has from fifteen to twenty-five violet petal-like rays.

336

ROBIN'S-PLANTAIN

Erigeron pulchellus

Composite Family

Robin's Plantain has a hairy stem which forms runners by which the plant spreads to make large colonies. The stem leaves are pointed and either toothed or entire. The basal leaves are widest near the tip, are hairy, and are bluntly toothed. At the top of the stem is a single flower-head or a small cluster of heads — each on its own tiny flower stem. The rays are pale lilac or magenta and the yellow disk in the center is very large.

COMMON FLEABANE

Erigeron philadelphicus

Composite Family

All Fleabanes have very numerous thread-like ray flowers in the flower heads. This species has as many as one hundred and fifty.

Common Fleabane is a slender, hairy plant with few to many deep pink, pale magenta, or white flower heads which are less than an inch across. The basal leaves are narrow, lobed, and spoon-shaped in general outline. The stem leaves are smaller and embrace the stem. The plant is from six to twenty-eight inches tall and grows in just about every type of environment.

SALT MARSH FLEABANE

Pluchea purpurascens

Composite Family

This plant grows best in salt marshes which are sometimes flooded by salt water at extremely high tides. It may be from four to thirty-six inches in height. Fleabane is a stiff, seaside plant which will grow in large masses

if conditions are suitable, but will not grow at all if everything is not to its liking. The plant is sticky and smells of camphor. It has many tight, flat heads of lavender-rose flowers and does not bloom until the last two weeks of August. The alternate leaves have no stalks. They are smooth, bright green, and are succulent. The tiny flower heads are one fourth to nearly one-half inches broad and are in leafy, flat-topped clusters.

PLUMELESS THISTLE

Carduus acanthoides

Composite Family

Plumeless Thistle is a much-branched, prickly biennial. It grows in waste places, fallow fields, and roadsides to a height of from two to four feet. The leaves extend downward from their axils. They are lance-shaped in general outline, but are cut into lobed segments which have spiny margins. Erect purple flower-heads are borne singly or in clusters at the tips of spiny-winged branches. Each head may be over an inch broad.

BULL THISTLE

Cirsium vulgare

Composite Family

This large thistle grows from two to six feet high along roadsides, in fields, and in waste places. It can be distinguished from the Pasture Thistle by the conspicuous *spiny wings* on the stems and the rigid, yellow-tipped spines on the flower bracts. The heads are reddish-purple and the stems are sometimes reddish or just tinged with red at the leaf axils. The spiny leaves are pale and wooly on the underside.

338

FIELD THISTLE

Cirsium discolor

Composite Family

This is a large thistle which grows in fields, open woods, prairies, and waste ground to a height of from three to five feet. The plant has numerous leaves which are very deeply cut and have prickles on the margins. Upper stem leaves embrace the flower head at the tip of the stem. There is white wool on the underside of the leaves. The flower heads are purple and the overlapping, sepal-like bracts at the base of it end in a long, colorless bristle. This prickle on the outer bracts is weak and bends downward, while the prickle on the inner bracts is colorless and soft.

SWAMP THISTLE

Cirsium muticum

Composite Family

Swamp Thistle grows in swamps, low wet woods, and thickets to a height of from two to ten feet. The smooth flower stem is soft and hollow. It rises from a basal cluster of long-stalked, deeply-cut, spiny leaves. The stem leaves are green on top, but are paler in color and sort of "webby" on the underside. The rose-purple flower heads are often in clusters. The bracts under the flower heads *do not have a spine* at the tip, but are somewhat sticky and cobwebby.

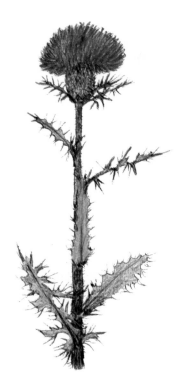

PASTURE THISTLE

Cirsium pulmilum

Composite Family

This thistle has the largest flowering head of any species in our area. It grows in dry soil in pastures, old fields, or open woods to a height of about one to three feet. The stems are very hairy, but are *not winged* as the stems in the next thistle. The lobed leaves are pale on the underside and have long spines. There are only a few flower heads on each plant, and many times there is only a solitary head from two to three inches across. The head is sweet-scented and purple-pink to white.

CANADA or CREEPING THISTLE

Cirsium arvense

Composite Family

This is a very leafy thistle which rises from a creeping, underground stem. It grows in pastures and fields, along roadsides, and has become a pest in some grainfields. It grows to a height of from one to five feet. The stems bear many small, curly, deeply-cut prickly leaves. They are dull green in color and have prickly, lobed margins. Upper leaves have no leaf stalks. Numerous clusters of small pink or pale purple flower heads are at the tips of the slender branches. Each fragrant head is about one-half to three-fourths of an inch broad. The pointed sepal-like bracts under the flower heads have a prickle at the tip of each bract. Usually these bracts are green, but on some plants they may be purplish.

340

TYROL KNAPWEED
or STAR THISTLE

Centaurea vochinensis

Composite Family

Tyrol Knapweed is a rough, more or less woolly, plant which grows in waste places, fields, and along roadsides to a height of from one to three feet. The firm-textured leaves are not divided nor toothed. The lower leaves have stalks and the broadest part of the leaf blade is at the tip. Rose-purple flower heads resemble flowers on thistles. These flower heads are about one and a half inches broad, and the marginal flowers are larger than those at the center of the head. An identifying feature is the dark fringe on the tips of the bracts at the base of the flower head. The fringe *does not conceal* the pale-colored base of bract above it.

SPOTTED KNAPWEED

Centaurea maculosa

Composite Family

This plant has wiry, much-branched stems with leaves that are very deeply cut into very narrow, thread-like leaflets. Spotted Knapweed grows in fields, waste places, and along roads to a height of from one to four feet. The flowers are pink, purple, or white and are arranged in numerous heads at the ends of the many branches. Each head is in a thimble-shaped receptacle which is covered with overlapping, black-fringed bracts.

OYSTER PLANT
or SALSIFY

Tragopogan porrifolius

Composite Family

This plant is often called Purple Goat's Beard because of its similarity to Yellow Goat's Beard on page 233. It grows in fields and waste places or along roadsides to a height of from

two to five feet. It has hollow stems and purplish, dandelion-like flowers that close by afternoon. The leaves are long and grass-like. Each showy flower head is from two to four inches broad and has spiky, sepal-like bracts which extend beyond the purple rays. The seeds form a puff ball similar to that on a dandelion, but much larger.

COMMON CATTAIL
Typha latifolia
Cattail Family

Cattails grow in ditches along the roads, wet meadows and swamps to a height of from three to six feet. There are many long, flat, narrow leaves at the base. A novice may not consider this a "flower" but the slender brown "cat's-tail" is actually made up of thousands of minute female flowers which are hardly more than a single pistil for each minute flower. Above the cluster of female flowers is a slender spike which is smaller, lighter in color, and which contains the staminate (male) flowers. When the pollen has been dropped to fertilize the female flowers, the top flowers die away — leaving only a grayish dry-looking stem.

NARROW-LEAVED CATTAIL
Typha angustifolia
Cattail Family

This cattail is similar to the one above, but can be distinguished by the separation on the stem between the male and female flower clusters. The leaves are narrower and a more yellow-green in color than those on the above cattail.

342

BUR-REEDS
Sparganum americanum
Bur-Reed Family

There are about ten species of Bur-Reeds in our area and all are very similar. It would be easiest for the novice flower collector to call them all Bur-Reeds, and leave the determination of species to those who study botany. Bur-Reeds grow from one to three feet in New England in marshes, shallow water, and along borders of ponds or streams. They are usually erect plants, but sometimes are floating on the water. They have grass-like leaves and pistillate (female) flowers which form bur-like balls when they have gone to seed. The staminate flowers (male) form separate and smaller balls above the pistillate.

HEART-LEAF TWAYBLADE or DOUBLE-LEAF
Listera cordata
Orchid Family

This twayblade grows in mossy woods or on mossy knolls to a height of from three to ten inches. It has a smooth, very slender stem with two rounded to heart-shaped leaves about midway on the stem. The flowers (see insert) are brownish-purple in a loose raceme of from four to twenty flowers. The oval sepals and upper lip are arched over the lower lip which is divided into two narrow, spreading lobes. The lower lobe has a horn-like tooth on each side of the base of the lip.

BROAD-LIPPED TWAYBLADE
Listera convallarioides
Orchid Family

This twayblade grows in damp peaty or mossy woods, thickets, swamps or shores. It is from four to ten inches tall and has a stouter stem which is

343

densely hairy above the two leaves. There are two pale-green, broadly-oval leaves mid way up the stem. These are smooth, not hairy. There are from three to twelve flowers in the loose cluster at the top of the plant. They are larger than the one above. The narrow petals and wider sepals are shorter than the lower lip. The lip is broad with two teeth at the base of the lip, and the tip is slightly two-lobed. The lower lip is clear-colored or whitish-green.

CRANEFLY ORCHIS

Tipularia discolor

Orchid Family

Cranefly Orchis grows in hardwood forests to a height of from fifteen to twenty inches. A single (sometimes two-colored) leaf is produced in the autumn. It has a slender stem and is purplish on the underside. This leaf frequently survives the winter, but disappears before the flowers appear the following summer. The nodding, greenish flowers are tinged with brownish-purple. They are in long, loose clusters at the top of the stalk. There are no bracts in the cluster. The three sepals are oblong; the two side petals are toothed; and the three-lobed lip has a very slender spur which is often twice as long as the flower itself.

PINESAP

Monotropa hypopithys

Wintergreen Family

This plant looks similar to the Indian Pipe, but has several dull yellow nodding flowers at the tip instead of only one. The entire plant is yellow, tan, or sometimes pale pink in color. It is quite hairy and grows in open or sandy woods. It is from three to twelve inches high. The stems have crowded scales which are up to one-half inch long. The upper scales are sometimes toothed. The dull yellow flowers at the tip usually have five parts, but the ones nearer the stem sometimes have only three or four petals. The petals are from three-fourths to one inch long and are slightly hairy.

FIGWORT
Scrophularia lanceolata
Figwort Family

This erect plant grows in thickets and at the edge of woods to a height of from three to eight feet. The leaves have petioles which seem to flow into the main stem. The leaf blades have a pointed tip, a broadly-rounded base, and sharply toothed margins. The curious flowers are arranged in a branching inflorescence at the summit of the plant. The calyx is cup-shaped and divided into five broad lobes. The corolla has two lips on a wide tube-like throat. The upper lip has two lobes which lean forward. The bottom lip has three lobes, but only the middle one hangs down. The corolla is a dull reddish-brown except for the lower lobe which is a shiny green color.

SQUAW-ROOT
Conopholis americana
Broomrape Family

See page 210 in the yellow section.

345

Indexes

INDEX OF COMMON NAMES

353

INDEX TO LATIN NAMES